THE ROACH PRINCESS

THE ROACH PRINCESS

HEALING WITH THE HOLY SPIRIT

Jennifer Rani Barham

DESTINY IMAGE® PUBLISHERS, INC.

P.O. Box 310, Shippensburg, PA 17257-0310

"Speaking to the Purposes of God for This Generation and for the Generations to Come."

This book and all other Destiny Image, Revival Press, MercyPlace, Fresh Bread, Destiny Image Fiction, and Treasure House books are available at Christian bookstores and distributors worldwide.

For a U.S. bookstore nearest you, call **1-800-722-6774.**

For more information on foreign distributors, call **717-532-3040.**

Reach us on the Internet: **www.destinyimage.com.**

ISBN 13 TP: 978-0-7684-3764-5

ISBN 13 HC: 978-0-7684-3765-2

ISBN 13 LP: 978-0-7684-3766-9

ISBN 13 Ebook: 978-0-7684-9001-5

For Worldwide Distribution, Printed in the U.S.A.

1 2 3 4 5 6 7 8 9 10 / 15 14 13 12 11

Dedication

To my husband, Brett, who fought on his knees with courage and faith. To my children Nathan, Brayton, and Jordan who show me the realities that forgiveness and love are like breathing for life, and Christ *in us* is the hope of glory (see Col. 1:27). May the five of us praise Him and give Him all the glory, in everything, until we meet Him at the end.

Gratitude and honor to: Vicki DeMoney, Vicki Weaver, Susan Richardson, Pastor David, and Nita Hale, who guide me to know God's way. You demonstrate His pure love as it is proved undeniably true through His saints.

Endorsements

I can hardly believe the stories in this book! In fact if it were not that the author's pastor is a friend of decades long, I would not believe it! Read and be amazed!

—Tommy Tenney

The Roach Princess is a powerful testimony of how Jesus can transform a life. As Jennifer's pastor, I can see how her personal testimony will become the foundation of all her future Christian ministry. Her passion for the Lord comes through the pages of this book and conveys a passion for others to find the same freedom and victory that she has found in Christ. This book is an incredible ministry tool for leading people to victory.

—David Hale, Lead Pastor
Christ Life Church of the Highlands

Having observed firsthand Jennifer's quest into the passionate heart of Jesus and genuine freedom, I know she has authority over the material presented. This transparent book of her journey will touch a vital place of need in the Bride of Christ and bringing people into the Kingdom!

—Vicki Weaver
Founder of Vicki Weaver Ministries and The Dwelling
Author of *Fleshly Saints in a Fallen World*
www.vickiweaverministries.com

Over the past years as a pastor to hurting women, it has been a blessing to see Jennifer take in all that God has given her and write a book that can help all women find a path to healing. I have watched this young woman walk from a broken place of confusion into an undeniable healing. As she stood in obedience to the Holy Spirit, she discovered a wealth of truth that every woman can grow from. *The Roach Princess* is a story of how one young woman came from the lie of who satan said she was to the truth of who Christ says we are—Princesses of the King of kings.

—Vicki DeMoney
Founder of CrossRoads Outreach Ministry, Inc.
Clergy Leader, Kairos Ministries
www.crossroadsms.org

Contents

Introduction   The Stairway to "Heaven" 11

                    Section I 21

Chapter One   Leave Behind the Masquerade of Pain.............. 23

Chaper Two   We Are Not the Ultimate Authority 53

Chapter Three   Submit to the King and Be Healed................. 71

Chapter Four   The Throne of Supreme Counsel 87

Chapter Five   Halt the Cycle of Defeat 105

Chapter Six   Deep Roots in Royal Ground 125

Chapter Seven   Obedient as a Palace Guard 147

Chapter Eight   Hear What the Spirit Says 169

                    Section II 189

Chapter Nine   Wielding Your Scepter With Balance 191

Chapter Ten   Vineyard by the Castle Court 211

Chapter Eleven   The Crown of Consistency 225

Chapter Twelve   Wisdom: The Moat Surrounding Your Fortress 241

Chapter Thirteen   The Topography of God's Love 257

Appendix A   Godly Steps for Healing 273

Appendix B   Life Application Actions for Healing 275

Appendix C   Read the Bible in One Year 277

The Stairway to "Heaven"

An Interview With the Devil

I have heard your prayer and seen your tears; I will heal you...
(2 Kings 20:5).

I accepted Jesus as my Savior when I was a teenager. Are you ready for a shocker? Here it is: In my free will, I still proceeded to pick up a variety of serious "issues" including alcoholism, depression, anxiety, panic disorder, mental torment, eating disorders, religious pride, drug abuse, shopping addictions, idolatry, almost divorce, and compulsive behaviors. There are more, but there is no need to list them all.

Although I wanted to do right, I could not seem to choose the path that would heal the pain. Instead, I chose to numb the pain with devices that kept me on the wrong road. I welcomed God into my territory, not realizing I needed to step into His Kingdom.

Surrounding me was a confederacy of people who did not walk with Him. I had no foundation on which to build and no builders to assist my growth in Christ. Often, when this is the case, the devil wins for a time.

In a moment, I will share with you an example of a typical day in my late teens and early twenties. (Sadly enough, those years were a cakewalk compared to my early thirties.) While this story is real, I choose to portray certain details of my interview with the devil figuratively. But, yes, I did wear a crown all day long. I was a princess of darkness.

A Day in the Life

On this typical day, I woke up, aware that dehydration had set in overnight. I could feel the deficiency making me sick. My sour stomach also ached from the overbearing emptiness caused by guilt over my addiction and actions. The emptiness even overpowered my hangover. The pain was unbearable. My head throbbed and my eyes closed at the slightest sound. My tongue was stuck to the roof of my mouth. I had been drinking heavily the night before. When I drank, I drank all night and consumed as much alcohol as possible. That is just how I thought drinking worked.

I gazed up through the sparkly, prismatic crystals set in my tiara. The crown had slid down onto my face while I slept. I strained to focus my eyes on the bumper sticker I had attached to one of the blades on my ceiling fan. My father kept asking me to stop sticking things onto his house and cars. I liked bumper stickers and found them quite revealing. On this day, when I was the only thing in the room that was spinning, I read the bumper sticker words aloud:

And she's buying a stairway to heaven.[1]

I always pictured the woman in the Led Zeppelin song as some kind of princess. With only a word, she owned all her heart's desires. No pain, no fear, no lack—she had everything. I was trying to mimic her by manufacturing a stairway to Heaven. My purpose was to find pleasure; but pleasure was hard to come by. I wondered why I was not like the princess in the song. Why did I have to hurt all the time? Why were my days devoted to finding ways to make the pain go away?

Dazed, I stared at the fan blade, singing the song in my head. I kept repeating:

*Yes, there are two paths you can go by. But in the long run
there's still time to change the road you're on.*[2]

I did not believe this statement at all. I misunderstood my situation and thought that I was trapped in my pain. Consequently, I stayed there too long.

As I lay there that day, I thought, "Regardless of their biblical knowledge, whoever penned this song had great wisdom tucked away in the lyrics."

I began to hum and realized that the song talks about a piper:

The piper's calling you to join him.[3]

To me, that piper was Jesus and He is calling us to join Him. I had ignored His call for so long that I was surprised that my body was not yet in a coffin six feet underground, awaiting the judgment.

As I read the bumper sticker on this particular morning, I felt more like a failure than a princess. I knew I was on the wrong road, but I did not know how to get on the right one. I did not know how to follow Jesus. My proclamation of accepting Christ had not led to my walking in a godly procession with His other saints. In fact, I was unsure whether I wanted to march for Christ all the time. How could He lead me home? I would have to give up and change so much. How was I even worthy? I had gone too far. I was too broken.

My hangover was awful, but before my feet hit the floor, I was already planning my next drink. I removed the princess crown from my brow, gently set it on the side table, and traded it for my smokes. When I was sober, nicotine made me more nervous than usual, but I smoked anyway. I opened my pill bottle and took two or three sedatives to steady my nerves and calm the fear and guilt.

I began to plan the rest of my day: I would shop all day and starve myself until dusk. Then, I would start the revelry all over again. I stepped out of my bed remembering how I had drunk and drugged throughout the previous night and early dawn hours at my favorite club, The Masquerade. As I reminisced, I stooped to pick up my shoes from the floor. Reaching for the side table to stabilize myself, I inadvertently pressed my hand into the points of my crown. Feeling the pain, I lifted my hand and peeled the headdress from my squashed flesh. I placed the crown back on my head, smashed my half-smoked cigarette in the ashtray, and cursed the hurt. (In case you are wondering, tiaras, nose rings, tattoos, dark makeup, blue hair, and even full costume dress was normal in my circles, whether day or night).

Having steadied myself against the hallway wall, I made my way into the kitchen. I felt the sting of glass penetrating my heel as my feet hit the kitchen floor. My head was numb, but my face winced at the pain. Not that pain was anything new; I lived in pain. I wanted to believe that I wandered into it most days but it was too obvious that I was choosing the torment, and ironically always wondering, "Why do I feel this emptiness deep inside?"

Juggling my thoughts, I began to sing again:

Our shadows taller than our soul....[4]

The lyrics rang true as I noticed a broken window and dried blood all over the tree and sidewalk just outside. I remembered that friends had come back to my house, done some cocaine, and gotten into a verbal altercation. The argument quickly became physical. Someone had a knife and someone used it. The sad part is that I did not care at the time. I had not even paid attention to the fact that someone had been stabbed.

As I pulled the glass from my foot, I realized it did not hurt a bit; the sedative had begun to kick in. Remembering that I had a job interview at The Masquerade, I reached up to remove my crown. Then I realized that, at a club as weird as The Masquerade, my tiara would probably improve my chances of being hired. I left my crown on my head and prepared to return to the club, where I would fill out all the forms and interview for the job.

Little did I know as my foot bled all over the floor, that I was planning more pain for myself. It was a mistake to apply for a job in a club I should never have even visited. Since I had numbed myself to reason, I was now ready for more things unreasonable. Isaiah's words had not yet penetrated my heart:

> *"Come now, let us reason together," says the* LORD. *"Though your sins are like scarlet, they shall be as white as snow; though they are red as crimson, they shall be like wool"* (Isaiah 1:18).

My sins were still red.

I cleaned up the glass, wrapped up my foot, and headed back to the nightclub. I had to see whether my friends could help establish a reason for me to be at The Masquerade every day. Knowing I was late, I drove 90 miles per hour on the highway into downtown Atlanta. I even passed the college that I had just quit attending.

On this typical day, I was dazed on pills. I wore my tiara, all black attire, and platform shoes. I smoked and listened to Led Zeppelin, still glazed over from leftover alcohol and tranquilizers. Somehow, I exited the highway safely, made it through the city, and turned into the club's parking lot.

As I opened my car door, I grabbed a pen and my purse. Before locking the car, I squeezed my pack of cigarettes to make sure I had an ample supply. I heard the rumble of a passing train echo through the mill equipment that was attached to the side of the warehouse that housed the bar. Meanwhile, small groups of people shuffled around behind the nightclub. I recognized the roadies from the night before; they were cleaning the equipment belonging to the rock band that had played.

Even in broad daylight, The Masquerade felt like an evil place. The freestanding building sitting on the outer edge of Atlanta looked like a deceptive gift from the devil lying on the Christmas tree skirt surrounding the city. From the warehouse area, I always noticed the buildings gathered together like a bundle of iron in the distance. The club was in a quiet, eerie district that most of society avoided.

With my dehydration now seeping through my temporary pill fix, I began to feel ill. I started to panic and searched my purse for another bitter comforter.

I entered the building by a side door off the gravel parking lot that held one of the two cars I was looking for. Inside, the club flaunted 20-foot metal doors, wooden beams, and high ceilings. I walked through the smoky haze of the bar, guided by the red glow of the exit signs. I grabbed a glass from behind the first bar and shot soda water into it to swallow my remedy.

My stomach ached. I could find temporary peace in my pills, alcohol, cigarettes, shopping, starvation, and the attention of others. Still, I wondered why I was the only person who hurt this bad. I wanted to know why my shadow of emptiness felt larger than my soul.

Sunlight pushed through the cracked doorframe. Leaving the rays behind, I went deeper into the darkness. The club had three levels. The Masquerade had titled them *Hell, Purgatory,* and *Heaven.* They counterfeited God's terms.

The friends I was looking for were most likely in the bar area called "Heaven." Our world so often relates the word *heaven* to anything that satisfies our flesh I thought as I remembered the song saying:

Cause you know sometimes words have two meanings.[5]

"Hell" was empty and "Purgatory" was closed. As I ascended the creaky, wooden stairs to "Heaven," I realized a small stream of sunlight had somehow found its way into the dark box. The florescent lights attached to the ceiling some 20 feet above led me up the stairs. Atop the stairs, a hidden door stood ajar, revealing the origin of the small stream of light. The sign on the door read *Office,* so I entered. Sitting behind a large mahogany desk was an even larger albino man with pure white hair and long fingernails. He hissed as I entered.

I was feeling ill from all the substances, smells, and lack of anything good in or around me. Muttering, "Excuse me," I turned and ran to the restroom, which was directly across the hall.

As I ran in, my foot slipped in a puddle of water in front of the commode. As I caught myself, my tiara fell and tumbled behind a trash can. Barely making it to the toilet on time, I vomited and began crying aloud.

Once I collected myself, I stood up, left the stall, and reached behind the trashcan. I grabbed my tiara, placed it atop my head, and turned the corner to exit while simultaneously glancing into the mirror to check my face. To my horror, a cockroach was caught between the crystals in my crown! It was half-dead, half-alive, and flailing desperately.

I froze, unable to even lift my hand and remove the headdress. There in the quasi darkness, I looked like a roach princess. In fact, I was *The* Roach Princess. My drunkenness, drug addiction, depression, fear, idolatry, and gluttony all screamed, "Nasty, rotten, hedonistic Roach Princess!"

I pulled air into my lungs with a deep breath and swallowed hard. I removed the tiara, threw it into the gloom under the stall, and then shivered the tingles away. I heard my crown roll along the wood floor and eventually fall down into something as I left the room. The hollow thuds sounded like aluminum sheet metal in an open-air vent. I wondered if the roach was still intact.

I stepped back into the albino's office, my skin still crawling as I thought about the roach. I did not like roaches. I had a history with them and it was not good.

"I'm sorry. I feel sick—dizzy—I'm here to apply for a full-time position. My friends are here somewhere," I said stammering. I was about to cry, but I would not allow a tear to fall.

He reached out, his nails so long they almost curled, and handed me a white piece of paper. I knew I should not have accepted, but I did. I succumbed to the weakness Paul described in Romans 7:19: *"For what I do is not the good I want to do; no, the evil I do not want to do—this I keep on doing."*

In the moment that I received the application, I could see into the albino man's eyes and realized that a color would have muddled the message they conveyed. His eyes spoke of the acceptance of alcohol, drugs, defective body image, endless gluttony, vanity, illusions of fame and idolatry. I did not respond with words, but my actions expressed my agreement to accept the job. I stood there noticing his pulse as the blood danced with his words. I had my eyes on the wrong person's blood. I suddenly felt like there were angels around me. They were humming, but never pushed me or prodded me. They never exposed me to any images, but the albino had. I was veiled to the truth because of my choices, giving ample room for evil persuasion.

The angels had joined me in the grossest place on earth so I would know that there is no secret too dark for them to help me reveal. They did only the Lord's bidding. My eyes kept searching the room, but I decided not to look to the angels, knowing they would not cross my will. I kept track of the light and noticed that the humming sound accompanied it.

In this instance, the angels relied on my heart and my hearing to function. Unfortunately, my heart was hard and I was deaf to God's call. Even so, He never gave up on me. When I finally chose His path years later, I heard and reacted to the angels' praise. Their humming became audible as "Holy, Holy, Holy is the Lord God Almighty."

And if you listen very hard
The tune will come to you at last.
When all are one and one is all....[6]

That day in the albino's office, I stood at the crossroads of two kingdoms and entertained the signals of both. What a double-minded woman unstable in all her ways:

> *And no wonder, for Satan himself masquerades as an angel of light. It is not surprising, then, if his servants masquerade as servants of righteousness. Their end will be what their actions deserve* (2 Corinthians 11:14-15).

Never Too Late

The Masquerade serves as a metaphor for my journey to healing. It illustrates my choice to travel the albino's fictitious steps in his deceptive world. I would remain trapped in that paradigm for more than 15 years. On a symbolic level, I eventually chose to step out of that room in order to step into healing in the Kingdom of God.

It took some time before I realized that we are all in a masquerade on some level and at some point in our lives. This is the place where we are deceived, whether we live in denial of our sinful ways or flat-out revel in iniquity. When we recognize the masquerade, admit our pain, and give it up to God, we step onto the healing stairway that leads to His Heaven.

Every time we choose evil over the ways of God, we allow satan to employ us for his purposes. However, we are always free to leave his masquerade. Isaiah prophesied to Hezekiah when his end was near: *"I have heard your prayer and seen your tears; I will heal you. On the third day from now you will go up to the temple of the LORD"* (2 Kings 20:5).

God gave me a third day and freed me from the bondage of tremendous pain and torment. This is your third day. Together, we can allow the Holy Spirit to guide us up God's stairway to the heavenly Jerusalem. Today, you can choose to step out of the masquerade of pain and into the temple of the Lord to receive your healing.

"Impossible!" you say.

Not true. Nothing—absolutely *nothing*—is impossible for God (see Matt. 19:26).

I am sharing my testimony with you. I felt wrecked, overwhelmed, and trapped. What I discovered is this: He has grace for us all, anytime and all the time. You can never say too much time has passed. How do I know? Because He fixed all of my pain. Today I am healthy, peaceful, and blessed. He has healed me and is healing me daily. Now, I have the peace of a constant hope and the victory of a true healing.

You may feel hopeless, defeated, and broken; but God can heal you and make you whole.

Let's Set the Table

I have divided this book into two sections. For the first eight chapters we will journey into healing, where true peace, joy, and health are found. With each step, we will learn why healing is a lifelong process and we will accept our fallible nature.

The last five chapters will help us understand how to stay consistent in our healed and healing state. There are a million quick fixes out there; they never last. This healing will lead you to the only fix that is eternal and infallible—as long as you are willing. I am living proof; all I could offer was willingness.

If He has grace for me, He has grace for you. You may not agree with this statement right now. You might not even feel adequate to receive His grace. However, you will see that as long as you are truly ready to let God help you, He will. Life always presents us with two paths. One is pain-free for the most part; one is filled with pain. Too often, we drag our sacks full of issues, struggling with the weight of it all, even as we travel down the wrong road.

Which path are you on? Which path are you willing to exit? How badly do you hurt? Is it bad enough to want to get better?

While being in pain may not be your fault, staying there is your decision. For too long, I decided to stay. In fact, I was downright terrified and confused. I didn't know how *not* to stay. Although there had been many reasons for me to step onto the wrong path, none of them forced me to stay.

The Piper—the living God—will soon lead us into the deeper reasons guiding our choices for pain so that we can heal from them as we journey. His forgiveness is available, as Isaiah 1:18 attests.

For now, we will simply recognize the pain and accept that we make the choice.

And I am not afraid of anything anymore.
And I am not ashamed, the masquerade has ended.
And I will stand for You even if I lose it all.
Cause nothing really matters,
You are all that matters, Lord.
As messed up as I am, still You bring me in.
You take me in Your arms and hold me.
The worthlessness I feel, You make it disappear.
You are always there, You're endless.[7]

Endnotes

1. *Led Zeppelin IV* (assumed album title), "Stairway to Heaven," Led Zeppelin, © 1971, Atlantic Records.

2. Ibid.

3. Ibid.

4. Ibid.

5. Ibid.

6. Ibid.

7. "Masquerade," Seventh Day Slumber, © 2005, BMC Recordings/EMD.

Section I

Chapter One

Leave Behind the Masquerade of Pain

Step One: Out of Denial and Into Hope

*Heal me, O LORD, and I will be healed; save me and I will be saved,
for You are the one I praise* (Jeremiah 17:14).

Rooms That Hold Our Pain

THINK back to the rooms you have traveled through. Some rooms bring back good memories; some bring back bad ones. You might remember a hospital room in which you heard and saw your child for the first time. You might also remember a hospital room in which you left a piece of your heart when a loved one passed away.

Do you remember a bedroom in which you felt safe? Or a bedroom where you lost something you feel you can never recover? Do you see a dark room where you were deeply hurt? A room in which you felt the hurt would never end? Perhaps it was a classroom where you were ridiculed and belittled. Or maybe, you left your heart in the kitchen where your husband told you about the other woman? Is a piece of your heart still held in a courtroom, a church room, a prison cell, a sanctuary, a bathroom, an office?

Is there a room that has walled in your fear, heartache, tears, and ultimately your heart, or part of your heart? Think about it. Allow your heart to be open and soft so that you can eventually allow God to repossess and heal you. Begin to establish the habit of letting His truth come into your mind to counterattack the lies.

We have to face the pain, with Christ's help, in order to discover what led us into the masquerade. I think of people in actual prisons and wonder what they go through. Yet, there are other kinds of prisons. I was imprisoned in my mind for way too long. Our world, media, and society try to imprison us daily with lies about who we are and who God is.

Are you in a prison? If so, in what way are you willing to let God help you out? Do you believe He really will?

A Step Toward Freedom

In my early thirties, when I finally decided to give God my whole heart, He led me up a stairway to Heaven. He took me out of what I thought was permanent entrapment in the masquerade of pain; He drew me out of my territory and into an enduring healing in His Kingdom.

It all began with my first step, which was to allow God to reveal the denial that kept me bound. When I stopped denying my addictive nature, my belief in the seeming impossibility of healing was replaced with the hope that there had to be something better. I remember leaving behind the scorching Mississippi heat to enter the building where a portion of my healing would begin. The cool, white hallway led me to a safe place to heal, a place where I felt at ease. A single lamp stand illuminated my footsteps as I entered the serene room. I was the first person to arrive at the treatment center that day. Regardless of my fear, the accomplishment of having shown up made me feel good, at least for a moment.

I scanned the room, admiring its simplicity. The only furnishings were the lamp and nine velvet armchairs arranged in a circle. I pictured myself sinking into the down-filled cushions and disappearing inside them. Although I felt safe upon entering the room, my heart now felt as though it were in a vice grip. Somehow, I was thankful for the clutch that kept my softening heart from pounding out of my chest.

My eyes leaked. I had to look up to balance the tears inside my lower lids, hoping they would evaporate before falling. By this time, I was OK with crying, but still a little hesitant. My breath was hard to pull in and let out. I felt dizzy from the lack of oxygen. Yet I was thankful for the soft room, because I believed that I really belonged in a hard iron and concrete jail cell.

God allowed part of my heart to be healed in that quiet room. It was the part I gave Him on that first step. Having finally decided to come down from the devil's staircase and leave the masquerade behind, I found the angels waiting for me with open arms. I still feared the unknown, but the fear had become a kind of willing trepidation.

Accepting the dread of the unknown was a significant step in my healing. God took the sickness in my life and, with each step toward Him, He healed me—right before my eyes.

You may be feeling the same dread right now. You might feel numb, unsure, and scared. These feelings are normal; accept them. Healing is not comfortable. That is why so many stay sick. Repeat this truth often: *If I heal, I will step into the place of comfort much faster than if I stay in my pain.*

You will be OK if you trust Christ. Embrace the pain so that you can overcome.

The Rooms

The room at the treatment center was my transition room out of the masquerade of my persistent sinful ways. Do you remember the rooms of your pain or of your positive transition?

When we accept Christ, we also have to accept the fact that our sinful nature will always beckon us back to the wrong path. Do you see where this has happened to you? To combat this relentless lure, we need healing and then training in righteousness. Unfortunately, my only training was in worldliness. What has your training been? What about the opposite, too much "religious" training? It is not God's intention but man's imposition that made you feel incapable of righteousness.

Another room I will never forget is the space in which I received salvation. As a young teenager, I accepted Christ into my broken heart at a friend's house. In John 14:6 Jesus said, *"I am the way and the truth and the life. No one comes to the Father except through Me."* Salvation comes through Christ.

I always felt a strong call from the Lord. I fought through the worldly web satan had woven around me by getting as much of Jesus as possible through my friends and friends' parents. As soon as I would get home to my room, the devil would steal any godly seed I had received. I kept trying to do right, but just could not live up to the standard I desired and deemed necessary. Do you see this conundrum in your life, a counterattack against whatever is good? I call this the Romans' seven syndrome.

My room as a teenager was The Roach Princess suite. The chamber sat atop three stories of bay windows that mimicked a castle tower. To get to my abode, I had to step four flights up a staircase adorned with pink shag carpet. The space was beautifully decorated, but beneath the surface it was infested with roaches; some were actual insects, but most were spiritual "bugs." We will talk more about my teenage years as we journey.

We will also visit another room off the stairway—the room that comforted all the hurt. It was just like the room in Damascus where Ananias laid his hands on Paul and the apostle's life was transformed (see Acts 9:15-18).

One Step at a Time

For now, we will focus on the primary process to our healing. But first, let's establish that *rooms* are representative of *issues*. We will use the two words interchangeably in that regard.

The first step up the staircase to healing is to acknowledge and release the denial of our pain. This process occurs as we remember the issues in our lives, realizing that they have hardened areas of our hearts and continue to hold captive parts of our souls. We will allow God to repossess and heal us as we step up into His heavenly temple where no walls hold us captive.

When we look to anything but Christ to ease our pain, the hurt eventually becomes too severe for earthly remedies to resolve. There came a point in my life when my only hope for healing was to give it all up to Him. Oddly enough, our pain sometimes becomes a place of comfort. It is not authentic comfort, but deceptive. We cling to it because we are afraid to leave.

Looking back, I realize that a series of steps toward God led to my healing. The stairs were not shaky or shaggy like the pink carpeted ones, but steady and still in Christ. These steps are perfect for fixing our pain because they lead us directly through His Word. (Remember that Jesus *is* the Word of God.) We can also use them repeatedly when any new pain arises.

Healing is a lifelong process. We must learn how to allow God to heal us. Then we need to know how to stay healed or receive further healing. I discovered—finally!—that issues are resolved by stepping onto the right staircase and following it all the way to the top.

The first eight steps of the 13 we will take together are designed to guide us into the state of healing. This outcome occurs as we gain knowledge of how we can be healed from hurts and tribulation. The remaining five steps "glue" us to God's hem so we become less apt to step back into our old ways more likely to remain healthy.

You can find healing on these steps if you are willing to keep heading upwards. The steps form a cycle of hope in a hopeless world replete with downward paths that lead to sickness and pain.

Jewel for the Journey

The hope for healing is our choice, and allowing the cohesion of each step up into the temple sets us free.

If you are hurting and feel as though you are on the wrong stairs, you are in good company. That is exactly where I was. I am thankful to have found the right stairway and I want to help lead you to the source of true healing.

First, allow me to share a few of my missteps on the wrong stairway. It will help you to see why I can say in all truthfulness: "You are not alone."

Addiction Denial

The addiction I suffered was my way of escaping pain. When I was hurting, I would consume 23 beers, some liquor or wine, and two packs of cigarettes per day. Many times, I tried to mask the depression and guilt with pain pills, muscle relaxers, sedatives, antidepressants, and sleeping pills.

For the majority of that time, I gossiped to friends about my troubles and desperately attempted to get their agreement with my victim mentality. I used this technique to excuse, sustain, and justify my behavior.

My "pain management" tactics were unhelpful; days like the ones I have described always ended in severe shame and hopelessness.

Emotionalism

Emotions stem from deeper issues. Pain was the catalyst for my emotions. I used them as a faulty coping mechanism. Severe anxiety attacks soon manifested as agoraphobia. I could not leave my house. Crowds and busy places terrified me. I stayed depressed and full of fear all day long; I was imprisoned in my mind and my home.

These issues made me angry, bitter, and frustrated. My pain caused me to feel estranged and different from everyone else. The panic trapped me in isolation. I, in turn, used seclusion to "treat" my sense of estrangement. That is not unusual; we often use pain to fix pain.

Controlled by Consequences

Instead of being fearful, drunk, and hurting, I wanted to be normal. I desired to live the "normal" life everyone except me seemed to be living. I wanted to be free of consequences like DUIs, identity theft investigations, lawsuits, and daily embarrassment. Being sober and healthy seemed impossible to me. I added fuel to the fire of my difficulties by making poor decisions from an inebriated mindset. The cycle kept going.

My desperate need to fix myself resulted in me allowing the world to influence me and shifted me into thinking I was somehow in control. When we try controlling what God intends to control, we are out of control. My chain of command was upside down, with me at the top. It resembled more of a shackle with a ball attached. I put the fetter on with the devil's help. My mind was the ball weighting the manacle in place.

Faulty Body Image

I starved myself on occasion, threw up, and sometimes took pills to stay thin. First thing each morning, I determined the path of my day based on the digits displayed on the scale. I began to realize that math and eating disorders are tightly intertwined. The figures on the scale, the tags on the clothes, the measuring tape, the body fat percentage, the reps required, the miles to run, the number of bites I would allow or disallow—these were just a few of the issues I struggled with daily.

To Struggle Is Human

We are human. We have struggles, issues, and sad days. What is not normal is for us to cycle in defeat and pain daily. Christ overcame on our behalf. He recognized our helplessness and intends for us to tap into His healing power.

God finds no dark corner too horrible for His Spirit to enter and pull us out. My corner was worthlessness and victimization. He did not require any worth from me. He taught me that no one's pain compared to that suffered by His Son, who came with gifts we could not earn. Shortly after He pulled me out, He impressed on me a gift of self-worth that surpassed my hopes and dreams. I became a victor. It was not a gift for me only; this gift is for *you*.

These steps into healing apply to all issues and all people. A healthy life may seem impossible now, but there *is* a way. At this moment, getting out of bed may be your first priority. That is OK. We can take this journey into healing one step at a time. We must only be willing to let God order our steps. He will give us the strength needed to take each step.

A wise man once explained the difference between traveling up the staircase and down: If you are heading up the stairs and trip, you will most likely catch yourself. You might end up one or two stairs back, if you descend at all. But if you stumble while traveling down the staircase, you are likely to land at the bottom, with bruises and maybe some badly broken bones to show for it.

We need to get on the right set of stairs and start climbing. The struggle upward is worthwhile. It leads to a state of healing described by Jeremiah:

Behold, [in the future restored Jerusalem] I will lay upon it health and healing, and I will cure them and will reveal to them the abundance of peace (prosperity, security, stability) and truth (Jeremiah 33:6 AMP).

Our Pain Is Real

Most people are familiar with emotional hurts. The damage done *to* us or *by* us year after year causes us real pain. The hurt hardens parts of the heart and fragments parts of the soul. We carefully box up that portion, only to find that, instead of healing, the pain grows. Our issues are made evident by our anger, fear, insecurity, guilt, unbelief, bitterness, fear of abandonment, loneliness, and worry. We cleave to worry even when Matthew 6:27 asks, *"Who of you by worrying can add a single hour to **his** [**or her**] life?"* (emphasis added). We will eventually step into a place of hope. On that step, we will learn how to release fear just like the widow at Zarephath did (see 1 Kings 17). She was facing death by starvation; she had a legitimate reason to respond in fear to Elijah's request for food. Instead, she stepped up to hope as God requested through His prophet. By taking that step, she learned about more than God's ability to produce limitless supply. She also found faith, life (for herself and her son), and healing for the portion of her heart that she had boxed in with worry. Like the widow at Zarephath, we are journeying toward God's unfailing provision and healing.

The journey involves choices, some of which can prolong unnecessary suffering. When we refuse to let God make us whole, our distress is driven into addiction, depression, performance orientation, judgment, rebellion, idolatry, eating disorders, and more. The longer we refuse God, the deeper we delve into issues of sexual and verbal abuse, rage, self-inflicted wounding, divorce, physical ailments, addiction to medication, codependency, isolation, and idolatry.

Most pain stems from events and issues in our lives that got suppressed. As a result, we feel a nagging deficiency; we are unsure of the origin of our pain or the nature of the missing piece we seek. This room of bondage and confusion (or denial) is exactly where the enemy would like us to stay. He wants us to believe that we are trapped in a place of defeat, suffering on the devil's cyclical staircase.

To break the bondage means to look to God, as Psalms 65:2-3 reveals: *"for You answer our prayers. All of us must come to You. Though we are overwhelmed by our sins, You forgive them all"* (NLT).

We are about to take the initiative in order to leave the masquerade of our pain behind for good. Our first step is to be without denial; we have to realize and accept the fact of our pain. We must admit it and trust God. We need to be whole-heartedly obedient to the healing process He laid out for us. We cannot quit after taking the first few steps and expect to experience the best outcomes of our lives on earth. We must climb all the steps to healing. Let us commit to the stairway to God's Heaven so we can experience blessed and complete lives.

It is easy to have a genuine desire for healing. It is common to get off to a great start. All too often, however, we give up, lose hope, slow down, or quit. Persistence and consistency are not automatic. I have found that without the fullness of God's Spirit, I am not consistent in anything but sin. Let us step into His Spirit and allow His Spirit to step into us. This is where healing begins. (We will learn how to do this through a combination of real-life examples and biblical exploration.)

We can step into the mindset of hope, which naturally leads us into the victorious, faith-filled place of healing. In your sadness, this might seem impossible; but all things are possible with God (see Matt. 10:27). Philippians 4:13 says, *"I can do everything through Him who gives me strength."* We *will* step out of denial and into hope.

We have to accept our God-ordained paths and not the faulty ones that lead us away from God. Jeremiah quoted God's command: *"Stop at the crossroads and look around. Ask for the old, godly way, and walk in it. Travel its path, and you will find rest for your souls..."* (Jer. 6:16 NLT).

Upward Steps

There are stair steps into His Kingdom. The same is true in the natural: the temple was elevated; each section rose higher than the rest. We will enter His gates with thanksgiving, His court, the court of women or the Gentile's court, with praise up into the holy place and then into the Holy of Holies. You can only arrive at the next level by steps. Each time we ascend in His purpose, we choose the right way—up not down; forward not backward—into healing and away from more sickness. It is important that we follow God's leading as Jeremiah explained: *"I know, O LORD, that a man's life is not his own; it is not for man to direct his steps"* (Jer. 10:23).

As we continue our upward trek, we will highlight certain truths or *Jewels for the Journey*. These are helpful as you read, but are also available for encouragement whenever you feel weak or sad. Jewels have many facets and continually cast new rays of light. These jewels will serve to reveal power and wisdom. They are symbols and guideposts for your upward course. They will direct you to the foot of the cross, where true strength is found. They will also remind you to step up and away from pain by allowing God to complete you through the blood of Christ.

We are traveling together and the stairs are safe. On each one, you will find a *Life Application Action* and several reminders called *Princess Principles* defined in the text by (PP). At the conclusion of each chapter, in *The Princess Principles Practice* or *P³* section, we will revisit the action and principles to reflect upon them further (*P³* means "P to the third power"). This is a biblically based set of rules designed to ensure a lasting healing. It will help us to become more aware of His Scriptures and more accustomed to practicing His truths and His ways.

At the end of this book, you will find clear-cut, bullet-pointed lists that will lead you upward. *Godly Steps* (Appendix A) will train you to stand firm in your call and healing; *Life Application Actions* (Appendix B) will help keep you in God's will. All of these guides originate from and point to and through our Bible.

When we realize and admit that neither we nor anyone else can fix our pain, we can begin to heal; we can gently step out of any unnecessary suffering; and we can enter the place of freedom.

By the grace of God, we are already free to make this choice. So why do we bolt ourselves into rooms filled with pain? Why do we shackle ourselves to the handrail on life's wrong staircase? Why, when we finally choose the right staircase, do we stop on the bottom steps?

We live in the age of grace! We are at liberty to choose life. Are you willing to release your pain? Then let the bolts be undone and the doors opened. My beautiful friends, let the shackles fall and the true path be revealed. Allow Him to have your whole soul and soften your whole heart. Then mindfully step toward Him. When we permit God to work in us, the healing ensues.

The Deadbolt of Denial

Pain is not the catalyst for our bondage. Denial is the primary issue that blocks healing. It is, in fact, the deadbolt on the door of healing.

Once we admit we want to leave the masquerade where our pain has been kept—to climb the stairs leading to temple to receive our healing—we are on our way! We step out of denial by accepting our responsibility for the duration and depth of pain that we allow (PP). We cannot heal if we cannot get the deadbolt undone. Ironically, all of us who have accepted Christ already have the key!

We have the key! If we fail to see the part we play in maintaining our pain, we will remain immersed in it. We control how pain affects us; we can stop the ache by accepting this fact.

This may be hard to recognize right now, but hold on to this truth. I am speaking of the fortitude that characterizes a victorious state. We can use this information as a springboard to get out, and stay out, of the pain. That is not to say that your life will be forever pain-free. Tribulation is inevitable as long as we live on this earth in emotional and fleshly bodies. The good news is that, if you believe, God can heal you.

Denial is the blatant rejection of an obvious fault in our character. It is hard to come to terms with denial, but it is not impossible (PP). This garment we choose to wear is a cloak that seemingly conceals many sins. It whispers to us, saying that hiding and excusing our transgressions is OK. Denial tells us that we can use pride, bitterness, and anger to mask our fear and pain. The Bible tells us differently. It says that pride comes before destruction (see Prov. 16:18). It feeds denial's defiance.

The shroud of denial is heavy, but once we throw it off, we will experience tears of joy. The load of life will lighten, because humility leads to blessing and honor.

The way to undo denial is to step outside of ourselves and look inside with humility, knowing that everyone has faults. Accepting our faults and the faults of others makes us better people. When we realize God loves us and is not accusing us, we begin to understand relationship with Him, stepping us into healing (PP).

We need to step out of the mindset called *victim mentality*. In order to fix our imperfections, we need to first accept them. All of this is part of the unfolding of our lives. Romans 8:28 says that *"...in all things God works for the good of those who love Him, who have been called according to His purpose."* If we are diligent to obey God's will, we will experience this truth. That means putting Him above all our trials and sicknesses.

Faults are normal. With Christ, they can be fixed and forgiven forever. Forgiveness is not a one-time event. Jesus said it is a seventy times seven process (see Matt. 18:22). Accepting our faults and relinquishing them to God renders them powerless over our lives.

At some point, each of us can relate to feeling like the Princess of "Always, Forever Hurting" in 'The Kingdom of Pain and Woe Is Me." Yet, we needn't stay there. God is no respecter of persons (see Rom. 2:11). That means He loves you and will heal you just as He did me. We like to think that the good stuff is for some other Dick or Jane out there and not for us. The healing and blessings of God are for *you*.

Revelation Bride

I felt incapable of coming out of my pain. I was sure I was stuck in it. Many times, we realize these insecurities during life-changing events: our college years, marriage, pregnancy, divorce, illness, sobering up, healing, the death of a loved one, or any other transitional situation. We allow life to overwhelm us with the sins of our past and the responsibilities of our future. Sometimes we need to be jolted out of going through our unhealthy motions.

Because I was so sick at the time, my own wedding was one of those jolts for me. Although I kept trying to look like a real princess and desperately wanted to be one, I was The Roach Princess. However, I was in complete denial of this fact. I kept trying to make the outside prettier, hoping that the prettiness would eventually sink inside somehow. A decade later, while watching my wedding video, I conceived the paradox of the *Roach Princess* title.

The shiny jewel sparkling out of a white gold setting on my finger represented a covenant I was unaware existed. I knew the term *marriage,* but had no idea of what God had intended it to represent. I didn't realize that it symbolized the divine relationship between Christ and the Church. The idea of an unconditional, eternal alliance with anyone or anything was beyond me. My hurt had caused me to become a skeptic.

While watching my wedding video, I remembered the gardenias' sweet honeysuckle smell and the sound of James Taylor playing softly as my husband and I strolled onto the dance floor, in the center of it all. My tiara sparkled; my white dress flowed with the music. Regally postured wait staff poured bubbly champagne into crystal goblets. There was laughter and children's crisp white clothes stained by splashes of Shirley Temple. The bridesmaids' ball gowns filled the room, swishing in the cool night air. The stage of the old rustic inn was set as though for worldly royalty. The scene gave the appearance of perfection. The appearance, however, was deceptive.

As I watched the video, I cried. I remembered the drugs, the alcohol, the insecurity, the uncertainty, the inability, and the lack. I felt so unqualified to love, so sick inside with the fear of knowing I did not love myself. The addition and expectation of someone else to love increased my apprehension and made me feel even more incapable of providing love. I was a wounded vessel—afraid, hurt, and filled with unbelief. How could I have even gotten married in denial of that much pain?

I have been married for a long time now. We have stepped a good distance from our wedding video and all of its hidden pain. My husband and I have even recommitted our lives to one another by reestablishing our covenant. This time we left out the dress, the flowers, the crowd, the feelings of insufficiency, and the alcohol. We included the all-sufficient Jesus, our acceptance of each other's imperfection, our desire for constant healing, and the eternal unity of the agape love God intended us to have for one another.

When we heal, not only do we get better, but so do our surroundings. Most times, the people around us will either follow suit or make their exit. Eventually, your healing encompasses you *and* spreads to those you allow God to love through you. I am not saying that others will definitely change just because we do. If we truly change, however, we will see others much differently. Our love will then lend itself to produce the same effect in those who are willing. We will not only become healed vessels; we will become healing vessels.

Room to Hold the Holy Spirit

It wasn't until many years after the tears fell and I recognized my pain watching the video that I was even ready to confront my defiance. Stepping out of denial in my early thirties was my first step into a radical life change. I allowed God to alter me and I literally became a new creation. He did not change me all at once, but there was a specific moment in which healing began—a moment when transformation became my path:

> *And be not conformed to this world: but be ye transformed by the renewing of your mind, that ye may prove what is that good, and acceptable, and perfect, will of God* (Romans 12:2 KJV).

I would call the change a death of my flesh because almost everything about me began to change. Second Corinthians 5:17 says: *"Therefore, if anyone is in Christ, he is a new creation; the old has gone, the new has come!"* God began to mold me into the image of Christ.

We cannot even begin to grasp the all-powerful capabilities of God. We rarely allow Him room to do the miraculous. His healing can exceed any and all of our expectations, if we allow Him.

This transformation occurred around the Thanksgiving and Christmas holiday season. It came after I had surrendered substances, gone through treatment, and spent about six months in absolute sobriety and obedience to the Lord.

I felt like Esther in her period of preparation before she could go in to the king. It was the season before she stepped into his court and received power as *"... he set a royal crown on her head..."* (Esther 2:17). She had to take some cleansing steps before she could make a request from the king. God cleans us out in order to fill us up.

The preparation served me well, but it was just the beginning of my cleansing. The day came when I walked into the church office, hesitant and irritated at having to step back into counseling so soon. Only four months had passed since my completion of a three-month period of intensive outpatient treatment. In my mind, I did not need this. I was sober and doing just fine. I was separated from my husband, estranged from my two children, working my fingers to the bone to make ends meet, and crying myself to sleep at night.

Despite my cynicism, this room would prove significant. In fact, of all the rooms I had passed through up to this point, the impact of this one was the most astonishing. My transformation was ignited in this very "Damascus room" of my own.

The passageway leading to this room had a bookshelf full of great Christian books. I began to scan the spines. I used my fingers to walk from book to book, reciting their titles as I went. My hand landed on *Christ in You*. The title made no sense to me, but it was about to be clarified. I had accepted Him as Savior, yet this phrase sounded strange. I tilted my head, shrugged my shoulders, and turned an unexpected corner in my life. Although I did not know it yet, Christ was about to step into me in a greater way.

That day, I walked into a room just like the room the apostle Paul entered in Damascus (see Acts 9:17-18). I did not even know such a room existed. My Ananias was a woman named Vicki D. It might sound silly, but that is what I call her. I did not know such power of impartation existed. There was no reference point in my life for it.

What we are taught or not taught so often limits us and keeps us in bondage. I was in denial of the fullness of God's Holy Spirit. I did not deny the existence, but I did not understand how the Spirit could live within me. If you are unsure as I once was, my desire is to make certain that you leave this book understanding the availability of the Holy Spirit in all His fullness. We are going to take each step up, hand in hand, and I will explain these truths all the way up the stairs.

Here in this room is where I received a healing that I was not aware was available; it was a healing I was sure I did not deserve. Yet, I emptied myself out enough to allow God to have all of me. That is the very beginning of our stairway: openness to God. It is the point at which the rubber tip of your shoe touches the baseboard below the first stair. It is the initiation of humility, the freedom to surrender in brokenness and begins our journey into healing.

Vicki D. opened the conversation. "Jennifer, I am so glad you decided to show up. I told your husband I would not call you. He told me he hoped you would come."

Her voice was soft, and when I crossed the threshold of her office, I got dizzy. It was not the same kind of dizziness I experienced at the treatment center. Now I was strong and physically healthy. I was dizzy because she carried the Spirit of the Lord within her in such capacity that His glory was overflowing all around her. I was love-struck by His Spirit and confounded, all at the same time.

I sat down and breathed deeply. I now knew how to combat anxiety with healthy methods, but this was not anxiety; this was new and mysterious. Even though my flesh was uncomfortable, I did not want to combat the unknown feeling. The most amazing thing, other than the obvious anointing or presence of God, was the love in her eyes. I had never seen anything like it. God in her was fascinating and comforting.

I knew the counseling systems well, so I cut through the small talk by getting straight to the significant part. "I am done, Vicki. I do not want to go back to that house or that marriage. But I miss my children and I feel like I am doing to them what was done to me."

My voice cracked. Once again, I had to do the eyes looking up thing to try to dry up the tears.

"What does God want you to do?" She looked into my soul when she spoke. Her eyes had Christ so deeply embedded in them it was difficult to think. She knew my passion for the Scriptures. In fact, she knew everything about me because it was not her, but Christ in her counseling me. I could not be anything other than surrendered in His presence and hers. My attempt would have been futile and defeating.

"He wants me to trust Him and adhere to His covenants." I knew the answer, but knowing the answer is nothing unless you are willing to live it.

"What is covenant to you?"

I only knew the flat definition, so she explained with power from her Spirit. "Covenant is what God promised you when He told you all your sins would be forgiven as He sacrificed His own Son on the cross for you; all of them. You have a representation of that beautiful covenant on earth with your husband." She was soft not an ounce of judgment in her voice.

A tear fell from my eye and in that moment something deep within me grabbed hold of that promise, that covenant and out of sheer thanksgiving I made a vow to reestablish my earthly one as well. With just a shred of hope that God would fix all the brokenness I stepped out of my flesh, goals, plans, fears, insecurities, needs, wants, dreams, life. It was the last surrender, that last goodbye to my flesh, and she knew it.

"Hmm," she said.

At the end of this particular session, Vicki D. stood to her feet and asked, "Do you mind if I lay my hands on you and pray over you?" As she spoke, she walked around her desk slowly; she hummed and rubbed her hands together; her eyes closed in prayer.

"Sure," I said weeping in my emptiness, surprised. I breathed in a sweet aroma.

"Jennifer, God sees your obedience and He will bless obedience. He knows your heart and He honors those who honor Him, His ways, and His covenants."

She hummed again after speaking. Her voice was always soft and filled with the genuine authority of God.

"I know God has me in His hand," I said. "I can feel the weightlessness."

As I spoke these words, I believed who Christ was; but I did not yet have the ability to understand what He intended for my life because my sin was keeping me veiled. We are not able to comprehend His ways without His Spirit. I was still in operation mode instead of flow mode. (This point will become clear as our journey unfolds.) In simple terms, I did not yet know what was meant by the words, "...Christ in you the hope of glory" (Col. 1:27).

I lowered my head, closed my eyes, and had no idea that I was allowing myself, that is my flesh, to die. Vicki placed her hands on my head and began to pray for me. Her words went from recognizable ones into a language I could not interpret. My spirit, however, was familiar with every syllable. I began to cry with no effort on my part. My tears dropped so fast and hard they splashed upward as they plinked off the thin pages of my Bible, which was open on my lap.

Vicki D. asked God to protect me and not let me be like Lot's wife. I had just privately studied that account the night before. She was praying for me, standing in the gap created by my lack of understanding. While I had followed the Lord's guidance to read that passage of Scripture, I had not yet known what to pray for.

She prayed in her prayer language for a while. In the midst of it came a discernible voice in English: "Jennifer, My beautiful daughter, welcome home. I have been calling you since I gave you ears to listen. Stay on My narrow path; each step will lead you closer to Me."

It was God's voice through Vicki D. I felt a rush of wind and warmth. In that moment, God allowed me to understand His fullness, the concept of Christ in me for eternity.

The Seal of Renewal

We will explain this fullness as we travel up the staircase. I can tell you now that this power has made healing possible for me. What I received from God, that day was the baptism of the Holy Spirit or the fullness of the Holy Spirit.

You may have already experienced the fullness in your own life and praise God, if not keep stepping because we are going to grab hold of this powerful truth. Luke explains this baptism in the Book of Acts:

> *Suddenly a sound like the blowing of a violent wind came from heaven and filled the whole house where they were sitting. They saw what seemed to be tongues of fire that separated and came to rest on each of them. All of them were filled with the Holy Spirit and began to speak in other tongues as the Spirit enabled them* (Acts 2:2-4).

From the examples I just shared in my session with Vicki D. you may have a fair sense of this promise. Or you may need more explanation and guidance. We will be diligent to cover this truth so that you and every reader will receive the teaching that is necessary to healing. Revelatory learning is imperative for the permanence of our healing.

> *He saved us, not because of righteous things we had done, but because of His mercy. He saved us through the washing of rebirth*

and renewal by the Holy Spirit, whom He poured out on us generously through Jesus Christ our Savior, so that, having been justified by His grace, we might become heirs having the hope of eternal life (Titus 3:5-7).

God desires for us to experience more than a "taste" of His goodness. He desires us to live and grow through a lifelong journey.

Jesus provided the Holy Spirit's miraculous infilling to equip believers for healing, power-endued ministry, and victorious living. I was ignorant of the fullness of God's Holy Spirit. No one ever taught me. Therefore, I did not understand how the Spirit could live within me. Little did I know at first that, as the new birth brings us into eternal life and prepares us for Heaven, so the fullness of the Spirit equips our present life with authority, power, healing, joy, and peace. A piece of heaven deposited into our being!

Jewel for the Journey

The Holy Spirit will transport us from knowing Scripture intellectually with an occasional spiritual encounter, to living Scripture intimately with the revelation of a spiritual perspective.

In order that we, who were the first to hope in Christ, might be for the praise of His glory. And you also were included in Christ when you heard the word of truth, the gospel of your salvation. Having believed, you were marked in Him with a seal, the promised Holy Spirit, who is a deposit guaranteeing our inheritance until the redemption of those who are God's possession—to the praise of His glory (Ephesians 1:12-14).

For a season, I was like an eager puppy following my "Ananias" around and draining the wisdom out of her. Vicki D. told me that I did not drain her. She told me I gave her as much as she gave me. She even told me God had placed me in her heart, and praise Him because if not, I surely would have run her off. So often, in our healing we unknowingly help others as well as ourselves. As long as we are stepping up, we are useful for God's Kingdom.

For two years straight, I read Scripture endlessly. It nourished me! The New Testament is covenant guaranteed. The Comforter or Holy Spirit remains available to the Church until Jesus' return (see 1 Cor. 1:7). The spiritual gifts have not ceased. The Spirit is the seal on the promise of healing that is inherent to His covenant people. Not everyone experiences these things exactly as I did. God ordains a spiritual journey custom-suited to each saint. The fullness of Christ in us, however, is available to everyone who receives Him.

Sometimes the infilling of the Holy Spirit accompanies our salvation. Sometimes, it comes later, as it did for me. Before I received the infilling, I definitely felt the Holy Spirit move in my life. But I had not yet come to a place where I had a limitless source; an overflowing well of God's love. I kept too many obstacles in place.

Upon receiving salvation, we have access to the indwelling of the Spirit. The Spirit's intent is to reside in us full time and overflow out of us. This is the completeness that requires us to surrender our desires and seek only Him. We do this by faith and with a willingness to receive what He offers.

Among the gifts of the Spirit are the *word of wisdom* and the *word of knowledge*. I have experienced both. These gifts and others are listed in First Corinthians 12:7-11. I also have a prayer language; Romans 8:26-27 supports this truth.

The gifts empower us to minister to others. Over the years, I have witnessed physical and emotional healings by God through His saints. Since that day in Vicki D.'s office, I received discernment and a teaching gift that surpasses my capabilities (see Eph. 4:11). I am not the only one to whom God has given gifts. I just believe God's entire Word and I remain open to His work in me.

The Hope of Glory

As I suggested earlier, the infilling of the Holy Spirit can occur 20 years after salvation is received. The promise of the Spirit relies on our surrender and God's order, which is specific to the need. Three specific examples in the Book of Acts teach us not to presume that everyone must follow the same order (see Acts 2:38, 8:15, and 10:47). We will break them down in our P^3 study.

God poured out His Spirit in all three cases. The truth that is fundamental to all three is this: we need the fullness of His Spirit to walk in freedom during our lives. This seal is a deposit, earnest, or a piece or promise of heaven on earth (see Eph. 1:14). As Matthew 6:10 tells us, *"on earth as it is in heaven!"*

I believe there is a healing for you; it is found in the pages of the Bible, in the power of the resurrection, and through the infilling to fullness of the Holy Spirit that can accompany you through life. I thought I understood this when I accepted Christ as a teen, but I was missing the power that was available. I also blocked that power with my choices. My salvation was a mixture of the right words and the wrong actions, including severe disobedience on my part. I was all talk and very little walk.

Sadly, if we are not vigilant, salvation can quickly become an event that happened in the past. When the Bible is just a story to us; when we pick and choose the parts to which we will adhere; we end up sitting atop a dunghill of denial. On that heap of hopelessness, we often inadvertently deny the deliverance of healing that we desperately need.

While the Spirit enters the believer upon salvation, few people release enough faith to allow the fullness, or infilling, of the Spirit to reside within them. Too often our Sunday schools get stuck in the comfortable zone of teaching about Noah's Ark, the whale's belly, and the manger. Few venture far enough to get the children filled up with the fullness of the Holy Spirit. I believe this is the very reason our society is hurting; we are missing this critical step. Therefore, we lack the capacity to understand His ways and bring healing. Without His Counselor, the Holy Spirit, we can do neither.

We need to be filled to overflowing. Raise your hands! Yes, right now—set the book down and raise your hands. Praise Him. Sing to Him. Love Him. Drink Him into your hurting heart. Then lie down with your face in the floor and tell Him you are sorry. Tell Him you want His blood covering, the fullness of His infilling and His healing. Believe, have faith, and let your emotions and mind play catch-up later. Many times, faith involves believing the truth of God's promises even before we see their truth in our life.

If you desire to be filled in this way, pray this prayer:

I believe in Jesus Christ. He is God's son. He died for my sins. He was resurrected. After He ascended to heaven, I believe God deployed His Holy Spirit, so the promise of His life can live inside of me. Seal me, Father. I no longer wish to tap into the power of your Holy Spirit. I want You to unpack the power inside my being and take up residence. Forgive me, Jesus! I choose to have my flesh die for You, Christ. Replace all of me with You. Baptize me in your Holy Spirit in Jesus name.

Allow your faith to meet His faithfulness. If you are still struggling with this death to self and the infilling of His Spirit, do not give up. "God things" rarely happen according to our plans. Feeling unsure or fearful is normal. This will make more sense as you gain more knowledge. We still have 12 chapters to go, and I promise to do my part. I know God always does His.

We are walking the steps of healing from death into life—my death into life and your death into life. As you read, you may remember having already experienced this transformation in some area of your life. You may be rejoicing and praising God at this very moment. You may also be in desperate need of healing in some other areas. I pray now that you will surrender the pain and allow your feet to step up, up, up into the Holy of Holies where Jesus lives within us— *"...Christ in you the hope of glory"* (Col. 1:27).

Your Worth in Him

The transition out of denial and into healing starts at the foot of the cross with our surrender and without denial to the fullness of God's Spirit. Our purpose in Christ is for a hope and a future (see Jer. 29:11). God has ordained everyone's transformation, but we must claim His promise and healing by refusing to deny that we have a sinful nature (PP).

We hinder the work of healing simply by choosing our own way. We need to notice and honor God's unusual way of doing things. For example, His Word reveals how He transformed dirt into life: *"The LORD God formed the man from the dust of the ground and breathed into his nostrils the breath of life, and the man became a living being"* (Gen. 2:7).

Just as God breathed life into Adam, He took my dirt, breathed life into the mess that I was, and turned my failure into purpose. His way of doing things is supernatural. His process leading to victory looks different from the way we do things. At the same time, His ways allow for us to come out from under the destruction in and around us. He gives us hope.

The key is to recognize where we are without Him and quit denying it. Once we realize our denial and let it go, we begin to see the whole picture more clearly. Suddenly, we catch glimpses of promise. The road might still look grim, but we have taken our first step in an upward direction. Hope is bred in these small successes. These small achievements are the steps that lead to the fullness of healing we desire (see Zechariah 4:10).

Defeating denial and practicing hope—these are keys to receiving a lasting healing. Check to see whether there is a flicker of self-worth beginning to glow. As it rises up in you, take hold of the power it releases (including, but not limited to, the sense of divine purpose that is revealed).

There is a call deep within you, and that beautiful purpose is real and will keep you moving forward even when you become tired (PP).

The first moment I felt the true worth of what God intended me to be was on this very step. The experience brings me back to the song "Masquerade" that I referenced in the Introduction. The lyrics describe what was going on in my heart when I began to catch those glimmers of promise:

> *As messed up as I am, still You bring me in.*
> *You take me in Your arms and hold me.*
> *The worthlessness I feel, You make it disappear.*
> *You are always there, You're endless.*[1]

Hope was beginning to rise up inside me. It didn't happen all at once. You might still feel hopeless. That is OK; you are in the process of healing. If this stepping upward were easy, you would have done it years ago. He can restore and replace what you feel you have lost. As He said in Joel 2:25, *"I will restore to you the years that the locust hath eaten..."* (KJV).

One day, my son came running in to the bathroom, gasping for air, and said, "Mom, there is a locust outside. He is blackish-green with wings and bulging eyes. What does he eat? Will he bite me?"

Jewel for the Journey

Here is a piece of hope: God can take what the devil purposed to harm you and make it into healing power for you.

I could not help but reply, "No, sweetheart. If he is in our yard he is very full from eating all of Mommy's years." I figured I would explain the conundrum later.

The point is that healing becomes obvious over time. The more your divine purpose peeks above the surface, the easier it is to make your way up the staircase. Inch by inch, you begin to realize that you have the faith you need to be healed and stay healed.

The more we see God's changes within us, the stronger our faith becomes. Increasingly, faith strengthens hope, as Hebrews 11:1 reveals: *"Now faith is the substance of things hoped for, the evidence of things not seen"* (KJV). This is when healing becomes real to us.

The Spirit does the work and we realize God is transforming us, not through our physical strength or ability, but by His Spirit. We begin to notice that being sober, healthy, or peaceful is easier with the passing of each successful day. Before this point, faith is similar to hope; both involve a belief in what is unseen. When healing occurs, faith becomes the substance or tangible truth of what Scripture promises.

God desires for us to live in healing. He gives so many gifts to those who love Him, accept His Son, and receive the fullness of the infilling of His Spirit. This is His desire *for you*. He longs to meet your specific needs and wants. If you will see healing as a process and begin to step up the heavenly staircase without denial, unbelief, unhealthy expectations, and fear, healing will become a fact—an achievement—in your life.

Well done! You are ready for your first *P*³!

The Princess Principles Practice

Introduction

For there are three that bear witness in heaven: the Father, the Word, and the Holy Spirit; and these three are one (1 John 5:7 NKJV).

Though one may be overpowered, two can defend themselves. A cord of three strands is not quickly broken (Ecclesiastes 4:12).

The Princess Principle Practice or P^3 (P to the power of 3) is a tool to improve biblical learning and, therefore, healing. The work and requests to journal are fashioned to build the habit of *practicing* God's truths and living out scripture.

The only way to heal and stay healed is to know His Word and walk in His ways. The itemized points listed at the beginning of each P^3 section are practical ways to climb each step of the staircase. Ultimately, the questions, actions, and principles covered will instill a strong biblical foundation in your life. You will not only know truth, you will *live* it.

I highly recommend dedicating a notebook to your P^3 exercises and any other writing you feel inspired to do as you take this journey. Also, feel free to jot down thoughts, underline words, circle ideas, and highlight the text in the book itself, as you read. Writing increases learning and awareness. As you read and reread the feelings and thoughts that come to mind during the healing process, even more healing will occur!

The journaling you do will help you to understand the Scriptures better and embed biblical principles and actions in your daily life. Only one Bible verse has been added to each action and principle. This is intentional. It is important for you to dig through the Word on your own and discover additional passages that relate to the text.

As you study the Scriptures quoted in this book, use your concordance and other tools to find other relevant passages. Referring to a commentary or study Bible is another good idea. If these extra tools are too much to contend with at the moment, just stick with the basics, one of which is to read your Bible daily. (I recommend three chapters a day to keep the devil away!)

Pray before you begin reading or journaling. Pray again when you close. Your time with the Lord in this daily stepping process is imperative. We are going to believe in faith for your healing. Be strong and when you feel weak do not give up. Always rest in Him (see Ps. 46:10). We are not and never will be perfect. Perfection is not even an expectation. We are human and dearly loved by a gracious God who heals us by His love and according to His will. But we must be willing to be healed, regardless of our imperfection. This is one of His inherent truths as it relates to receiving anything from Him.

If you are depressed, fearful, and unsure, keep moving closer to Him. With every step, you will get better. Let us now step into His healing by beginning a friendship with Him through His Word. We will learn all about His ways, expectations, fruit, and above all else, His love. May your travels be blessed.

Pray this prayer:

> *Lord I seek Your face and give You my life. I accept Your Son, Jesus Christ, as my Lord and Savior. There is no other Lord and no other Savior. I am struggling and I have sinned. I surrender my life and transgressions up to You. Please forgive me. Take my mind and make it new. I want to step up and away from the things of this world. I ask You, Father, to fill me with Your Holy Spirit and to guide and protect me on this journey. Give me the ability to understand and live Your truths as You heal me. I love You, Lord. Amen.* (See John 14:6.)

Step Out of Denial:

⁊⁊ Recognize your pain and any unhealthy behaviors.

⁊⁊ Accept the fact that the issues are yours to overcome with God, no matter who is to blame.

⁊⁊ Assign proper responsibility for what caused your pain. Leave others to deal with what they did, while accepting full accountability for your part.

⁊⁊ Take your pain and your deeds to God, asking for His help alone.

⁊⁊ Trust that He is sufficient, knowing that, if you let Him, He will take care of you.

⁊⁊ Know and believe, with hope, that He has a good plan and purpose just for you!

You might think this is impossible, but *all things* are possible with God (see Phil. 4:13). It is time to step out of denial and into hope. Accept your God-ordained path and not the faulty path that leads away from God. Let Jeremiah 6:16 guide you:

> *This is what the LORD says: "Stop at the crossroads and look around. Ask for the old, godly way, and walk in it. Travel its path, and you will find rest for your souls..."* (NLT).

Life Application Action

Hope

Even youths grow tired and weary, and young men [and women] *stumble and fall; but those who hope in the LORD will renew their strength. They will soar on wings like eagles; they will run and not grow weary, they will walk and not be faint* (Isaiah 40:30-31).

Dissect this scripture and notice God realizes our struggles; list the promises He gives us with just hope. Journal about hope in your life. Where do you see a glimmer of hope even in your pain?

Dig deep and ask God for hope regardless of how the landscape of your life looks. You might feel as I did at the base of the first stair: lacking even the energy to hope and without a clue as to where resources or strength could be found. Isaiah 40:30-31 says that, if we can muster hope, God will give us the energy we need to take the next step.

Summary of Princess Principles

 We step out of denial by accepting our responsibility for the duration and depth of pain that we allow.

I will exalt You, O LORD, for You lifted me out of the depths and did not let my enemies gloat over me. O LORD my God, I called to You for help and You healed me. O LORD, You brought me up from the grave; You spared me from going down into the pit (Psalms 30:1-3).

A healthy primary response is to realize that, all we need to accept full responsibility for our healing is to get alone with Christ. A common unhealthy response is to seek a "partner in crime" or a wounded buddy who can help us feel "normal." This is codependency. On this journey, you are responsible only for yourself. List the people you need to release:

 Denial is the blatant rejection of an obvious fault in our character. It is hard to come to terms with denial, but it is not impossible.

Why do you look at the speck of sawdust in your brother's eye and pay no attention to the plank in your own eye? (Matthew 7:3).

Consider your pain and determine which of your behaviors is serving to keep the pain intact. When you begin to understand that you have the ability through Christ to stop the habit, you begin to see your role. Often, we continue bad routines because we do not want to stop or we feel helpless to stop. This is where Christ and His truth come in: they reveal truth so we can recognize any lie under which we are living. Write a prayer accepting *your* fallible nature:

 When we realize God loves us and is not accusing us, we begin to
P P **understand relationship with Him, stepping us into healing.**

> *Therefore, there is now no condemnation for those who are in Christ*
> *Jesus, because through Christ Jesus the law of the Spirit of life set me*
> *free from the law of sin and death* (Romans 8:1-2).

He not only sets us free from the pain but He sets us free from condemning ourselves. You have not gone too far this time. When you come to Him the old is gone and the new begins. We can always start over and step toward freedom. Pray aloud for God to show you freedom from condemnation. Circle the word *in* and write what He sets us free from. Journal about the difference between conviction and condemnation:

 God has ordained everyone's transformation, but we must claim His
P P **promise and healing by refusing to deny that we have a sinful nature.**

> *Do not conform any longer to the pattern of this world, but be*
> *transformed by the renewing of your mind. Then you will be able to*
> *test and approve what God's will is—His good, pleasing and perfect*
> *will* (Romans 12:2).

For some reason our flesh and sinful mind love details and drama; God wants us to stay above them. They are tactics from the devil to keep us sick. Journal any areas that you know are unnecessary patterns in your life, mind, and actions:

There is a call deep within you, and that beautiful purpose is real and will keep you moving forward even when you become tired.

"For I know the plans I have for you," declares the LORD, "plans to prosper you and not to harm you, plans to give you hope and a future" (Jeremiah 29:11).

During your healing, you will begin to recognize that your weakest points are often just a counterattack from the devil to hide your strengths. Write down the good Christ has for you. If you are so sad that you cannot see good yet ask Him in prayer to help you see what He is promising you in Jeremiah.

Before we take the next step, let us summarize:

First, we will take full responsibility for our pain. We can accept and acknowledge our pain and stop hiding. We do not have to take responsibility for stuff we did not do, but we must allow God to fix our issues whether we caused them or not. That is our responsibility.

Admit your specific pain. Now journal about what you cannot fix in your life. Tell God aloud that you are releasing it all to Him; you know He is not condemning you and you know He loves you. He created you, of course He loves you!

Congratulations! You have successfully navigated your first step. You have *stepped out of denial* and into *hope*. I am so proud of you. Next, you will discover how to release control with faith and step into submission to God. This next step should produce a release of some of the pressure you feel—so keep going.

Step up Kingdom princess, step up!

Endnote

1. "Masquerade," Seventh Day Slumber, © 2005, BMC Recordings/EMD.

Chaper Two

We Are Not the Ultimate Authority

Step Two: Relinquish Control, by Faith

And I will put My Spirit in you and move you to follow My decrees and be careful to keep My laws (Ezekiel 36:27).

Fear: Breeding Ground of Control

TRYING to control your world is as helpful as attempting to exit the room of your pain by stepping out of a window: If the window is high enough, control is exactly what you lose. If the window is low enough, you could end up under the control of a briar bush.

We need to realize that when we think we are in control of things or people, we are actually making self-sabotaging and even life-threatening decisions. Control has no upside. God intended us to permit only His control in our lives. His control is real power. When combined with our faith, it is the force that brings healing (PP).

In fact, the window in The Masquerade was inoperable, hidden, and too small to get through. Any windows that are part of our pain will always be too small to serve as exits. We stand at these openings and holler for help. In reality, the deadbolt has already been unlocked with the key of our salvation in Christ. Yet, there we remain, stuck screaming in satan's employment pool.

We refuse to do the very thing that would free us: we refuse to release control and let God help us turn the doorknob. As long as we refuse, the unturned knob prevents us from leaving.

There are as many ways to stay in control as there are people. A few methods I used were justification, pride, depression, blame, judgment, false opinions, and a victim mentality. To these seven I added a twist of manipulation and stubbornness. The sad part was my failure to realize that I was operating deceitfully. We rarely see our sin.

My irrational need to control people, my emotions, circumstances, and surroundings was rooted in deeper issues like fear and anger. It was keeping me sick. What I thought was holding everything together was the very thing tearing me apart. The devil is an expert at keeping us tied up in the incidentals so that we overlook the real issues and the bigger picture of our purpose.

Eventually, I recognized that I was the one keeping me sick. I stepped out of the denial; but I was still so overwhelmed in sickness that the root cause seemed impossible to fix. This is the place where we so often give up because, until we accept the fact that we are incapable of fixing ourselves, we will not release the pain to God.

Which methods do you see yourself using to control your pain? Do you employ any of the methods I mentioned? Look deep into your heart and allow God to reveal any devices you are using. And know this: At some point, we all depend on something to stay in control. If that something is not God, then the hurt will resurface.

The Blame Game

I was convinced my pain was justified. There was always a good reason: the way my parents raised me, or my husband's behavior, or the weather that day. I could not assume blame. My pride had to stay intact. The shell of arrogance was the only thing holding me up. So often, we find an overinflated ego attached to severe pain. I see anger and pride as the reverse of depression even as far as to say it is our evil nature attempting to create depression in others; yet we use both to hide and control our hurt.

When we point fingers, we operate in a false sense of control. We think that blaming someone or something else frees us from responsibility for our actions. We even think hurting others will somehow relieve our pain. Never the case! Therefore, we believe we are still in control. The only thing we are still controlling is the duration of our pain. We keep the pain from healing and ensure a longer battle! In our ignorance, we think we have found a scapegoat who will accept the guilty verdict for us. It is one of satan's favorite methods for keeping us in bondage.

Opinions that do not line up directly with Scripture keep us bound. The certainty of God's Word is where we must base our claims. That is where we can experience freedom. We also need to realize that the people in our lives have no control over our healing. As long as we listen to God, He can heal us—even if their behavior defies our standards and His.

God has our best interests at heart. We are responsible for choosing His ways over ours and the devil's. The devil wants us to think letting go is scary; but it is not scary to let God heal you. Either way, Second Timothy 1:7 (NKJV) says, *"God has not given us a spirit of fear, but of power and of love and of a sound mind."*

Accepting Jesus was the beginning of my healing. Inviting the fullness of His Holy Spirit activated the actual manifestation of healing in my life. This is the subject many churches and Bible studies do not cover. The infilling is where true healing and power reside.

Jewel for the Journey

Replacing a victim mentality by giving God total control of our lives is true empowerment.

It comes down to being willing to let go completely. We need to be totally emancipated from our control if we are to obtain God's healing, gifts, and power. We cannot expect to remain in ultimate authority over our lives *and* be healed.

Same Ole, Same Ole

It was the same old routine. I had been there before. I knelt and then fell to the floor in tears. With my head on my hands, I rolled myself up into as tight a ball as I could. All I wanted was to protect myself from any more pain. The problem is that, for the most part, the pain I was feeling was on the inside.

Unable to withstand any more hurt, I ached and felt like life had ripped my heart out of my chest. My tears fell. Hyperventilation hindered my breathing. My body was in the fetal position that innately I knew I needed to take as a representation of a new birth, but every time I uncurled to go back to the dog's vomit instead of my Father's love. I found myself in this position too often, especially when the substances wore off.

"Why me?" I asked. Another syndrome is the all too popular why-me syndrome. "Why do I have to endure this awful pain and depression? Why do I have to feel paralyzed by fear every day? What can I blame? Whose fault can it be? How can I keep the bad feelings from surfacing again?"

I sincerely wanted answers to these questions. I think we all do at times, especially when we are unaware of where the pain is coming from and confused as to how to get rid of it—for good.

Instead of remaining prostrate before God, knowing I was causing most of it and that He had the rest under control, I would eventually get off the floor, stand up, and answer my own questions. Then I would find a worldly method to sweep the pain under the rug and keep it there for as long as I could. It was a vicious cycle that stole almost two decades of my life. Do not let your pain steal any more years from you. He loves you, and your place in the Kingdom is important!

I would remove the cloak of depression (or so I thought) by embracing the cloak of pride and arrogance. It wasn't enough, however. Even at the height of my control as the reigning Roach Princess, I still felt exposed, as though everyone knew about my pain, despite my mask. I still felt vulnerable and sick.

Our improper, calculating attempts to fix things over which we have no power keeps us powerless. Ironic, isn't it? Satan and our need for control has us trapped in the masquerade, hurting behind a closed (yet unlocked, unlatched) door. Although denial is gone, we still find it hard to release our hold. It is tough to let go.

We have claimed ownership, yet we are shocked and rightfully intimidated by the issue. The fear of our lack drives us to "manage" our feelings of inadequacy by quitting. In fear, we attempt to shift even deeper into control. Instead of steadily moving upward, we step off to the side and withdraw from the fight.

What we fail to realize is that we will always lack *something*, but God is sufficient. With Him, we need never give up. He created us. He knows how to care for our every need.

The only thing we accomplish by giving up is to create a mudslide next to our step. It is a bad place to be. The footing is treacherous and we can slip back into denial if we are not careful.

When the desire to quit in fear rises up inside, we need to stay alert. Instead of choosing to control the situation; we must choose to trust God to heal us. We need to opt out of taking control. The truth is, we have no control; but God does.

Do you believe God can handle all the details of your healing? Are you willing to trade your control for His power? Do you understand only your free will can keep the door to freedom closed?

Orange Bottles of Pseudo Peace

I reached into the tiny opening in the pill bottle and pinched a pill between my first two fingers. I could do it in the dark, and most times did. My fingers went too far into the bottle. That meant my supply was dwindling. When pill shortages occurred (and they were often), I immediately felt panic sweep over me. My chest tightened, my stomach soured, and a breathless, threatening fear set in.

I struggled to pull in some air, knowing I would now have to manipulate somebody in order to get a refill. The insurance company monitored the timing of my refills, but I did not care. I would pay out of pocket, if necessary. The doctor stood between me and my supply; I would have to get her to agree with me, even though the insurance and pharmaceutical laws backed her up.

The obstacles were plentiful. All I wanted was to be in control. Control would quiet the panic. I would feel safe, if only for a time. Control is deceptive. It provides a sense of healing that is nothing more than a counterfeit (PP).

Acknowledging the devious and debilitating nature of denial and control will help open the door to healing. Be aware, however, that denial and control will try to weave themselves into every issue that comes up. We need wisdom to recognize and eradicate bad habits that attempt to surface or resurface. We must be aware that satan whispers in our ears. We must be quick to shut him down.

I did not know what to do with the symptoms plaguing me. My "solution" (a wrong, unhelpful approach) was to numb myself with substances and guard the mess with pride. It was my feeble attempt to control my out-of-control situation. These attempts were exhausting. Manipulation always causes more damage, more pain, and more issues.

Do you see similar tendencies in your life? Can you identify areas which you attempt to control? Are they typically related to your emotions, physical appearance, surroundings, circumstances, or other people? When the devil comes calling, are you willing to resist him and wait on God, in faith?

Afraid to Be Free

There are so many memories from the years of my captivity—the hiding... feelings of inadequacy...fear of weakness...the destructive behaviors designed to camouflage my overwhelming insecurities.

There was never a shortage of control devices in my arsenal. Smoking was one. I remember how my nervous hand shook as I inhaled the smoke into my lungs. My fear of being seen smoking made me nervous. When sober, I could never have a cigarette without feeling guilty.

Like any other vice, there is always the issue of supply. Just like the pills, my cigarettes kept running out. I remember buying them more than I remember smoking them. The same was true for the beer I bought at the convenience store. The smell of gasoline and the shade of the gas port became as familiar as home to me.

This was the life I was used to living. It had become a kind of comfort zone—so much so that when I arrived at the door of freedom and noticed that the deadbolt was disengaged, I wanted to reengage the lock. I would not relinquish control of my habits. I refused to allow God to open the door. I was afraid of all the pain that would manifest the minute I became sober. I was not trusting God to be my comfort.

Do you believe that God can comfort you and protect you as He heals you?

It sounds hard to believe, but we are often more afraid of healing than we are of being sick. We see the sickness as a safe place, an evil cushion of familiarity, if only because the unknown is intimidating. Please let me give you hope: Familiarity is not the answer. We have a far better solution in God. His Holy Spirit fills and heals us. It is the closest thing to Heaven on this earth. There is no reason to give up. Healing need not frighten us!

Jewel for the Journey

Have you ever asked God to fill you to fullness or baptize you with His Holy Spirit?

In this world, God's truths are often disregarded or forgotten; that is the reason sickness is so prevalent. If you have not received the fullness of His Spirit, ask Him. Keep asking Him until you get it. The Gospel of Luke assures us of His desire to fill us:

If you then, though you are evil, know how to give good gifts to your children, how much more will your Father in heaven give the Holy Spirit to those who ask Him! (Luke 11:13)

Having received from God, you will be better suited for your journey—freer to be healed and better able to share the healing power of God with others.

As we said, this process is individual; it is different for everyone. Do not expect your life to follow the same diagram as someone else's. Your neighbor's vision is not your vision.

We need to let go of some stuff before the abundance can reside. When I held onto my pain on those first few steps, I made little "room" for the fullness God offered. Yet, I still made it up the flight. He knows if your heart is right. If it is, He will heal you and fill you to overflowing.

Remember, He does not expect us to be certain about those first steps. I wasn't. I proceeded with trepidation and uncertainty, not really wanting to move. We are not supposed to be certain. This is the step where faith comes in and fills the gap.

Freedom From Alcohol and Nicotine

The garage in our second home is a room I will never forget. God got my attention there. It was several years into my marriage, but before I discovered God's fullness; I was in the worst stage of my alcohol and nicotine addictions.

One evening, during my late twenties, I stood in that garage, inebriated and listening to the radio. I had already told God, a bazillion times, that I had taken my last dance with the devil. I kept promising to get sober. This time was different: I admitted my inability to get sober and asked Him to do it. The only station I could get in that garage was a Christian radio station. A praise song came on and I began to dance, this time with God. I praised Him and thanked Him for the life I did feel in those moments when I allowed it. I cried with hands raised and thanked Him for my children and husband. I danced, wept, laughed, and jumped for my Savior.

Worship comes before warfare. Ground was about to be taken. I did not know at the time that Jesus had already gone to hell and paid for this exact sliver of my life. I did not realize He had already done the work for me—but He had.

In our weakness, He is strong. I screamed out the name that is above all names: "Jesus! Jesus! Jesus! Heal me. Save me. Make me OK with You. Help me to understand You. I release the control of alcohol and cigarettes on my life."

On that night, I gave that part of my heart to Him. Loving Father that He is, He gave it back to me healed. I was free from the addiction to alcohol and cigarettes, in an instant! Like a child, I sought God's face. I worshiped Him at one of the lowest points in my life. He knew I was steeped in brokenness, wallowing in the pit of addiction, control, anxiety, and fear. It was then that He turned the tide.

Notice that I spoke aloud to the exact hurt that needed healing. Speak to *your* disease, issue, or pain directly. Command it to leave in Jesus' name and by the power of Christ's blood.

Now, I was ready to let go of the alcohol and cigarettes. He took them; I was healed from the very thing I was ready to give Him. All we have to do is be ready to let go of the issue and then release it fully. Whatever piece we hold on to in an effort to control the situation will keep us sick.

How many times had I cried out to Him before this eventful night? I cannot say. But all of my pleas cumulated in this very precious moment. Somehow, my wrong way of dealing had shifted; I moved out of control mode and into humility. I allowed my hunger for help and healing to be seen. I trusted His ability to provide for me. I believed that He was enough for me and able to replace the habit with wholeness.

My trust in Him and my releasing of control were all that were necessary for God to deliver me in that moment. It was a beautiful step into faith. God was real and so was His healing. We were building a bond of trust together. Several years later, I allowed Him deeper access to soften my heart, which gradually gave Him access to more of my broken soul.

I did not realize at that moment, still in my late twenties, that my garage deliverance was a miracle. I still had stuff in my pocket that I was not ready to give up. Until I decided to give it all up in my thirties I was keeping myself hindered from seeing the fullness of what had occurred. I entered the right process, but continued to hold out on God. I allowed a partial work, which we all so often do, but He promises us in Philippians 1:6 if we allow Him, He will finish the good work.

Step Forward by His Spirit

Each time we take a step forward, He is pleased. His yoke is easy and His burden is light (see Matt. 11:30). Often we say, "I could never please God, so why even try?" That is another form of control. Giving up and perfectionism—the all-or-nothing approaches to life—are control issues. They have no place in the Kingdom. Giving up or trying too hard with the arm of the flesh is why we are sick to begin with. Jesus is the only example of perfection; the rest of us fall short (see Rom. 3:23).

Now, we are not to disregard the command of Matthew 5:48 to *"Be perfect, therefore, as your heavenly Father is perfect."* There is a difference between perfectionism and the godly striving toward Christ's likeness. The latter is about allowing the Holy Spirit to sanctify us. The former is about us trying to paint the perfect picture of self.

Zechariah 4:6 warns: *"'Not by might nor by power, but by My Spirit,' says the* LORD *Almighty."* I will remind you of this verse often. We must accept our imperfection as we navigate up the stairs. Healing happens when we release control for refinement into His image, knowing that we are incapable of succeeding without His Spirit (PP).

In that garage, God and I had a moment of healing and trust that superseded anything I had ever known. He gave me a taste of freedom and I held that flavor in the understanding of my heart. This step defined my faith for the next level of healing.

In the exuberance that freedom brings, it is important to remember that the timing must always be God's. We know healing is a process; yet we can manipulate it to suit our comfort level or expectations. On the one hand, we can make excuses for dilly-dallying on a certain step. Equally unhealthy is the attempt to get ahead of God. We need to let Him finish before we move on; until God is finished, we must stay put.

I was not ready to die out yet and still quite blind. What an example of trying to be in command of our destiny. There is always this resistance to allowing God to rule it all. You can see how many wrong methods I used to attempt to break free and how hesitant I was to release total control. I had a crowbar wedged in the door that led to freedom; but I also had my head hanging out the window hollering, "Victim!" On both sides of the issue, I tried to exert my control over God's.

Looking back, my sin seems so obvious, sad, and strange; but in the midst of the battle, I was either oblivious or scared of my failure to please God. Now that alcohol and cigarettes were abandoned, I attached my foolish affections more strongly to the orange opaque bottles full of temporary peace.

The Sandcastle

Finally, I had left the denial and control around my alcoholism and smoking at the foot of the cross. Those sins had been visible to all—and they were ugly. The ones I still had were more subtle and easier to hide. Therefore, I kept them and the mindset of sickness and death that accompanied them.

First Timothy 5:24 explains: *"The sins of some men are obvious, reaching the place of judgment ahead of them; the sins of others trail behind them."*

My knee-jerk response to confusion and pain was to foolishly assume that I had control of my environment. I was confused as to what happened with the alcohol and I was scared to accept it as a miracle from God. If it had been a miracle, then I would have to trust God with my other issues. So I decided to cope with my remaining "stuff" by managing my surroundings. Instead of getting better, my husband and I decided to buy a better house. We were not yet trusting the truth that His power is sufficient.

Too often, we purchase boats, cars, planes, houses, clothes, vacations, club memberships, and countless other things as a way to fill the void only God's fullness can satisfy. Now I know we need some of these things but we are all aware there is also a stuff syndrome. When we buy to supply satisfaction, we are attempting to control our pain by altering our surroundings. Ignorance works temporarily, at least until our nagging pain reveals that the only thing we changed was the wallpaper.

My husband and I purchased our third home just as I was sobering up, by God's grace, from my 14-year bout with beer, wine, and cigarettes. However, I was knee-deep in the medicine chest and neck-deep in my own power. It was like being in the purgatory room at The Masquerade; I wasn't in hell yet, and a long way from Heaven.

When we are mired in transition, we need to keep forging ahead remembering His scripture, *"being confident of this, that He who began a good work in you will carry it on to completion until the day of Christ Jesus"* (Phil. 1:6). Only He can bring us out of life's purgatories and into Heaven on earth.

As I tried to fill the void left by the departure of alcohol and cigarettes from my daily routine, I made sure my bag contained a variety of colored pills and my credit card. Drugs, shopping, and a bigger house were suddenly my addictions of choice. But, even the house did not hold up. Like me and my husband, it was sinking. Our home seemed as broken and messed up as our hearts and minds.

Matthew described the condition well:

The rain came down, the streams rose, and the winds blew and beat against that house; yet it did not fall, because it had its foundation on the rock. But everyone who hears these words of mine and does not put them into practice is like a foolish man who built his house on sand. The rain came down, the streams rose, and the winds blew and beat against that house, and it fell with a great crash (Matthew 7:25-27).

Our new home was not built on a solid rock. Over the period of mere months, the front of the house separated from the front porch. New cracks were forming before our eyes. Our kitchen ceiling rippled like waves of sand on a beach. Every corner of the house had separated. The brick was cracked all over.

When I bathed, I looked up at an actual cardboard box top covering a hole in our ceiling and prayed no rain would drive it into the tub with me. We had to remove walls and portions of the roof and cover them in plastic. When I got out of bed, the cold from the concrete floor shot up through my legs. I almost longed for the warm soft carpet that had been in place before the toxic mold infestation required its removal.

The shower in the master bath sank downward along with the foundation. It was unusable for almost two years. Both the kitchen ceiling and the driveway parted like the Red Sea. Tiles cracked and the mortar fell away. The huge front palladium window shattered and stayed that way for several years. Like my attempts at control, the inoperable window served as a weak substitute for genuine protection. I stood vulnerable behind that window, both literally and figuratively.

Many times, you have to look hard at the outside of a structure to detect damage; ours was not one of those cases. The calamity was self-evident. On a spiritual level, the life of denying our idolatry and the effort to control sin without God's power did not create pictures of calamity as profound as the sight of our dying house. Nevertheless, that which happens behind the scenes eventually shows up on some level. We will sink if we do not allow God to ground us in the Word and build us upon the solid rock.

The Parallel of Restoration

This physical illustration also applies to what happened when we turned from our sins, reestablished our covenant with each other and God, and moved forward with nothing but hope and faith in Christ. Starting with solidifying the foundation, God sent laborers who fixed our home. He mended every crack, hole, and break.

The entire structure was made complete. The sheetrock went back up, new carpet went in, the shower fixed, broken windows restored, mold removed, roof leaks sealed, nothing left out because we were willing to trust the process laid out for us. We were on the path God had ordained—and finally, I might add.

We must constantly take heed and step carefully. Moving forward without God is costly. Missteps always lead downward—down and back into control and denial. We need to release control of our emotions and environment; we need to trust God. When we head in His direction, focus on our responsibilities, and stop blaming others, we heal. God then restores, rebuilds, and renews.

> *Give us gladness in proportion to our former misery! Replace the evil years with good. Let us, Your servants, see You work again; let our children see Your glory. And may the Lord our God show us His approval and make our efforts successful. Yes, make our efforts successful!* (Psalms 90:15-17 NLT)

Faith Is the Action Piece

Our Life Application Action for stepping out of control is *faith*. We will have faith to believe that God is in control and will take care of us. We will base our lives in the faith described by Hebrews 11:6:

> *And without faith it is impossible to please God, because anyone who comes to Him must believe that He exists and that He rewards those who earnestly seek Him.*

Trust is not an all-or-nothing virtue. It is one that grows and develops the deeper we go into relationship with God. As we step up, so does our faith.

Your transitions are individual, yet they share certain characteristics with those that occur in the lives of believers across the globe. The bottom line is to accept and serve Christ in everything. If the window keeps us half in and half out of the fullness He offers, why not trust God to see us all the way through in all the right ways? When we leave the need for control behind us for good, we can move on to the next step of the journey.

For now, let me say that I am so proud of your perseverance! You are moving up and being healed. Be patient; do not give up. With your newfound faith, God can now answer your prayers. Believe me, He is faithful!

THE PRINCESS PRINCIPLES PRACTICE

Step Out of Your Control:

- Understand the difference between what you can do and what only God can do.

- Release the demand to do it yourself.

- Step out of the victim mentality and recognize your sinful nature.

- Give everything to God with faith.

Life Application Action

Faith

Now faith is being sure of what we hope for and certain of what we do not see (Hebrews 11:1).

Be sure your release of denial is complete; realize your surrender of control has created blessings you do not see yet. Sometimes, when we hurt the last thing we can find is faith adding to our defeat. Break Hebrews 11:1 down listing what faith is to you:

We eventually understand how our feelings and limited sight interfere with what God wants us to see. The scriptural essence of faith is this: We believe even when we do not see anything. Believe in your healing right now, even if walls of fear and pain are all you see. You are not trapped; I can attest to this fact.

Summary of Princess Principles

 God intended us to permit only His control in our lives. His control is real power. When combined with our faith, it is the force that brings healing.

And if the Spirit of Him who raised Jesus from the dead is living in you, He who raised Christ from the dead will also give life to your mortal bodies through His Spirit, who lives in you (Romans 8:11).

Ask God in a written prayer to reveal His resurrection power to you:

 Control is deceptive. It provides a sense of healing that is nothing more than a counterfeit.

The mind of sinful man is death, but the mind controlled by the Spirit is life and peace (Romans 8:6).

List ways you can assure you have the mind of Christ in order to discern any counterfeit "operations" keeping you bonded:

Healing happens when we release control for refinement into His image, knowing that we are incapable of succeeding without His Spirit.

"Not by might nor by power, but by my Spirit," says the LORD Almighty (Zechariah 4:6).

We need to store this verse in our memory banks (I will assist by repeating it often). Accepting our imperfection and remembering His perfection keep us grounded as we mount the stairs. Journal what you have experienced so far by allowing control of His Spirit's work in your life:

 His Power Is Sufficient

But He said to me, "My grace is sufficient for you, for My power is made perfect in weakness." Therefore I will boast all the more gladly about my weaknesses, so that Christ's power may rest on me" (2 Corinthians 12:9).

Do you understand that we have received by grace, but in order to hold on to the healing we need to diligently step His ways out for life. Pray for God to give you His power to walk in His ways.

It is time to learn about His power! God sent His only Son to die for our sins. We know He is the only way to Heaven. Once Jesus is in your heart and life, you are saved and indwelled by the Holy Spirit. You have the ability to tap into His power—so tap in!

Scripture says there are three who testify in Heaven: the Father, Jesus, and the Holy Spirit, who are one (see 1 John 5:7-8 NKJV). These three form the Godhead or Trinity.

This is an imperative truth—a bit basic, but we need to focus on the basics if we have pain issues. We have talked about the infilling of the Holy Spirit and the deeper walk with God. The baptism of the Holy Spirit is this infilling. It means releasing everything to Him so we can allow the fullness of His Spirit in us. This is not a theological argument or a denominational preference. This is a biblical truth (see Acts 1:5). We will learn more about it in Chapter 8; for now we know that this infilling facilitates our sanctification into His likeness—hence our healing.

We need this for our journey, but if you have not yet experienced this impartation, don't stop here. Keep going. Keep asking for understanding along the stairs. God knows exactly when you are ready for His fullness. He freely gives and He never gives a moment too soon. He is an on-time God. So hope in faith, believe in the unseen, and discern the Scriptures for yourself, with His guidance.

God opens our eyes in the midst of our brokenness and desire for Him. As we learn to walk humbly into His love with repentant hearts, we begin to heal. What we are willing to release is in direct proportion to what we are able to receive from Him. If you want power, freedom, joy, and peace, you must let go of everything that is contrary. Keep a contrite heart and a willingness to change into His likeness. Know you are fallible and know that is OK; keep reevaluating your sin and asking for forgiveness.

If you still feel unsure about the things we are discussing, you are normal. Let me share a secret: Just love God with all your heart and trust that He will work in your life. It is OK to wonder about what has happened in your life so far and to be a bit timid of your future if you are hurting. As you release your sin and pain to Him, it will all begin to make sense.

Be willing to step up; also be willing to retrace the previous step if you need to. Whatever you do, please do not stop! Keep releasing yourself into His hands and trust Him. You are healing!

Congratulations! You have *stepped out of control*. You have also added the Life Application Action of *faith* and are aware of the baptism of the Holy Spirit (see Acts 1:5). God sees your hard work. He is proud of you, and so am I. You are beautiful and getting stronger every day!

Step up mighty princess, step up!

Chapter Three

Submit to the King and Be Healed

Step Three: Surrender to God in Prayer

But He gives us more grace. That is why Scripture says: "God opposes the proud but gives grace to the humble." Submit yourselves, then, to God. Resist the devil, and he will flee from you" (James 4:6-7).

Afraid to Close the Patriarchal Umbrella

GOD intended for us to be friends with Him. So often, we revere Him to the extent that we are willing to prepare an Easter basket or place a manger on the mantel. As we blaze through life in our fury and all on our pagan calendar we forget God. When Christmas ends, we take Him down, the same way we do the pilgrim doll when Thanksgiving is over. On December 26, we store the healing power in the attic for another year.

This is not God's desire for our relationship with Him. He wants us to take Him off the mantel and allow Him to *be* our mantel every day. In order to be healed and stay healed, we must deepen our intimacy with Him.

When we do this, our friendship with God comes to life. The free-will door on our masquerade is always ready to open, if we are willing. We are free to welcome His ways and gain access to the narrow stairway leading to the holiest place on earth, The Holy of Holies, God's presence. If you will get into an intimate place with God, He will heal you.

It hinders our healing to pretend that God cannot be our friend. We revere Him, of course. But is our version of reverence pleasing to Him or to us? The issue is whether or not we have cultivated an intimate daily relationship with Him. Why is it so hard to believe that He wants to know us personally? Why do we attempt to regulate our relationship with God according to secular or "religious" expectations and rules?

Jewel for the Journey

Evaluate your beliefs and allow God to deconstruct and reconstruct them as He sees fit.

God is the great I AM. He is perfect and He is perfect love. Many of us have been hurt, abandoned, rejected, smothered, or controlled by our earthly parental figures. As a result, we project their characteristics onto God. It is a fallacious view, because God's love is flawless. If a family member inflicted pain, your intimacy with your Heavenly Father is the only cure for the sting. As I was healing and being filled with the fullness of God's Holy Spirit, I could not understand why I felt so bothered by the way my parents raised me. I honor them and love them for the provision and love they provided. However, I had to work through my pain for years. I needed God to restore the lack of spiritual truth presented in our home (even though, from a worldly perspective, the deficiency looked normal).

My frustration made sense when I found three key Scriptures:

> *Fathers, do not exasperate your children; instead, bring them up in the training and instruction of the LORD* (Ephesians 6:4).

> *He who spares the rod hates his son, but he who loves him is careful to discipline him* (Proverbs 13:24).

> *Train a child up in the way he should go, and when he is old he will not turn from it* (Proverbs 22:6; see also, Deuteronomy 6:7; Proverbs 14:26 and 22:15.)

Feeling cheated and upset because your parents did not raise you in the knowledge of God is scriptural. However, we must not hold resentment in our hearts or sin in our anger. We must forgive and move past our irritation, knowing that God can make of our pain a blessing to help others who have struggled with the same issues. Many people need to know they are not alone. In order to heal, they need to understand their feelings of frustration. Your journey up the stairs is for you *and* for others.

Whatever our spiritual heritage (even if there seems to be none) we tend to perpetuate the religious design our family established for us. We then attempt to relate to God according to their rules and expectations. But what if their ways are not pleasing to God? Often in Scripture, we see that God desires a remnant who will return to His ways and establish a line that pleases Him.

Our lack of godly guidance can restrict our ability to go deep with God. I even have friends who grew up with weekly doses of "religion," but their problem was their "religion" was missing God's heart. On this third step, we will learn how to surrender our preconceived notions through prayer. We will then discover the freedom to receive the godly guidance we once lacked.

First let me say this: God is my best friend ever. Let Him be yours. Put on no pretense; render no judgment; and subject His love to no human ideals. Do not allow anyone else to define God for you. Embrace Him by reading both Testaments, by praying, and by walking with Him in friendship daily.

Take to heart Paul's admonition about the "religious" people of his day:

> *Since they did not know the righteousness that comes from God and sought to establish their own, they did not submit to God's righteousness. Christ is the end of the law so that there may be righteousness for everyone who believes* (Romans 10:3-4).

The White Flag of Surrender

Surrender shows humility. It reveals your willingness to be exposed to God. Humility will cause you to open the door you thought protected you. God tells us that humility comes from wisdom.

We need to capitulate to God's love with godly sorrow, opening our hands and releasing our grip on our lives. We can then place our palms on the door of self-protection and push through. Surrendering to Christ and to the fullness of God's Holy Spirit will lead us into an intimate relationship with Him. This is where healing is accessible.

Once we release our grip on our lives, we can surrender our lives to Christ. That means releasing *everything* to Him. This humility will bring the realization that we need to yield to Him daily, if not hourly.

Paul described the yielding this way: *"I die every day—I mean that, brothers— just as surely as I glory over you in Christ Jesus our LORD"* (1 Cor. 15:31). If freedom is what we desire, we will surrender our ownership of the whole lot. We will give in to God's authority and we will let Him fight for us.

This walk is one of continually submitting and resubmitting to Christ. We may feel that we have already done so or at least done so in a particular area, yet, we may need to surrender again. When pain persists, we must find the area in which we have not yet chosen Him over the pain.

The time to choose Him is today—every day. There is always another opportunity to surrender to Him again. Make it a daily habit, just as Paul did.

As long as we surrender, He will guide us up the steps at His speed. We might wish we had surrendered earlier, but He is patient and forgiving with us. We need to be open to Him on this step. From our salvation experience, we know what surrender feels like. Now we need to get used to living in a surrendered state. We can do this through prayer; therefore, we will birth a healthy prayer life on this step.

God should be your best friend. He has an intimate plan for you; that plan is bound by love. All Kingdom relationships are based in love, as Colossians 3:14 reveals: *"And over all these virtues put on love, which binds them all together in perfect unity."*

Walk hand in hand with Christ and share every trial with Him. Do you long for His company? In what ways have you surrendered to Him? Are you still unsure? Ask Him to comfort you and help you. He will teach you how to let Him in so that you can be healed.

More Walk, Less Talk

As we to begin to implement Life Application Actions, it is important to understand the power behind each act. We need to have our hearts open when we do them. These foundational biblical techniques are designed to build gradually, one upon the other, to ensure healing.

You have already accomplished two actions, hope and faith, each connected with their respective steps. Now take them with you on each subsequent step, along with the third action, which is *prayer.*

Life Application Actions are employed throughout your lifetime: hope, faith, prayer, reading, worship, rest, fasting, listening, giving, serving, studying His Word, functioning in your purpose, and functioning in His love (PP).

During this surrender step, I will stress the importance of a consistent prayer life. Prayer will help us to remain faithful to the remaining actions. The life of faith is one of knowing and doing. We have to walk the talk. As James wrote, *"Don't just listen to God's word. You must do what it says. Otherwise, you are only fooling yourselves"* (James 1:22 NLT). Do what it says! James does not tell us what to believe in. He tells us what to do because of what we believe in.

Part of walking the talk is to surrender ourselves daily in prayer asking for His will to be done (see Matt. 6:10). We need to understand that prayer deals with situations in the spiritual realms first. Our trials are of a spiritual nature and begin in the heavenlies. Paul taught as much:

> *For our struggle is not against flesh and blood, but against the rulers, against the authorities, against the powers of this dark world and against the spiritual forces of evil in the heavenly realms* (Ephesians 6:12).

The heavenly realms are where satan, the accuser of the brethren, resides (see Zech. 3:1-2; Job 1:6-12). When we pray, spiritual warfare is activated in the heavenlies first. Then, as God releases His angels, power, and truth, the healing (reconciliation, resolution, restoration) filters down into the natural realm. His order, which is opposite to what our flesh desires, is thereby reestablished.

We begin our prayers by requesting His forgiveness for our sins and then asking Him to reveal the things we do not see. He needs to reveal the hidden areas that have arisen from our sickness, the areas that are not pleasing to Him. The attitude we need to assume is reflected in Psalms 139:23-24: *"Search me, O God, and know my heart; test me and know my anxious thoughts. See if there is any offensive way in me, and lead me in the way everlasting."*

The binding mechanism in our prayer is faith. Our last Life Application Action gave us exactly what we need to reach God. Faith is inside you. The disciples did not ask Jesus to teach them to preach; they asked Him to teach them to pray. If all you can do is recite the Lord's Prayer from Matthew 6:9-13, then do that. If not, just talk with the Lord and ask Him to teach you to pray.

When you arrive at this step, you have admitted your need for healing and our responsibility to seek it. The door to your heart and soul is open and ready for God to work. After mastering the first two steps, you should feel a release of some of the pressure you were under. It may be only a small improvement, but take note of it. Do not allow the devil to subvert your healing by diminishing it. You *are* progressing. With God, the progression is real and the healing is gradual, because He is working to heal you from the inside out. It takes time.

We move upward by asking forgiveness and submitting to God's order through prayer. Here we begin to establish useful, healthy habits for a fruitful life. We are submitted only to the battles God would have us fight, a cease-fire for the devil. (Have you raised a white flag in any areas of your life yet?)

Vulnerability is not comfortable, but it is a good place to be. There we can cut loose of all the junk that has hardened our hearts, fragmented our souls, and caused bad roots to take hold. The hand of God holds us up and is cleaning us out. We must relax, rest, and allow Him to work in our lives.

God will take us up and through each step. Challenging emotions may surface; we may not even understand them all. But they will subside. Be prayerful not to allow the emotion to rule. Choose to be still. God will shape and change us in this molding stage. As far as God is concerned, where there is willingness, there is a way.

We must be vulnerable and open to God. That is part of walking the talk.

The Saint and the Sinner

After more than a decade of popping pills, I stuck my hand into the rays of sunlight and watched as the dust scattered and jumped around me. Everywhere, there was dirt, filth, and impurity; but, I could not see even a speck of it until the door opened and the light came streaming in. Immediately the light grabbed the filth, and held up the impurity for me to see.

Jewel for the Journey

As our surrender to God creates vulnerability in our flesh, a strange openness arises that is foreign to us accept that place with Him.

I was amazed at the conditions surrounding me. I had been living in this mess for years, but not until this very moment did I realize how the dust had owned me. The rays exposed the air that was full of grime. It was one of the toughest seasons of my life; I had to surrender to the belief that God would clean up the atmosphere because I finally knew I was incapable.

I was almost 33. I had an array of drugs in different types, shapes, and colors. I had one to make me strong, one to make me happy, one to make me sleep, and one to wake me up. All I was missing was the White Rabbit and her "muchness."[1] The remedies would run out of the bottle and out of my system. They never lasted; they never healed anything.

I realized that the drugs were temporary at best; the more I took them, the more I found myself habituating to the dose. More pills were necessary to obtain the same level of manufactured peace. The vicious cycle had me trapped. I wanted out, even if it meant total defenselessness. My habit was getting dangerous and difficult. That is how sin functions; the slope of our sin gets steeper and more slippery. In fact, my slope was giving way to a treacherous mudslide. There was not so much as a crag of rock on which to catch a foothold.

I accepted my pain and was familiar with my specific level of hurt. I was not familiar with the hurt of the unknown, but resolved to believe it could not be worse than this. This revelation made me aware and willing. Spiritually speaking,

I was free of drugs in that moment of surrender! As is true of prayer, everything happens in the spiritual realm first; then it manifests here.

We will always be able to acknowledge a specific moment, a mere millisecond of time in which the transformation began. So often, the "fog of war" obscures these tiny but important details and accomplishments, but we need to recognize them.

Jewel for the Journey

We make things much too complicated.

Surrender is one of those very precious moments. I believe angels stop and dance for us when the healing begins. They sing. They laugh for our freedom because they see our futures with hope and purpose arriving. God smiles down on us and utters the words, "My good and faithful servant" (see Matt. 25:21). In that instant, we release our will so that His will can be done (see Matt. 6:10).

In my moment of surrender, I was physically sick. I weighed nowhere near what I should have weighed. I was a faint shade of green and unable to sleep for months after taking my last pill. Instead of sleeping, I would read my Bible and stare at the walls. I was not sure which words, if any, were sinking into the abyss that was my mind.

I was the most vulnerable I had ever been in my life so far. I had opened the door and placed my toes at the edge of the threshold, waiting for God to gently lift me up and set me on His side. I was too tired and too vacant to move on my own.

All I could do was pray. It was enough; the Lord gave me His hand to hold. He had scheduled a divine appointment for me. On that particular day, I managed to get dressed and meet with a woman who had played tennis with me for years. I paid little attention to the fact that her husband was a pastor. I just knew she had something that I needed.

That day, I wore a tennis dress that fit perfectly several weeks prior; now it looked like a sack on me. My stomach felt raw and my nerves were jittery. I was cold and sweating at the same time. I had spent a lot of money; my husband was unaware of it. When the pills did not fulfill the emptiness, I tried to fill it with stuff. I needed help fast. I had decided to stop taking the pills, and when I did the reality of my condition and guilt came rushing in. I wanted to get better, but had no idea what was next. I was scared.

In my fear, I turned to God and He sent me a saint. She did not look down on me from her sainthood. She was with me and for me, for no apparent reason. She allowed Christ in her to see me through His blood. We talked for hours. Her counsel was biblical and godly. She housed the Spirit and served the Lord, so she was obedient to interrupt her schedule to do His work. She told me to whisper the name above all names and then she prayed for me.

Whispering was all I could do. Jesus was doing miraculous things in my life, but I was not quite seeing them yet. I stood in a dense fog at that moment with only hope, faith, and prayer.

If you are diligently pursuing Christ and you feel like you are not doing much, He is doing things you are not capable or aware of, so keep allowing Him to sculpt. Our allowing God and others to help, pray for us and see our surrender is another one of those moments where we deepen our friendship and trust with the Lord.

In my most vulnerable hour, I got godly advice because I chose to pray, seek, and surrender. In allowing only God to lead, I not only received advice, I received healing, because God's answer trumps every request. Not only did that woman pray and believe for me but her husband became our pastor years later. Only God can ordain such an umbrella of blessing.

She walked in Christ's likeness in order to walk me to Christ. I whispered "Jesus" to get up, to get to meetings, to take a shower. Sometimes I asked Him to help me breathe. I replaced my pills with that name.

God picked me up, held me for a time, and was about to move me across the threshold of my surrender. I remember during this period being very aware that I was resting in the arms of the Lord. During this time, my husband placed me in a Christian treatment center. I spent months there. Do you remember the room I described at the beginning of my healing, the one with the circle of chairs and only a lamp? It was in this facility.

Being in treatment was not easy. Believing for the strength to get dressed and go to meetings was not easy. We cannot expect healing to be easy. Healing is good, hard, laborious work that will reap great rewards. The choice remains ours: We can allow or block God from handing us our healing and our blessings. We have free will. We need to surrender to God's will and ask Him in prayer to make His will ours (PP).

Please do not give up (PP). I did not. I did, however, cry at times. I missed my children. My emotions were strained. The tunnel looked long and dark; funny thing, I realized after passing through it was only a half-foot door casing. By the grace of God and through faith, I stood, I stepped, and I trusted. It was so worth it!

Surrendered as I was, I looked like a deer in the headlights of life. I had never experienced life sober. I had always resorted to the escape hatch. The devil kept telling me to go back. I had spent a lifetime believing that avoiding surrender meant avoiding pain and hurt. That is the way of the enemy; he deceives us into believing the exact opposite of God's truth.

Take Heed What You Hear

We must be careful, because satan does not want us to get better. He will tell us that because we have not conquered all the steps or all the issues, we need to give up. He suggests that there are too many steps or the journey is too hard. I was unaware at the time that the enemy was planting this advice in my mind. Nor did I realize that I was the one letting him enter. When I refused to listen to the lies, the enemy's scheme in certain areas was finished. God replaced the devil's lies with His truth.

I still had not surrendered a few areas of my life; I gave quite a foothold to the devil. How I related to my husband was one of those areas. It was a rollercoaster of a journey. I felt very vulnerable as I journeyed down and then up for many years. Scriptures like Colossians 3:18, which says, *"Wives, submit to your husbands, as is fitting in the Lord,"* left me feeling defeated.

The counselors at the treatment facility told me to move out and separate from my husband. When we are healing, we are vulnerable. This emotional state lends itself to the acceptance of bad counsel as well as good. In some cases, the advice of the enemy is cloaked in an angel-of-light-costume. It is an effective masquerade.

I received this poor advice and did not even realize I had accepted the lies. The effects were not immediate, but I eventually lived out the lies. That's what happens when you embrace the wrong words.

Make no mistake, the decision was ultimately mine; the problem was that I lacked a sound foundation from which to pull good instruction. During the healing process, the right guidance is critical. The discernment you need comes by surrendering only to God. Can you accurately choose whom you should listen to and whom you should shut down? If you are uncertain, pray.

Before my infilling, and during my vulnerable post-treatment state, I attempted to separate from my husband. The fighting that ensued in the midst of that much pain was intolerable. Because I could not manage him, I thought I had to get away from him. Sadly, I was exchanging one kind of control for another: the control of my environment once again.

My husband was hurting just as much as I was, but in a different way. Ridiculous as it sounds, I wanted to fix him. Of course, I could not even get myself together. I was stubborn about letting God do the work. (Are you trying to fix someone?)

Thankfully, God has dealt and is dealing my husband as powerful a healing as He has dealt and is dealing me. Truly, God is no respecter of persons. And, in this grace-filled dispensation, He is never offended or busy. With His help, I eventually surrendered my marriage and my husband to His throne; I did it kicking and screaming, but I did it. That was when I began to heal in this regard; both my marriage and my husband began to take the shape God intended.

During this time, my husband could easily have moved on. Instead, he decided to seek God-fearing counsel, submit to their authority, and pray. He won! The devil had parts of my heart so hardened that I could not see the light. However, my husband stood in the gap, as Ezekiel did, for our covenant. Because of his surrender, faith, and prayers, my husband heard the right voice, and the devil lost.

God never leaves us nor forsakes us during our trials (see Heb. 13:5); we often leave or ignore Him but He never leaves us. My husband fought. I love him for emulating Christ for me and drawing me that much closer to knowing my God through his obedience, faith, and love.

Keep Up Your Spiritual Guard

Wholeness is a lifelong journey of warfare and resting in God. The enemy operates cyclically, cleverly repeating and morphing old patterns to keep us in bondage. When we get freedom in one area, he tries his tricks in another. He did the same with Jesus. When satan left Jesus in the desert, he did not leave for good. He planned to return at a more opportune time (see Luke 4:13). Stand guard and allow God to fight for you!

We are conceding control to God. By allowing Him to remove the roots of sin and replant His seed in the soil of our hearts, we will make sure that God is the protector and healer in our lives. The denial we once accommodated was a hardening agent that made our hearts impervious to God. With denial left behind, our hearts become more pliable and open to Him.

We have relinquished control and entered into surrender, which we are mastering. We are allowing Him in to heal our souls. The reason people remain in bondage is that they stop surrendering. Upon salvation, we recognize our need for Christ. Sometimes at this point, we are not yet mature enough to see our deeper needs and God's corresponding provision. It is OK to walk with Him awhile before we see the contrast between His ways and ours. In time, we realize our need for a deeper level of commitment and surrender (PP).

We need all the provision God offers as we travel through His healing steps! Often, the process will dictate the need for others to nurture us and help us along. That is not always comfortable for us. Yet we cannot skip over His provision; it would be akin to turning around and walking back down the stairway or stopping mid-flight.

Often, we are too embarrassed to share with others or too busy to take the time. Then again, the things of God take effort; they always seem to rub against the grain of our comfort level. We are flesh and bones. He is Spirit and Truth. Let us remember to do things His way.

The next step is imperative. God will not let us graduate to higher levels until we walk out the step we are on. The process becomes more natural the more we adhere to His leading. There may be some pauses, but the path upward is becoming smooth.

Take the most from what He is teaching you. Take a look around; assess the areas in which you are receiving healing and those in which surrender is not yet complete.

It is time for P^3.

The Princess Principles Practice

Step Into Surrender:

- In order to receive from God, let go of everything in your heart and mind that you think you need.

- Give in to God's work in you.

- Be still and willing to wait on Him.

- Spend time in prayer. Voice your need for His help.

Life Application Action

Prayer

Do not be anxious about anything, but in everything, by prayer and petition, with thanksgiving, present your requests to God (Philippians 4:6).

I have realized as I climb upward that when I hit a roadblock, the only way to remove it is to pray and surrender in obedience to God's Word. Meditate on this truth in the above passage as you circle the words *anything* and *everything.* Now journal about thanksgiving (I know somewhere you have something to be thankful for!):

Summary of Princess Principles

 Life Application Actions are employed throughout your lifetime:
PP **hope, faith, prayer, reading, worship, rest, fasting, listening, giving, serving, studying His Word, functioning in your purpose, and functioning in His love.**

Do not merely listen to the word, and so deceive yourselves. Do what it says (James 1:22).

Do you realize that most times if our actions go opposite of our will/feelings they will actually teach us how to surrender to God. List the actions presented and a way in which you can attempt to accomplish each this month; this will begin to employ them into your life:

We listen to increase our faith, but we accept the fact that action is also necessary. God causes truth to produce fruit in our lives as we release our control and naturally become more Christ-like. While grace is the conduit of salvation, healing results from God's works in us—the outgrowth of sanctification or infilling.

We understand that we must not operate on the basis of our assumptions. Just because salvation comes purely by grace that does not mean that everything comes easily. A healthy life takes hard work. It is worth it! Adherence to God's Word moves us into closer relationship with Him and farther away from our pain.

We must ask for God's help and it will be given to us (see Matt. 7:7-8); we must then do what He says (see James 1:22).

We have free will. We need to surrender to God's will and ask Him in prayer to make His will ours.

> *for it is God who works in you to will and to act according to His good purpose* (Philippians 2:13).

Mark this scripture by underlining what God says He does and why He does it.

 Please do not give up.

> *During the days of Jesus' life on earth, he offered up prayers and petitions with loud cries and tears to the one who could save him from death, and he was heard because of his reverent submission* (Hebrews 5:7).

Submit in prayer and realize that Christ also got worn out and tired. Journal about Christ's amazing surrender to His Father:

 It is OK to walk with Him awhile before we see the contrast between His ways and ours. In time, we realize our need for a deeper level of commitment and surrender.

> *In all my prayers for all of you, I always pray with joy because of your partnership in the gospel from the first day until now, being confident of this, that He who began a good work in you will carry it on to completion until the day of Christ Jesus* (Philippians 1:4-6).

Pray about your purpose realizing you are so precious that you take time. Relax and thank God for completing you in His perfect time by writing Him a note:

Congratulations! You have successfully made it up one more step. By *releasing control,* you have *allowed surrender.* This is a good place to be because, until you are truly surrendered, you are not truly free to be healed. He will never trespass against your free will. But you *have* surrendered, so stand ready to receive healing, blessings, gifts, and best of all, His love.

You have also added a new Life Application Action: *prayer!* You are getting ready to experience a new level of freedom and joy. Soon, you will know a new level of His liberty; it is what I call passing from *the know* into *the flow*—the place where you understand the Scripture that says His burden is light and His yoke is easy (see Matt. 11:28).

Keep truckin'; expect His angels to rally and dispense His will in His perfect time. You are doing a great job and stepping into a healthy life. Take a breath, and step up!

Endnote

1.   Lewis Carroll, *Alice's Adventures in Wonderland* (London: Macmillan and Co., 1866, multiple reprints).

Chapter Four

The Throne of Supreme Counsel

Step Four: Godly Guidance by His Word

*You guide me with Your counsel, and afterward
You will take me into glory* (Psalms 73:24).

Godly Guidance Into Glory

THE threshold you are about to cross is the acceptance of godly guidance. As you cross it, you allow fresh air to envelop you. You are finally ready to greet your guest, your God-ordained guide, The Word of God.

Let us recount our current position: We have stopped denying the existence of our imperfections and control issues. We are no longer hiding without hope behind the closed door with the open latch. We are faithfully surrendered and have prayerfully arrived at the perfect time and place to seek a hand to hold.

Once the door is open and the threshold is exposed to view, we pray for our healing and pass through the door at will. The door is open. We welcome help into our heart and stop hiding.

This is a place where individual accountability and responsibility for our healing are critical. Our independence to this point has served a purpose. It has allowed us to build relationship and trust with Him alone. We learned to accept our responsibility without blaming others. We know that He alone is enough.

Humans naturally tend to glorify earthly counsel or counselors. It is important to remember that they are only willing vessels; this helps us to praise God and thank Him for the ability of these people to exhibit the love that comes from only Him. When we understand the source of their goodness toward us, we can receive what He offers through their participation.

Our Life Application Action for this step is *reading*. Understanding our responsibility to read God's Word helps us to "own" the godly guidance He provides. When we meditate on His Word, we find our daily bread and our sword of protection.

God tells us in Romans 10:17 that faith comes through hearing His Word. His Word is truly a powerful weapon (Hebrews 4:12)! Proverbs 30:5 says, *"Every word of God is flawless; He is a shield to those who take refuge in Him."* We come to Him as little children. Children are flexible, open, and hungry for truth; they are the perfect example of openness to guidance (PP).

Our prayer for faith every morning increases our gift of faith. Hearing God is what strengthens us, although we might not realize it immediately. I did not realize the magnificent power of what my daily dose was doing until years later.

Remember, it is normal when you are hurting to feel weary, overwhelmed, or unsure about what you are gaining when you read the Bible. You are not alone in questioning the meaning of Scripture. He tells us clearly that it is a mystery until we are converted (see Col. 1:26). Did you know that one of the devil's favorite tactics is to make you feel overwhelmed or confused when you read?

We step into the Word the same way we do anything with God, the very way we have stepped into healing so far. First, we get rid of doubt. We dismiss the fear of not understanding and we choose to reside in faith. Daily doses of the Bible, preferably three or more chapters each day, provide protection for the journey. Three chapters a day keeps the devil away (PP)! (*See the chart at the end of the book.*)

Heaven's "Medicine"

Take small doses of Scripture at first. Read just a verse, a parable, or a chapter. If you are having a hard time understanding, pray that God will interpret the message He wants you to receive. Slow down and rest as you read, believing there is power in the intake. Our reading serves as medicine for an empty soul, healing

Jewel for the Journey

When we allow godly counsel to nurture us up the stairs, we have assistance to better understand and receive God's healing.

every part of the mind and heart. As we progress, we move from the simplest truths (the milk of the Word) to the meat of deep revelatory meaning (see 1 Cor. 3:2; Heb. 5:12; 1 Pet. 2:2).

Hearing and reading His Word will combat the enemy's attempts to keep us sick and vulnerable to the wrong things and people. Through our reading, God will teach us to discern godly versus ungodly advice. Not all secular advice is bad; but all secular advice that fails to line up with God's heart is bad. The words may sound innocent or even kind, but so did the devil's spouting of Scripture in the desert with Jesus (see Matt 4:6; Ps. 91:11-12).

Jesus was not fooled by the desert battle of biblical poetry and law. He saw how the devil's wrong motives were couched in what seemed to be the right words. Jesus responded with Scripture, but without manipulating its meaning. He quoted Deuteronomy 8:3: *"...man does not live on bread alone but on every word that comes from the mouth of the LORD"* (see Matt. 4:4). He also quoted Deuteronomy 6:16 and 13, reminding the devil of the dangers of putting God to the test.

Let us pray always for the meaning in the Word—the manna or substances of it, the life within it—to fill our minds and hearts. We pray for God to speak to us through His Word, that the Scriptures would guard us and that we would remember what we read, never allowing it to be stolen from us (see Matt. 13:19). We implore that the Word be transformed from *logos* (divine words) into *rhema* (life-giving power).

As you continue in the Word of God, stop and consider the following questions: How has God's Word offered you hope during tough times? Do you have faith that He will help you understand it as you read?

Ask Him for the desire to read the Bible daily, craving it more than you crave TV and fruitless desires. He is our hope. He is our healing. Only to Him and His Word can we be safely surrendered. The Word precedes the foundations of the earth! John 1:1 says, *"In the beginning was the Word, and the Word was with God, and the Word was God."* His Word is everlasting!

Notice that prayer and Scripture are part of every step from now on. If you need to refer to earlier steps again, always take prayer and Scripture with you.

Doctor Feelgood & Co.

The realization that sickness had hardened my heart came to me the tough way. When I was sick, I was the Princess of Excuses. I had surrounded myself with a court of sinners. It was my way of disguising my excuse making: I used satan's little elves to agree with my sin.

After my transformation, I was shocked by my unsaved family and friends. I realized how ignorant I had been, not only of my dilapidated condition, but of theirs. Now I was willing to surrender and do what was necessary to expel evil from my life, but they were not.

They were stuck where I had been stuck: in the place where drinking, smoking, and other vices are the worldly norm. Just as my guidance for them had been bad, my friends' guidance for me was bad. I had used my social circle to help me stay in my comfort zone.

My circle was filled with physicians who guided my medication use. Media and advertisers endorsed my shopping habits. Movie stars nurtured my eating disorder and added the element of delight to my idolatry issues. My addictive nature (what I called *passion*) and the failing marriages of my friends provided the perfect cover for my suffering life and marriage.

I was slopping around in a big mud pit with a bunch of people just like me. Like the blind leading the blind, we mimicked one another. No one was holding anyone accountable on a biblical level or any other level. In order to prevent any light being shed on my darkness, I excused my own sin by surrounding myself with as much sin as possible. I was comfortable with the lousy guidance I gave and received. The devil was comfortable with it too; his plan was succeeding famously.

Let me ask you, in case nobody else has: How many people in your circle would give you a Scripture reference if you needed advice? How many of your friends are willing to lay down their lives for Christ? Are they carrying their crosses? How many of them are producing the kind of fruit that demonstrates a journey up the stairs rather than down? Do you see in them *"...love, joy, peace, patience, kindness, goodness, faithfulness, gentleness and self-control..."* (Gal. 5:22-23)?

I am not asking whether you have a sweet Auntie Annie or a nice neighbor named Mr. Robinson. Some people are just naturally nice. That does not make them godly. Jesus told the Pharisees that, even though they were evil, they still did some positive things.

The kinds of friends and family members I am talking about are God-fearing without compromise, Bible-reading daily, Holy Spirit-filled, Spirit-led followers of Christ. These are the people worthy of being listened to and mimicked. Interacting with people who seek God's wisdom and hold God's power will help promote healing in us.

Counsel and Truth

Paul warned: *"Do not be misled. 'Bad company corrupts good character'"* (1 Cor. 15:33). Accountability and help from the right people are important in the healing process. God is our ultimate authority; He has fashioned us to love and balance one another. *"As iron sharpens iron, so a friend sharpens a friend"* (Prov. 27:17 NLT). You might need some new friends. You might even need to separate yourself from some extended family members at this point (see Matt. 10:34-39). To keep stepping upward in our journey, we must travel with those who are willing to do the same.

Paul instructed his spiritual "son" Titus to separate himself from ungodly counsel:

> But avoid foolish controversies and genealogies and arguments and quarrels about the law, because these are unprofitable and useless. Warn a divisive person once, and then warn him a second time. After that, have nothing to do with him. You may be sure that such a man is warped and sinful; he is self-condemned (Titus 3:9-11).

During my less than honorable years, I found that the resolution of my pain was not to be found in the counsel of man. The right counsel would come from

God through man. I learned that *"It is better to take refuge in the* LORD *than to trust in man"* (Ps.118:8)

Man without God is in the business of fixing things by way of his own understanding. Scripture clearly states that we are not to lean on our own understanding (see Prov. 3:5). All the 12-step programs, books, and methods are only temporary fixes if they do not lead us to the power Christ Jesus offers us. The only way to be permanently healed is to experience God. He is the only one who can set us free (see John 8:36).

Some of the best, most professional earthly counsel I received came from those who worked according to their own ability and their best was not sufficient. They gave advice regardless of their lack of biblical knowledge, godly experience, and life experience. It seemed as though many of them were in denial themselves. The true healing method was of no interest to them. Most had not experienced anything close to what I had been through. They had not walked the dark alleys I had walked. They matured while safely tucked away in university libraries. Their well-worn library cards and psycho jargon were not helping me.

I became numb to the counseling "system." I chose to deny the ability of the counselors I was seeking. Fear and unbelief kept me there. I had convinced myself that because no one had helped me thus far, no one could help. Every time I entered a new office I would divide the hour into quarters and count how many times the counselor used the terms *cognitive, inferiority complex, relational stability, behavioral accountability,* and *medicine.* I cannot remember them using the term *the blood of Christ*—that is, until I met the saint who eventually helped me out of my sickness.

Vicki D. had the goods. She had covered more ground in hell in a single day than most had experienced in a lifetime. She always came out fighting for the cause of Christ and is qualified in wisdom and worthy of many crowns in Heaven.... The degrees were not on her wall, but several doctorates hung on her heart. No man could have given her the glorious resource of counsel that God had so graciously bestowed upon her. I knew brilliant seminarians with multiple doctorates who could not even come close.

Genuine guidance comes when God directs the vessel. Most often, we seek guidance when we feel bad emotionally and are vulnerable. Many times, we do not even realize we are in the wrong office. This is dangerous ground.

The pursuit of godly counsel is just as important as coming out of denial, releasing control, and stepping into surrender. If we are to move forward, we need a system of accountability that is based in Christ. We need to allow godly counselors to know us. That does not mean that we are comfortable with their knowing us. But if God has sent God-fearing, trustworthy ministers to help us, they need to know the good, the bad, and the really bad parts of our life. What we keep hidden will keep us in bondage.

Vicki D. is a terrific mentor. She always tells me, "Jnfer" (that is how she pronounces my name), "be very careful when you counsel anyone who is requesting help on subject matter you have not literally walked through." In other words, if I have not stepped up the stairway into healing from grief, I tell the person seeking counsel in that area that I am sorry for their loss and will pray for them. If my counsel is sought by a woman who feels trapped in drug addiction and anxiety, I will take her hand and walk all the stairs with her as God leads.

When I was in trouble, I needed someone who had actually walked in and out of shadowy corners—someone who would not fear going into the dark rooms to help me retrieve parts of my soul. I needed someone who had actually been to war. A degree qualifies someone by man's measure. In my life, man's measuring device was powerless, at best.

Of course I understand that research, study, and knowledge are tremendous blessings. I am not discounting them; they serve us well. In the end, however, doctrine without the Spirit and love of God will leave you feeling incomplete, sometimes to the point of destruction.

By way of much prayer, I try not to seek in a textbook what I should be seeking at His well. In John chapter 4, while sitting at Jacob's well in the heat of the noonday sun, Jesus offered the Samaritan woman living water. He explained that, if we come to God's well, we will never thirst again (see John 4:4-13).

In our flesh, we idolize things and people according to standards that are not God's. We esteem worldly knowledge and leave little room for God. In Jesus' day, the counsel of the Pharisees and Sadducees was killing people. Why? Because the center of healing is not man's theory; it is God's truth. If we base our hopes for healing in worldly hypotheses, we should not then wonder why our healing does not last.

You may need a warrior like My Vicki D. (her formal name). God will provide. You will not find most true godly warriors in the yellow pages. The way to dial God's number is by prayer and supplication. Seek out His "wise owls."

Meditate at the Right Well

"Hurry, hurry, Brett! Hurry up!" I yelled to my husband. "Come out to the backyard fast. There is an owl in our tree, and he is staring at me!"

I hollered up the winding staircase, hopeful the message made it around all the corners.

God sent us an owl that literally took up residence in the oak tree in our backyard. He stayed for several weeks and would watch us, not like an owl, but like a hawk. We were clueless at the time; but five years later, wisdom and God-fearing counsel arrived.

God was letting us know what was ahead. Watch your surroundings. God can use anything He chooses to keep you on track and point you to the promise of blessings to come.

Jewel for the Journey

God filters our knowledge by His Spirit. He quiets the sting of our pain with His perfect guidance.

> *Blessed is the man who does not walk in the counsel of the wicked or stand in the way of sinners or sit in the seat of mockers. But his delight is in the law of the LORD, and on His law he meditates day and night* (Psalms 1:1-2).

God creates many opportunities for wise counsel for those who are attentive to what He is doing in their lives. Likewise, the enemy offers many "wells" of ungodly counsel. Where are you spending your time? What are you reading and watching? How are your indulgences helping in your healing?

Whom do you revere? Why do you respect them? Honestly, just look at the entertainment industry. They advertise their sins. Everyone recognizes their need for counsel. They get help, but after a few weeks, they are either divorced or back on drugs. Round and round they go on the merry-go-round of earthly pleasures. They keep ending up sick; most never receive a lasting, divine healing.

Yet, our flesh-driven souls flock to monetary comfort, movie stars, secular counselors, liquor stores, magazines, the "next craze," and other sources of gratification. It is all escapism! There is another escape that you need to be aware of: prescribed medications. Too often, pills become substitutes for wise counsel. We do well to question them and to refuse them, unless we are clear that God has ordained their use in our healing.

What may seem to be my opinion here is actually based in truth concerning the condition of our fallen world (see 2 Tim. 3:1-9). Too often, we seek answers from a dry well, an evil structure that is void of truth. Without the counsel of Christ (see John 14:16) that is poured out for all, no true healing can occur.

You may find something appealing, something that looks like healing. Things may look better for a while, but what is really happening? Remember that deception has to look appealing enough to get you hooked. Then the mask comes off and the real game is on, and probably again.

Just like the masses, I claimed to want healing. What I really wanted were enablers who would pay attention to me and provide an excuse to continue in my sickness. I was the one who was going to the wrong well. Whether we find it because of a lack of knowledge or a sense of trepidation, the wrong well cannot help us.

That is why, with God as our guide, we have stepped out of ignorance and fear. We choose to surround ourselves with godly guidance: pastors, mentors, friends, church family, and counselors. The newfound strength and faith that we are building through our healing allows us to accept our imperfections. We realize we are not and cannot be perfect; Christ is perfect. Our character is not in our ability. Our distinctiveness is found in His ability working through us, by His Spirit.

Through prayer and godly communication, we are connecting with others who know which well is the right one. James said, *"Confess your sins to each other and pray for each other so that you may be healed. The prayer of a righteous man is powerful and effective"* (James 5:16).

We are positioned to make progress, in part because we are ready to come clean where sin is concerned. Proverbs 28:13 warns, *"He who conceals his sins does not prosper, but whoever confesses and renounces them finds mercy."* You will find that when you disclose your sin issues to a God-fearing vessel, he or she will pray for you. In time and with your submission to God's guidance, you will find relief.

Try not to keep secrets; the devil loves to manipulate us with hidden stuff. This is the very reason why guidance is so important. When you have an ear to hear true wisdom, you are not looking for attention or pity. You are looking for prayer and healing; you want to be well. When your identity is in Christ, you are free to be yourself, without condemnation. Suddenly, you can handle constructive criticism and welcome genuine guidance. Your craving for empty words of flattery disappears.

When you desire wisdom from the right well, you are satisfied to hear from God. You no longer need approval or affirmation from man. Instead of trying to get agreement through gossip or manipulation, you find peace from God through prayer. The only intermediary you need is Christ.

Do you have good counsel right now? If not, will you stop, open your Bible, and read a Scripture regarding counsel? Will you ask God in prayer to send you help? Feeling overwhelmed is OK, but please keep stepping upward. It is fine to feel unsure about this new territory. Just trust that your feet are on holy ground and you are blessed.

The Whitewater Undertow

The exact moment in my very early twenties that my drug habit began was in the office of a secular counselor. A single, small, white sheet of paper was gingerly inscribed with a dosage. There was no warning about the frantic nights I would spend pacing the floors or the countless mornings of sickness that were ahead. There was no godly counsel regarding the fact that I would never be able to get enough of the drug or that its power would leave me feeling shackled in a bottomless abyss. No biblical caution about sorcery was offered.

The addition of numerous other drugs would hopefully balance the addiction. Which is exactly the problem; the very nature of addiction lies in the evil, endless cycle that leads, not to resolution, but to perpetuation of the problem.

Did I want to be warned about the crying jags, the weight loss, and the constant dizziness from the chemical imbalances that the medicine caused? Probably not. Would I ignore the red flags of feeling abnormal and broken every day? Yes. Would I have honored the prediction of the potential divorce, children scattered with a broken foundation, generations of pain, and on and on? No. If I had, I would have stopped in my tracks. I was too afraid to acknowledge any of it.

Are you ignoring what you know is true because of fear?

If you dig deep enough, you will find that we birth most of our own trials. Sometimes, we do it out of genuine ignorance. Mostly, we choose to stay sick because the right way seems too hard or too scary. I was ignorant about seeking proper God-centered counsel; I was also looking for a convenient quick fix and a posse to support my campaign. All this because I was petrified of getting better and had few resources for finding good help.

That is not the case now. We have the tools; the method is unfolding. We just need to keep stepping forward. You are precious to God and your work is precious to Him. I am here to tell you that you *can* do it and I am proud of you.

The process is not quick or easy. We need to be OK with that. I have a tendency to want it all right now. Immediate gratification is very often the issue; *everything right now* often ends in *nothing good forever* because hasty methods are just not God's way. He is in the business of miracles, but as far as lasting healing is concerned, we must walk it out.

Man specializes in immediate gratification. It is not God's way of doing things. The choice is clear: We can summon up a boatload of patience and pay the price of healing now, or we can look for a quick fix and pay with interest in the years to come. I would rather be the proud owner of the boatload of patience!

That brings me to my whitewater rafting story and the boat I had loaded up with fear. A group of us went whitewater rafting one summer, helmets and all. We rode Category 3 rapids. Because of the intensity level, we were required to sit through a guidance session on safety techniques. Unfortunately, I did not pay attention.

It is so sad when you can hardly enjoy life for fear that you might trip on your shoelace at the park and fall to your death. Granted, riding the rapids has its dangers, and such activities call for a natural fear. God put an innate fear in each of us to keep us safe. But I was the princess of irrational fear and always had been. It was detrimental to my life.

In this instance, everyone else seemed quite thrilled about the ride. Everyone had concerns for safety, but for the most part, my companions were excited. While they looked forward to the ride, I concocted my waterproof prescription protection plan and carried my bundle of fear to my side of the raft.

Jewel for the Journey

Stepping up is impossible alone; we are entering the impossible to find the only source of possibility.

We piled in, all stiff from the life jackets. While grabbing the oars, our guide hollered, "Everyone in. Cast off!" I wanted to vomit, cast myself off the side, and climb back to shore, but we were afloat *quickly*, even before I could activate my evacuation plan.

The rapids moved the raft at angles so unnatural I felt like the guide must have secretly glued himself to the orange rubber. I was shocked that he did not fall off. At the midpoint of the excursion, the rapids intensified. There were seven of us on the raft. I was on the front. The bow of the raft pitched up over a rock as the back swung around from the pressure of the enormous wall of water.

The motion finally tossed me and only one other person into the churning, frothing, racing, waters. All I could see was black water with white foam. I did not know if I was up, down, or sideways. I began to panic. My lungs ached as the current kept me under and pulled me downstream. I was completely disoriented. Everything was dark and bubbly.

An oar handle hit my helmet with a thud. I frantically grabbed at the stick as I pushed the only other capsized person down under the water, using her head as leverage to hoist myself to safety. I love Maria. She is not a fearful woman. I do not know why she went over; but at that moment, she was my means of escaping danger.

When we are fearful, we cannot be faithful. Nor can we help anyone else. Most times, we inflict damage on others and neglect them. If I had operated in faith, I would have responded as the guide had instructed: I would have pointed my feet downstream, crossed my arms, and ridden it out. Not only that, but I would have been able to help Maria.

Instead, I crunched up in a ball, turned upside down, almost drowned, nearly bashed my head on every rock in the river, and then used my best friend as an underwater step stool.

We use wrong methods and fear tactics because we prefer to carry our Bibles rather than read them. Too often, instead of carrying our cross on our shoulder, we wear one that rests gently on our collarbone. Emulating our godly guides with action is the key to shouldering our cross and eliminating fear (PP).

Jesus Is Our Guide

What results in a deliverance and healing is for the counselor to have been through more than the sick person. The only One who always fits that bill is Jesus. We can look to His cross because He suffered it all. He is the Healer, Jehovah Rapha (see Exod. 15:26).

Let us take another step into healing and another step closer to our godly purpose in this life. If the steps seem impossible to accomplish in your own strength, then you know we are right on track.

God's plan is underway. He is working in and through us. *"For we are God's workmanship, created in Christ Jesus to do good works, which God prepared in advance for us to do"* (Eph. 2:10). This is not the time to quit; it is the time to press on!

You are loved and purposed for greatness. Keep stepping. You will see. I promise. I did not believe it until I stepped it out either; but His healing is true. Remember to read your Bible. That is our Life Application Action for this step. We need to read The Guidebook in order to stay healthy on our trip. Let us pray and ask the Lord to help us find proper godly guidance with a pure heart (PP).

Keep these words: *"A wise man has great power, and a man of knowledge increases strength; for waging war you need guidance..."* (Prov. 24:5-6). Our travels will not be easy, but they will be blessed, and we will not be traveling alone. We will now move on to the next step: stopping the cycle of the enemy. I always compare this to pulling weeds out of my yard, especially after a dry season when the ground is hard and impossible.

The weeds' gestation cycles are inevitable. Every year at the same time, the same types manifest in clusters. The hardened soil holds the offending root firmly in place. Pulling it out is hard work. But after a good rain, the ground is soft and pliable and the root comes right up.

We have to open up and allow God to pour out His rain, His cleansing, His power, and His covering. A softened heart will accept His ways. Surrendering to His guidance is what we need to ensure God's removal of the roots and the restoration of our souls.

THE PRINCESS PRINCIPLES PRACTICE

Step Into Godly Guidance:

- Pray that God blesses you with the pastors, mentors, teachers, counselors, and prophets He has ordained for your life.

- Develop a willingness to submit to God's guidance further, to take constructive criticism, and to make appropriate changes.

- Cultivate the ability to step outside of yourself and look in objectively.

ॐ Adhere to total honesty and strive to be transparent.

ॐ Surrender to reading God's Word as your ultimate daily guide.

Life Application Action

Reading

Consequently, faith comes from hearing the message, and the message is heard through the word of Christ (Romans 10:17).

Journal and meditate on how much time you allocate to hearing/reading the Word of God:

Summary of Princess Principles

 We come to Him as little children. Children are flexible, open, and hungry for truth; they are the perfect example of openness to guidance.

He said: "I tell you the truth, unless you change and become like little children, you will never enter the kingdom of heaven" (Matthew 18:3).

Children are willing to learn and to be guided. We need to take lessons from them. Somehow as adults, we come to a point where we feel we have arrived and that is an open gate to sickness. List measures you can take to assure you never feel you have "arrived" and list why this is a good thing:

 Daily doses of the Bible, preferably three or more chapters each day, provide protection for the journey. Three chapters a day keeps the devil away!

All Scripture is God-breathed and is useful for teaching, rebuking, correcting and training in righteousness, so that the man of

God may be thoroughly equipped for every good work (2 Timothy 3:16-17).

List what Timothy tells us Scripture helps us with: Meditate on this verse.

 Emulating our godly guides with action is the key to shouldering our cross and eliminating fear.

We know that we have come to know him if we obey his commands. The man who says, "I know him," but does not do what he commands is a liar, and the truth is not in him. But if anyone obeys his word, God's love is truly made complete in him. This is how we know we are in him: Whoever claims to live in him must walk as Jesus did (1 John 2:3-6).

God's complete love casts out all fear. The world's way perpetuates fear. Circle the words *in him* and notice their repetition denoting their importance. Now journal where you see that fearing God, following guidance and biblical methods by reading biblical truths casts your pain out and draws His love in:

 Let us pray and ask The Lord to help us find proper godly guidance with a pure heart.

But when He, the Spirit of truth, comes, He will guide you into all truth. He will not speak on His own; He will speak only what He hears, and He will tell you what is yet to come (John 16:13).

Where can you find counsel that hears from God, list some places and ways:

Here is a mini practice to get you excited about *reading* God's Word! The fourth chapter of Paul's Epistle to the Philippians is powerful! We touched on it briefly in Chapter 3 regarding our action of prayer. In this Scripture, he gives clear instruction about how to find and follow God's counsel:

*Rejoice in the Lord always. I will say it again: Rejoice! Let your gentleness be evident to all. The Lord is near. Do not be anxious about **anything**, but in **everything**, by prayer and petition, with thanksgiving, **present your requests to God**. And the peace of*

*God, which transcends all understanding, will guard your hearts and your minds in Christ Jesus. Finally, brothers, whatever is true, whatever is noble, whatever is right, whatever is pure, whatever is lovely, whatever is admirable—if anything is excellent or praise-worthy—think about such things. Whatever you have learned or received or heard from me, or seen in me—**put it into practice**. And the God of peace **will be with you** (Philippians 4:4-9, empha-sis added).*

This chapter guides us as to how to combat fear. It was written to two women in the church, Euodia and Syntyche, who are misbehaving. Paul had to guide them back into proper fellowship. Notice how he shepherds them in love. Godly guidance is so important. We also learn from this passage that praise and gentleness guides us into peace. List the things we are suppose to think about, and journal about how they combat fear and unbelief. The latter portion above challenges us to actively practice the truths in order to receive the peace we so desire. We will go into more depth on this in Chapter 7. As you read the Word, take a look around and notice all the ways in which God makes things work together.

For now, congratulations! You have *accepted godly guidance.* You have also added a new Life Application Action: *reading!* You are healing, and God sees your diligence. You will not give up. You are climbing higher into a healthy life.

Take another step up!

Chapter Five

Halt the Cycle of Defeat

Step Five: Worship Ceases the Cycling

*Trust in the LORD with all your heart and lean not on your own understanding; in all your ways acknowledge Him, and He will make your paths **straight** (Proverbs 3:5-6, emphasis mine).*

Praise Away the Pain

YOU have stepped up so far that you might feel overwhelmed. If so, rest in God's command: *"Be still, and know that I am God..."* (Ps. 46:10). Be still and focus on Him. Allow your healing to settle in and praise Him for who He is.

Remember that God's healing takes time; there is no set calendar. You are healing and moving progressively toward blessing; it rarely manifests as fast as you expect it to. Just keep standing and keep up the good work. Take Paul's advice from Second Thessalonians 3:13 *"As for you...never tire of doing what is right."*

Look down at your feet and realize they have been stepping for and toward Him this whole time. We are moving toward awareness, breaking cycles of abuse, and pulling up bad roots. We have come so far! Every prior step was necessary to get to these higher ones. Do you feel good about what you have accomplished? You should. You have put effort into healing and God sees your heart.

Remember to deflect the devil's lies with the truth in your reading and praying. That, too, is a form of worship. The enemy knows exactly which buttons to push. He waits until you are weak or have let your guard down; then he pushes them. I know, because I kept falling into the same cycle. Every time I failed, it felt like I got the results I deserved, instead of the ones I wanted.

Jewel for the Journey

If we let Him, God will reclaim and restore the portions of our soul that have caused us so much discomfort, gradually likening us to His Son.

The irony is that, even so, I was shocked at the results. It has been said that the definition of insanity is doing the same thing repeatedly, but expecting different results. Some of that was evident in my approach! Our best defense is a consistent offense: continuous stepping up on the staircase of healing to combat the devil's cycle of bondage (PP).

Where do you see repetitive behaviors in your life? What harm are they causing? Do you want to stop? Do you feel powerless over the pain? If you answered *yes* to any of the last three questions, then boldly step up and let God stop the pain.

Let me explain further. God tells us in Genesis that every inclination of man's heart is toward evil (see Gen. 6:5). That is our fleshly nature. You can see the iniquity historically. Every dispensation has ended in apostasy due to man's sinful nature. If we do not step in tune with the Spirit and crucify our flesh, we will act and react in fleshly ways. Not only is the human character marred, but our souls are not whole. We need to allow God to fix both.

When we notice the same arguments, problems, habits, and issues arising day in and day out, we know the devil has us in a cycle of bondage. We must allow God to stop the escalator in satan's funhouse so that we can step off and into God's arms. He will then help us go back in our memories to find the origin of the pain.

Pain fragments portions of our souls, making them vulnerable. The devil then captures and guards our souls with gatekeeper such as denial, control, pride, and anger. These gatekeepers are the things that we have been working to dismantle in previous chapters. Once we are aware of their role and realize they are not working for our good, God can go in and preside over our territory.

Restoration is the very reason the fullness of God's Holy Spirit is necessary. We are incapable of restoring our souls without Him. With Him, we can restore anything willing. Even in the midst of our pain, we will begin to worship Him. This is our Life Application Action for this step. He inhabits our praise.

We need His transforming presence to heal and stop the cycle of our pain (see 2 Cor. 3:18). We can usher Him in through our adoration; in His presence, He heals us. We are going to cover some basic housecleaning rules in order to purify ourselves for worship. Then we are going to learn to praise Him.

The World Is Going Downstairs

Having reached this step, we are strong enough to allow God to raise our spiritual consciousness to much higher levels.

The world is in a downward spiral. At the same time, personal issues and situations cycle all around us. Whatever we face in this life hails from one of two sources: good or evil, God or the devil. We must discern one from the other.

As you get healthier, your surroundings need to change. If they do not, staying healthy will be more difficult. How will you change your environment to accommodate your healing? How much does being healthy mean to you? How deep are you willing to go to see your purpose in Christ fulfilled?

When we allow God to clean out our homes, cabinets, drawers, cars, offices and closets, we stay healthy. If there is anything tempting you to sin in your home, toss it in the trash. You may need to ask God what offends Him and chuck it all. For sure, if you are an addict, clean out the bar and medicine cabinet. If you have issues with wearing inappropriate clothes, take a trip to Goodwill and replace them. If your vice is watching bad channels on TV, protect yourself by getting rid of them. You know what you need to do. Do not make excuses, because satan will use as a tool any items you do not address. Leave him no room to tempt you. We cannot heal and stay comfortable at the same time (PP).

To ensure your continued healing, establish accountability and avenues of prayer, notify your church that you are in the healing process. Study Scripture and become aware of the spiritual chain of command that is in place to protect you. Sit down with your pastors and make sure they are covering you. Reassess your affiliations with clubs or organizations; be discerning about whether they fit into your new healed and healing life. Are they Christ-based? If not, are they healthy or unhealthy? Look beyond the surface. When God healed me, He removed me from activities that many of my Christian friends are still involved in. Never assume that what is acceptable for them is good for you, and never ever judge.

My husband and I had to learn these things as we began to heal. We had reestablished our marriage, received the infilling of the Holy Spirit, and were stepping up the heavenly stairway. It did not take long to realize that we were swimming upstream in relation to most everyone else. We even had family members and neighbors who were working contrary to God's plan for us.

With pure hearts, we began to pray for our surroundings and the people in our lives. "Lord, change them, save them, make them new," we would plead. Their hearts were hard, as ours had been. They were hurting and not helping us.

We went on a vacation, and while we were gone, we prayed again. "Lord, if they will not turn to You, please remove them from our lives," we would pray. When we returned from vacation, both our neighbors had "For Sale" signs in their yards. And our misguided family members had moved states away.

God is in everything; He protects His saints. He commands even the wind; He can certainly answer our prayers for a healthy environment. You can pray your way into a healed environment just as surely as you can be healed body, mind, and soul.

Awareness of the Cycle

The cycles of healing become obvious when you examine them with spiritual eyes. Awareness is a must as you climb the stairs to freedom.

Maintain constant awareness, knowing your surroundings either glorify God or satan. Historically, currently, and in the future, society is tilted against the Body of Christ. There is always the call to fight the good fight, both for what is going on internally and what is going on around you. Pray with discernment asking God to expose the evil order and its cycles.

It is time to end the cycle of unhealthy behaviors, emotions, and environments. God will help us prevail through supernatural warfare (PP). The psalmist encourages us to be open to God's scrutiny, knowing that His motives are pure:

> Put me on trial, LORD, and cross-examine me. Test my motives and my heart. For I am always aware of Your unfailing love, and I have lived according to Your truth (Psalms 26:2-3 NLT).

With so many issues in our lives being confronted, we may be amazed at the peace that we find in the process. Often, when the process slows down or God momentarily refrains from raising any new red flags, we assume that our healing is finished. We are never finished as long as we are still stepping on this planet. We are, however, moving upward toward freedom!

Satan comes to steal, kill, and destroy (see John 10:10). Just as is true in The Masquerade, where the stairs cycle endlessly downward, we tend to revolve around our pain. He will keep us spinning in the same sick patterns as long as we allow it. Right now, we are going to learn how to interrupt his cycles.

Unearthing Old Roots

I got off the phone with my father. Another year had gone by without a visit from him. We got along well and I just refused to accept his avoidance. I knew my lifestyle had been a thorn in his side. I had cost him endless amounts of worry and money.

"He would rather stay away," I guessed as I swallowed another pill to blunt the pain of inadequacy and rejection.

I had poor coping mechanisms for my immediate pain; but in reality, the source of this pain was the childhood abandonment I felt when my parents divorced. Feeling abandoned again in adulthood reinforced the negative cycle. Distancing was part of my father's way of dealing with difficulty. My limitless issues were just too much for him.

My father was not the real issue, however. His decisions may have been the initial catalyst for some of my pain, but I was the only one who could resolve that within me. I needed to put the pill bottle down, track back to the original hurt, the root, and ask God to help me.

On our current step, we come to grips with vicious cycles and gain understanding of the embedded patterns that support our sickness. This is also the step where we allow God to eliminate the cycles implemented by satan to protect the bad roots in our lives. These take work to uncover because the devil installs gatekeepers to stand guard over these roots.

Over time, our habits and behaviors develop around the issues and cycles that plague us. Our reactions form patterns that bring us deeper under the control of evil.

Alone, we are incapable of removing these issues. It is difficult to uncover the depths to which roots become implanted, or the time and place when habitual cycles began. Without God, a root is impossible to remove. But once we allow Him to reveal the reason behind the pain (and if we surrender with forgiveness), He will take the pain away forever. God must be the gardener here.

Once again, it is imperative that we cry out for God's fullness in us. We must be able to tap into something larger than ourselves in order to access the resources needed to do the work. The resources are divine; only divinity can combat this type of evil order. We have given the devil freedom to till the ground of our souls for so long that he has established colonies of demons and instituted the bad habits they bring. We need holy hands to wield the shovel, unearth the roots, and overthrow the cycles of hell.

When a plant takes root, it produces successive harvests of fruit. There are battles that we fight over and over again, because the root is intact under the soil and may have been for generations. We cannot see the root, but it guides us into the same arguments, the same offenses, the same hurt feelings, time after time. It reminds me of the way children act. They remember the last altercation with their siblings and they pick up where they left off. Here is an example from our home:

"He got the front seat last time!" she whines.

"She did, and she called me *dumb* and pushed me," he retaliates.

Then comes the crying and, in our house, the inevitable rebuke and sometimes spanking. I will not listen to the quarreling.

From the outside looking in, the cycle looks ignorant. Yet, I confess that my husband and I do not act much differently when we argue. We think our children's spats are silly, but ours are no better. It is what I call "plank-in-eye syndrome." We see the flecks in other people's eyes, but fail to see the telephone poles sticking out of our own (see Matt. 7:4).

More dangerous than our judgments is our ignorance of our own cycles. If we remain ignorant, the spinning continues, arguments or no arguments. Our stance needs to be: *"...as for me and my household, we will serve the LORD"* (Josh. 24:15). Serving the Lord is about what you do; it is about your reverence and regard for Him. Cycles and roots are combated in worship as God's love penetrates our hate.

About two years after my "Pentecost," I became aware of the cycles in my life. You may be shaking your head and wondering how I could be so "asleep at the wheel" after being filled with the Holy Spirit all that time. The truth is that healing is something we cannot rush. I had stepped into sobriety and was learning how to live sober. The idea of a healthy life was just sinking in. God was preparing me for the higher steps.

We have to be ready for God to break us down, clean us up, and make us aware. Then we have to let God ready us again. This succession is the cycle of hope. God's truth will replace the sick cycle that has kept us hurting so long. Satan operates in a similar but contrary way; he replicates and counterfeits God's order in an attempt to destroy our destinies.

The roots were working in my life. I kept seeing the same arguments and I was sick of them. Sometimes, we are too tired to fight; sometimes, we are just too tired to do anything about it. Neither circumstance applied in my case, so I prayed, stood, believed with faith, and fought all this on one step. I felt like I was beating my head into a brick wall *repeatedly*. I would watch the same demonic cycles resurface and I would react in godly ways. Weeks later, the same evil mess would crop up again.

"What on earth?" My shout came from a heart so passionately trying and yet so desperately failing. My question answered itself. The earth is satan's turf; he is manipulating the logistics around here.

Yet, we have protection. Our protection just happens to be where the real battle is raging—in the heavenly realms. We rarely travel far enough in our hearts and minds to realize it. But we need to go there and we need to take the right road: we will wage war in *worship*.

The Realm of Battle

Through worship, we enter the field on which the battle is being waged. We elevate our awareness to the spiritual realm where we can arm ourselves with effective weapons designed to defeat our real enemy—satan. Paul described the realm of battle beautifully in Ephesians 6:10-12:

> *Finally, be strong in the Lord and in His mighty power. Put on the full armor of God so that you can take your stand against the devil's schemes. For our struggle is not against flesh and blood, but against the rulers, against the authorities, against the powers of this dark world and against the spiritual forces of evil in the heavenly realms.*

When an argument arises in my marriage, I have to remind myself that I am not arguing with my husband. I am arguing with the demonic cycles he and I have allowed satan to implement in our lives. We need to rise above the physical details and not glorify the drama. When we rise above the physical level, we know that we are growing spiritually. We are stepping higher and getting closer to God. There we reside in the heavenly realms with praise. This upward mobility puts our weapons, purpose, protection, and healing within reach.

This does not mean we will never again be tempted to fight in the flesh. We will always be tempted to do so. We can, however, raise our chances of nipping temptation in the bud.

I remember a night when the room was dark and I was almost asleep. Brett had a Christ-centered speaking engagement at the local college the next day; I was scheduled to speak at a community worship service that same night.

Many of the churches in the area were invited to the worship service. I was prayed up and prepared to minister, but I was not ready for the warfare that was about to erupt. The most ridiculous part of this story is that satan did not even need to use a new technique to get this thing going. No, the devil dipped into the same old cycle; familiar words came out of my husband's mouth; they did not have to be mean words or nasty words, just the same old words.

We fought all night. To this day, I could not even offer a reason for the fight. Whether it was satan's attempt to make us feel unworthy and keep us quiet, or whether we just happened to be tired, unguarded, and fleshly enough to tangle, I don't know. I know this much—we wasted a good night's sleep and we allowed our joy to be stolen.

The speeches went over without a hitch. By that time, we were totally dependent on God to carry us; all we could do was let Him speak through us (which is the only way to speak for God, anyhow).

You reside in the heavenly realms above these battles of the flesh. Rise up! It took me way too long to realize God never intended this power struggle with satan. What many call warfare is merely a lack of spiritual conditioning and a deficiency in knowledge of their placement in the Kingdom.

Dig deep and notice any repetitive behaviors that make you sad, fearful, or angry. Even after years of healing, one of mine was the inability to fight fair with my husband. This is not surprising, really. Satan wants to dismantle marriage because it is God's covenant. There is amazing power in our marital unity. God, through Paul, likened the bond of marriage to that shared by Christ and the Church (see Eph. 5).

Find the cycles; look deep under the soil of your heart so that you can cut them loose and release them to God. The point where my cycle began to break was where I accepted the fact that my husband was not the enemy. The devil is the enemy and he comes at us through the closest vessels possible, even after we receive healing. Once I identified the enemy, I also recognized the cyclical behaviors that had been birthed out of root issues in each of our lives. These roots had been keeping us tormented; we did not know what the roots were, but God allowed us to see the cycles they produced. This revelation came when we were surrendered and ready to break the cycles.

Once we become determined to arrest the cycles in our lives, God steps in and gives us a place to rest in Him. He literally stopped me in my tracks. For a time, I felt like I was on hold or in slow motion. He had to slow me down so that the spinning top that was this cycle in my life could stop. When it did, I saw writing on it. It said, "Rejection, worthlessness, shame, and abandonment." That was what I needed to know and be healed from so that I could exit the cycle.

When we allow God's rest in us, the cycle has to rest too. In this rest, the ground opens up and exposes the root for easy removal.

Power and Peace

Worship is the central truth in this chapter. I believe it is no accident that the topic comes up near the center point of this book.

Praising God keeps us in a peaceful place of healing where we can grow steadily into Christ's likeness. Here we can love others from a godly perspective, alleviating a lot of our pain and protecting ourselves from further external hurts.

Worship is the vessel that takes us into the Holy of Holies to reside with Him. Only there can we experience fullness of joy and completeness in Him. It is the place of tranquility and healing that surpasses anything imaginable on earth. Behind the veil, He guides us into a mindset of Heaven and teaches us of His Kingdom on earth. This is the place that heals, delivers and imparts God's love.

We are responsible to learn about the role of worship because God created us to worship Him. How powerful is the truth that satan himself headed up the praise team in Heaven and his current work of control is the very reason we are hurting down here? We need power, not control. Find that power and know that, just as satan's relationships sent him south of the third Heaven, so do ours. (See Ezekiel 28.)

As long as we are sick and hurting, why wouldn't our relationships be a mess? Our relationships reflect our own condition. Everyone is involved in some type of relationship, whether with friends, spouses, children, siblings, parents, coworkers, church members, or extended family. Whatever the relationships, each of us is aware of arguments and disagreements that follow cyclical patterns.

Regardless of whom we argue with, these patterns are common to human beings. One of satan's major tactics is to capitalize on our habitual patterns. Our healing needs to encompass our need to crucify old patterns, not only within ourselves, but within our dealings with others.

Once we enjoy internal freedom in Christ, the enemy will attack us through our associations. We must deny all of his attempts. As God broke down and destroyed my personal cycles (addiction, depression, and anxiety), new hurts started coming in from the outside. Just as satan used other people to plant some of the original bitter roots in our lives, he will attempt to reestablish outside influences to inflict fresh pain. He sees that our healing has undermined his original plan, so he initiates new ones.

God's plan is for godly relationships on all levels. In the following passage from Ephesians, Paul addresses the Jews and the Gentiles. However, because the power of God's Word operates on multiple levels, I also see this passage as instructive to all godly unions: church and state, marriage, relationships, etc.:

Jewel for the Journey

We have to experience true worship before we can experience true freedom.

> *For He Himself is our peace, who has made the two one and has destroyed the barrier, the dividing wall of hostility, by abolishing in His flesh the law with its commandments and regulations. His purpose was to create in Himself one new man out of the two, thus making peace, and in this one body to reconcile both of them to God through the cross, by which He put to death their hostility* (Ephesians 2:14-16).

Unity and peace are God's relational prescription.

My Hurt Plus Your Hurt

His dark, thick hair moved as he swung his head to remove the hindrance from his eyes. He was tall, tan, and handsome. I remember seeing my husband for the first time when I was 22. From the outside, we appeared to be happily partaking of life together. Our looks in no way represented the state of our hearts. Our hearts had been hurt and were about to enter a cycle that would wound us both for the next decade.

We were inseparable and inseparably sick. I loved to listen and talk to him. We were so similar and at ease with one another. Both of us were in the same place with Christ, thinking we had arrived, but in reality resisting sanctification and His love. God had a strong call on both of our lives. To equal degrees, we were ignoring the call.

The profitable side of the similarity my husband and I shared was our love for Christ. In the design of satan's evil counterbalance, we shared destructive similarities: addiction and denial. Look around. If you are like the rest of us, you will notice that you have surrounded yourself with likeminded people. This tendency can profit you or cost you dearly (PP).

My husband did not mind my disorders or addictions; he was not a threat to my habits. Nor did I threaten his. We were perfect candidates for satan's circular plan. In fact, we enabled his schemes against our lives and our relationships. If the enemy can keep your family sick, he can keep you out of godly agreement with each other. That is a seriously destructive strategy, because agreement is power:

> *Again, I tell you that if two of you on earth agree about anything you ask for, it will be done for you by My Father in heaven. For where two or three come together in My name, there am I with them* (Matthew 18:19-20).

Do not let the enemy convince you that you and your spouse are not compatible. Unless your mate is rejecting the Gospel, the problem is likely a lack of awareness of the cycle. You be the strong one and defeat the enemy. You are defeating the cycle in your own life. Now stand in the gap for your marriage. The two will synch up eventually.

Pray for your mate. Do not allow the devil to prod you into waging war against the one you love. And remember this: God will only heal the willing party, and then the healed party must pray and stand in the gap, not run away. We have to be strong enough to recognize the cycle in our lives before we can see its manifestation in our relationships and the lives of others. We do this by worshiping God and seeking Him in prayer.

My marriage cycled through seven years of hell because we were sick and choosing sickness. That season ended with our surrender to God in everything we could see. Then we stepped into an entire year of individual healing and transition into God's ways. When that year concluded, we were shocked to find that we still fought.

We are human and we have flesh. This fact is irrefutable; it is the reason this book not only tells you how to get healthy, but how to stay there. His love is working in you and His love works best through consistent worship and praise of Him.

The same healing steps that I climbed for deliverance from my pain, I still have to tread for anything else that hurts me. We also need God's loving sensitivity to heal our associations and our surroundings. Call on Him; ask His guidance. He is willing to heal all things.

We can finally see the cycle. We are still climbing; remember, it is a beautiful, lifelong journey.

Baby Girl "Blue"

I sat up, bent over on the gurney and pulled air and prayer into my body. I kept my head tilted toward the cross of Christ on the wall. I said His name aloud as the anesthetist inserted the epidural. "Jesus, my Jesus."

I felt the sting and soon the medicine begin to numb my toes. The anesthetist lowered me back down to the gurney and taped my arms straight out like the Messiah on the cross. My knees, my waist, and then my neck began to prickle and buzz. I thought how amazing it was that I could lie awake while a doctor literally cut open my body.

I rested in Christ.

"She's numb; we are ready," the doctor said with authority.

I took one last breath before he cut and lifted a prayer to Heaven silently, "Please, Lord, have her be healthy. Do not let my sins affect her. Forgive me, Father, for my weakness and sickness; do not allow the pain to fall on her physically or mentally. Please have her be healthy."

The doctor touched my abdomen with the scalpel and applied pressure; the blade began to penetrate my flesh deep and deeper.

"I can feel the knife. I can feel the pain. I can feel it and—please—it hurts! Help me! Stop cutting me! Please!"

I could get no more words out before he inserted a tube into my throat. Suddenly, I was unaware of the precious birth that was about to occur. I felt I deserved the void. In all the commotion, they neglected to ask my husband into the room. He could hear, but not see what was going on.

Our baby girl was born without her mommy or daddy's comforting greeting. We did not deserve her. God gives us gifts sometimes that we do not deserve because He knows we will eventually arise to the occasion.

I call our precious, middle baby girl *Blue,* not because I spent the years surrounding her birth literally in sickness and tears, but because our whole family has dark eyes and she is the proud owner of two huge crystal-blue ones. Whenever I read the passage about Moses on Mount Sinai seeing God standing on blue sapphire, I think of my daughter's eyes.

So often, during times of great joy, warfare develops. I was my most depressed and vulnerable to the devil and his cycles during this time period. The doctors had medicated me during my pregnancy; I was terrified that my child would be born sick. She was born alone, but very healthy.

My sadness had nothing to do with my baby girl. She is perfect. My sadness was because the cycle was so evil. I felt like I could not break the fear and medication off my life. The spinning got worse before it got better. The cycle of addiction during those transitional years became almost unbearable. I could feel the pressure, and so could the enemy.

While, in reality, I was moving closer to freedom, everything seemed to be getting worse. I did not realize that my experience was common to those who are verging on a breakthrough. When you press through the pressure and get a glimpse of what God has in store, the devil knows that he is losing the reins on your life. Healing has arrived.

In what areas have you begun to recognize the evil cycle on your life? Are you ready to allow God to stop the spinning? If so, do you believe He will? Please do not forget to hope, have faith, pray always, read three chapters a day, and worship Him! Remember, worship takes us into a safe place where God protects us from everything and everyone.

Consistent Pressing Into The Asphalt

Do you remember my purgatory stage as I crawled out of the hell of addiction back in Chapter 2? God literally split that year into two halves: six months of my own might and six months of baby steps in His Spirit, neatly divided by my infilling of the Holy Spirit.

That year started with the release of the pill bottles I held so tightly. After five months without pills, and having just graduated from treatment, I separated from my husband, moved out of my home, and into an apartment. The cycle in my marriage was too much for me.

I did not understand. So often, we don't. We are healing and making great changes, but the relationships surrounding us are often exactly what satan uses to draw us back into sickness. Relationships are part of life, and that is why we are covering associations on this step. While we are going through an individual healing process, we must be aware of our links to other people.

When we are sick, we need to accept the fact that our friends, spouse, family, and kids are having a rough time, too. Our hope lies in the fact that, just as God is healing us, He can heal our relationships. In my healing, He healed some friends and family and took some away from me. Either way, I had to surrender the cycle and them unto Him. Sometimes, following Christ means letting go of people and things we love:

> *Peter said to Him, "We have left everything to follow You!" "I tell you the truth," Jesus replied, "no one who has left home or brothers or sisters or mother or father or children or fields for Me and the gospel will fail to receive a hundred times as much in this present age...and in the age to come, eternal life* (Mark 10:28-30).

Notice that Jesus mentions everyone except spouses here, because we are one with them.

Where our opposition is the strongest, God will do the most transformational works. We can pray for healing in our relationships, our spouses, our marriages, and in our children. God sent us a double rainbow the day I came home to my husband. He sent a double promise right outside our kitchen window!

He also gave us a physical manifestation of His promise, one that we could hold. We were both sober, awake, and right there to welcome her—our third child was born on our ninth wedding anniversary. If you know basic math (which is questionable in my life at times—I love calculators), you know that nine is divisible by three, three times, and three is the number of the trinity. Not to mention there are nine gifts of the Spirit, which we will cover, and nine fruit. God is in every detail, pay close attention.

She is delightful, loving, and joyful. Her eyes sparkle and she emanates peace. God has allowed us to see His pleasure in her. The love is beyond words. Our other two children are just as much of a blessing. They are precious gifts from the throne room. We just recognize the timing of Jordan's birth and realize that we almost missed her. Let us not miss our glory. God has it saved up in Heaven, but He shows up down here in amazing ways.

If I had not surrendered to stop my own cycle and the cycle the devil had imposed on my relationships, I would have missed many blessings and stopped blessings for my husband and children. If we are not aware of our vulnerability to damaging cyclical patterns, we will ignorantly pass them through our generations. Let us stop the spinning top and rest in Him.

Place of Praise

Take a look around; you are standing on higher ground. If you feel a tad dizzy, it is OK. I felt the same way. Denial and control have been released. We have stepped into surrender and guidance. We are protecting ourselves with constant prayer and the daily reading of the Word. We are aware of our relationships and recognize negative cycles.

On this step, we add the Life Application Action of *praise*. If you are unsure as to how to praise and worship God, just put in a praise and worship CD. During this very step in our own lives, my husband and I received a book on shouting to the Lord. It actually asked us to stand in our living room and shout out praises to Him. We did what the book said. We found out that words *work,* especially when they are heartfelt cries!

He made us to extol Him. If we do not praise Him, the rocks will (see Luke 19:40). When I have good news and call my Vicki D., she will say, "That is tambourine shaking revelation." Get one, shake it, and jump up and down while singing, "Thank you, Jesus, for my healing!" I am not kidding or better yet, go get you a shofar (if that is foreign to you make it an indigenous blessing).

Get before Him with a humble and contrite heart with nothing but glory for Him. Remove thoughts and requests from your mind and heart. Ask forgiveness; enter His gates with thanksgiving and His courts with praise (see Ps. 100:4). Ask Him to take you from the outer court into the Holy Place and then behind the torn curtain into the Holy of Holies. Then bask in His presence and might. Worship all the time and everywhere.

I have a prayer room in my home. Some days I spend hours in that space dancing, singing, and thanking Him. People do that for football teams that have nothing invested in their lives once they leave the stadium. Why do we cap our excitement for and from God who is willing to come into the same room as us upon the mention of His name? Lift Him up in worship and watch His presence fall. We need His presence to heal us, fix our families, and restore our surroundings. If we have relationships, we must honor those who are honorable and allow them to heal right alongside us.

Once we recognize the cycles that hinder us, we need to find the initial hurt, the root that generated the cycle in the first place. The next step is to allow God to destroy the root. This is how the cycle is broken. We become aware and God Himself eradicates the underlying issue and restores that portion of the soul. Suddenly, we notice that we have stepped off the escalator careening toward hell. Now, we are moving in a new cycle called *hope*.

THE PRINCESS PRINCIPLES PRACTICE

Step Into Stopping the Cycle:

- Develop an awareness of repetitive behaviors that are causing pain.

- Become willing to quit those behaviors and prayerfully wait on God to uncover the catalyst that activated them.

- Motivate yourself to worship God so that He can bring a stop to the very thing over which you are powerless.

- Release others from being responsible for your healing.

- Be diligent to change social structures.

Life Application Action

Worship

Worship the LORD with gladness; come before Him with joyful songs (Psalms 100:2).

Do you know the true power behind worship and that He actually made us to praise Him. He inhabits our praise. He enters the very room you are in when you exalt Him! Get some good prophetic worship music and invite Him in.

Summary of Princess Principles

 Our best defense is a consistent offense: continuous stepping up on the staircase of healing to combat the devil's cycle of bondage.

Resist him, standing firm in the faith, because you know that your brothers throughout the world are undergoing the same kind of sufferings (1 Peter 5:9).

Knowing you are not alone, list some simple ways you can resist the devil:

 We cannot heal and stay comfortable at the same time.

I have told you these things, so that in Me you may have peace. In this world you will have trouble. But take heart! I have overcome the world (John 16:33).

List some things you know are going to make you uncomfortable to release: Do not feel powerless, re-read the above Scripture and know you have the comfort/peace in Christ to overcome.

 It is time to end the cycle of unhealthy behaviors, emotions, and environments. God will help us prevail through supernatural warfare.

The weapons we fight with are not the weapons of the world. On the contrary, they have divine power to demolish strongholds (2 Corinthians 10:4).

Worship comes before warfare! List the weapons listed in Ephesians 6:10-18. Draw a picture to remember them if you need to (I did—a little stick figure with tons of armor on, silly but quite helpful!):

 Look around. If you are like the rest of us, you will notice that you have surrounded yourself with likeminded people. This tendency can profit you or cost you dearly.

So then, just as you received Christ Jesus as Lord, continue to live in Him, rooted and built up in Him, strengthened in the faith as

you were taught, and overflowing with thankfulness. See to it that no one takes you captive through hollow and deceptive philosophy, which depends on human tradition and the basic principles of this world rather than on Christ (Colossians 2:6-8).

Pray for discernment and protection. List the people you know that you do not need to be around:

Congratulations, you have successfully made it up another step—and with a bit of artwork this time. You are *aware of the cycles* in your life. You have also added another Life Application Action to your day! You are *worshiping* the Almighty God.

Step up, my healthy friend!

Chapter Six

Deep Roots in Royal Ground

Step Six: Excavate the Roots by Resting in Him

They are like trees in autumn that are doubly dead, for they bear no fruit and have been pulled up by the roots (Jude 1:12 NLT).

Then Christ will make His home in your hearts as you trust in Him. Your roots will grow down into God's love and keep you strong (Ephesians 3:17 NLT).

Rest and Release

WELL into my healing, I was disobedient, bitter, and angry. I had overcome a lot through Christ; yet, in some circumstances, I had released symptoms, but not the root issue. Once we allow God to destroy the root, the nasty feelings begin to subside and we feel an indescribable and undeniable freedom in our healing.

Think of it this way: When you go the doctor for a cough, the doctor looks for something deeper than your symptom. He listens to your cough, but looks further, knowing that there is a root issue causing it. He looks into your mouth, down into your throat, and sometimes even checks your lungs.

On this sixth step, we have made ourselves vulnerable and allowed God to help us find the reasons for our poor behavior and choices. He resolves the bad feelings we have by exposing and removing whatever caused them. As we trust Him for healing, the symptoms or unhealthy behaviors disappear.

When I arrived at this point, I was off drugs and alcohol. My feelings of depression and anxiety had resolved, so no more medicine was prescribed. My shopping addiction was over, but my personality still had some hitches in it. That made me frustrated and angry. I surrendered these areas to God and began stepping through each of the levels again in an effort to peel back and expose both the cycles and roots of my pain.

Many times, we eliminate our addictions, eating disorders, harmful decisions, and idolatry, but hold on to guilt, bitterness, depression, and anger. We wonder why we still feel rotten even though we are acting right. The trouble is that we still own the problem and are still sick. Satan still has legal ground in the soul; therefore, we are still in bondage. This is the point at which we must choose to let go, not only of the pain, but of the burden. Our life application actions so far are hope, faith, prayer, reading, and worshiping. Now we will add rest to our worship. These two things seem like apt counterbalances to one another; they actually necessitate one another. We need God's presence to rest in Him. Usher Him in and rest in His arms. Worship Him in Spirit and in truth, knowing that God inhabits our praise.

Steps matter. We want it all at once, but we can only do it a step at a time. We must be careful that by the time a step is accomplished we are not too exhausted. We can rest and should always rest in Him; yet we cannot stop. If we stop and give in or up, we stay sick. If we use our exhaustion as an excuse not to do more, then we have stopped healing. The resting I am talking about is getting into His presence to receive from His Spirit what you need to continue the journey. It is quiet time alone, allowing God to move in you.

The Lord Himself took time to rest from His labors (see Gen. 2:2). He rested on the seventh day and still calls us to rest on the Sabbath. He asks us to take a break once a week, so rest must be important. The journey you are on is hard work. Not only do we need rest to gain strength for the next step, but often we also need an interval of time while we process and understand more fully what He has done.

God is concerned for our well-being and promises to be our rest:

> *Come to Me, all you who are weary and burdened, and I will give you rest. Take My yoke upon you and learn from Me, for I am gentle*

and humble in heart, and you will find rest for your souls. For My yoke is easy and My burden is light (Matthew 11:28-30).

When we are in between the stairs, we are typically in one of two states: walking out the healing or taking God-ordained rest. The rest is when He fills us and readies us for the next challenge; it is mainly spiritual. Paul tells us of His travels to the third level in Heaven as an example of resting in Him (see 2 Cor. 12:2).

Rest does not always mean sitting in a lounge chair and sipping a fruity beverage. The rest we are discussing here is a kind of soaking submission to God. It is letting go of our thoughts, actions, schedules, ways, habits—*everything*—up to Him as we trust Him to move us in the direction we need to go.

Being still and silent when you want to scream and run is an example of soaking unto sanctification. It means relishing His renewing and refreshing. While respite is a beautiful truth, it is also difficult to find. When Adam and Eve listened to the wrong voice and disobeyed God, the consequences marred our lives. In our fleshly state, it is hard to take proper rest in God. We seem to either be workaholics or TVaholics.

Yet the psalmist assures us that God has provided it: *"The LORD is my shepherd; I have all that I need. He lets me rest in green meadows; He leads me beside peaceful streams"* (Psalm 23:1-2 NLT).

Rest is a delicately designed, vulnerable state that requires great faith to enter. The rest demands we trust completely. It usually goes against everything we think or feel or want to do. Adherence to the state of rest seems to run opposite of our will.

Scripture explains that *not to rest* is to be disobedient:

> *There remains therefore a rest for the people of God. For he who has entered His rest has himself also ceased from his works as God did from His. Let us therefore be diligent to enter that rest, lest anyone fall according to the same example of disobedience. For the word of God is living and powerful, and sharper than any two-edged sword, piercing even to the division of soul and spirit, and of joints and marrow, and is a discerner of the thoughts and intents of the heart* (Hebrews 4:9-12 NKJV).

Let us be diligent to enter His rest, lest we fall.

Only God Can Untangle It

Resting is good especially before we begin to excavate roots out of our lives. Roots are the epicenter of our pain. They are the festering source from which the pain began. A root is born from a life hurt; we saw, felt, heard, tasted, or touched something that wounded us deep down. Some hurts are hard to face, but God will always cushion us and carry us to victory (PP).

We need to relax and let the Lord gently lead us back to that place of pain so we can be healed. Going back there helps us to see whether or not the sting was our fault. Either way, we can then strip it of its control over our lives. Once God heals it, the issue is over, never to return. As the prophet said, *"Forget the former things; do not dwell on the past. See, I am doing a new thing!..."* (Isa. 43:18-19).

Sometimes we may not remember the action or event that precipitated the painful issue. We may have blocked the starting place and do not even know where to look. God's Spirit can find any hidden pain and release our hurt. He will get to the pain and we will allow Him to plant new roots in place of the old ones—roots of self-worth, security, love, peace, health, and a sound mind.

Most of my roots developed as an only child of divorced parents. I was the reason the earth rotated and revolved around the sun. My parents rarely disciplined me. I liked this plan. It suited me well, until I realized that the rest of society was not on board with it. I went from delusions of grandeur right into being The Roach Princess. It was a very abrupt and brutal transition. Have you experienced being a victim to your upbringing?

Even if our pain originated from somebody else's transgression, we have to choose to get out and get healed. I dug deep with God to get out. I was determined to find the catalyst that activated my pain, so that I could step back and let God remove it. To have played the victim would have put me right back into the devil's hands; I am convinced that he can destroy someone simply through the victim mentality.

I had collected several roots and buried them deep down in tightly packed soil. The evil shoots began to intertwine and twist into a tangled ball. Roots like insecurity formed inside me due to a lack of biblical foundation, family instability, disobedience (from lack of discipline), rejection (from the divorces and my father's departure from the home), perfectionism (from performance mentality and the absence of foundation in Christ), sadness (from a lack of acceptance), and fear (from a lack of belief, wisdom, and knowledge).

To make matters worse, I hardened my heart and covered it really well with a hopeless, controlling, stubborn disposition, and a heaping dose of denial.

Stop, Look, and Listen

This step is difficult. We have to go as deep as we can for now and we may shed many tears as we shed the pain. We will also realize many times that the pain was caused by something of which we were not even aware. Sometimes, we need godly counsel and intervention through deliverance ministries, another form of deeper guidance. We may need someone in front of us to wipe the tears away. God sends saints to stand alongside us—people who can look at us and connect to us spiritually during our healing (see Rom. 1:11; Acts 19:6).

If you feel as though you are going through your journey alone, make sure you are not alienating yourself. God gives abundantly, if we remain in Him. He will provide company for us when we trust Him and trust ourselves. Remember, you must walk up each step and you must grab hold of His provision.

When God directs saints to enter your life, you will know their presence is divine and precious. Looking back on the company He sent into my own life, I can see how amazing and instrumental they were.

You don't need just anybody's help; you need the right people to walk you through your healing. You can go to your pastor and pray together for God to reveal the people who have been there, who have stepped up themselves, and who now carry the Holy Spirit as a sounding board, to guide us back through the memories of our lives. *Please do not seek counsel with unfilled vessels.*

I came out of the denial of addiction, depression, anxiety, idolatry, eating issues, and many other things. I surrendered them and dug deep to figure out where the issues came from in the first place. The roots can be wide-ranging: the gamut runs from childhood molestation to someone taping a nerd sign to your back on the school bus. Life deals us all kinds of pain coming from a wide variety of roots.

What I have learned is this: If something hurt you, pay attention to it. Deal with it head on in prayer.

Remember that no matter who hurt you, God is bigger than they are and vengeance is His (see Rom. 12:19). If you love Him, He will protect and comfort you.

Follow God's "Program"

As different roots were exposed in my life, I asked forgiveness for my part. I repented for not trusting God sooner and I obediently walked out the next leg of healing. Whatever bad behaviors resulted from those roots, they vanished with a swipe of God's finger. I do not know where they went, but they are undeniably forever gone.

The emotional stress in my life was subsiding, but I still suffered with some strongholds. There was a moment in which I had an epiphany; I realized that stepping up the heavenly staircase was a lifelong process. We want it all at once, all now. Accepting this fact was like accepting the fact that I was evil, and they both are key!

That does not mean we should tolerate strongholds. They are demonic and you need to let God remove them. They are the negative areas in your life that seem to be chronic, as though they were glued to you. Hear this: they are *not* stuck to you and you are *not* trapped. You have, however, allowed them to reign. You have ceded to the devil some legal ground in your soul. He is opportunistic and operates from that patch of territory.

When we know God is willing to recapture that ground for us, yet we refuse Him the room to operate in our lives, we are allowing the pain to reside in us. Do you see knots or tangles in your pain and healing? Where are they? Some areas clean out

Jewel for the Journey

Your pain is never too great or small for God to heal. Don't be one who builds a great a wall around the pain; invite Him in to help.

more easily than others. The devil has caulked in and duct-taped over the resistant ones. This is because you keep trying to fix the tangle.

What you need to know is this: Only God can undo the tangle.

I want us to see that not all the roots can come out at once. While some may be released, we need to be aware there may be more left in place. If we are obedient, God will remove all of them in His perfect timing. We need to have hope and faith for complete healing. We also embrace the reality of this being a process, a beautifully planned one, at that. Our garden may not always be weed-free but it will be glorious and fruitful as long as we are stepping in tune with the Father.

In my case, the weeding involved getting to a powerful root: anger. I had a great deal of frustration from childhood pain that had formed a tangled knot of anger in my soul. Aggravation became a learned response to not getting my way. It was an unhelpful response that cycled throughout my life.

Uncovering the root was a key to healing, but healing can be messy. Often we feel stuck in habitual states of recurrence; sometimes we are. Check to make sure you are not trying to skip any steps. Remember that God will not let you graduate from something you have not yet learned. Refinement continues until you get the message.

God wants us to get the message and act on it. That means actively understanding Scripture, taking corresponding actions, and successfully applying truth to our lives.

He holds us accountable for the action part of the healing. But remember that God's timing does not conform to ours. I was healing, praying, and studying God's Word daily; yet I kept failing in some areas and still could not figure out why.

Just as falling while going down the stairs lands you at the bottom, running up the stairs usually involves skipping one or more of them. That was a revelation for me, one I am still trying to master. So many times, God extends His hand to me so that I can step back down and complete a step I raced past in my fury for the finish line.

He demands rest from us during this step. I felt like I was in slow motion on this stair. God had taken His hand and stopped me in my tracks. I was trying to outrun Him. I thought that if I just kept trucking, the pain would eventually disappear. Unfortunately, the pain was trucking right alongside me.

When I relented to believe He would provide if I stopped, God taught me true rest. He did this so I could see every move; each bend in my healing needed to be considered. He wanted me to be meticulous and allow Him to identify all of the roots so that I could resume my upward journey. He loved me enough to slow me down and clean me out again. It was uncomfortable. I felt vulnerable; the stopping seemed odd.

What I failed to realize is that, when we are sick, we are so far behind God that getting ahead of Him is not an option. Ironically, trying to jump ahead of Him is just as defeating as living in the chariot's dust. Promotion without God's endorsement is not a promotion at all. In our newfound freedom, we need to be extremely careful not to strive for achievements that are outside of God's purpose.

Stepping into healing is hard; postponing what we think is progress is just as hard because we see it as a denial of our vision. We must rest in Him and allow His lead, His unction, and His progress in us. We must abandon the versions of progress that we generate from our limited thought capacity.

His version will undo the tangle, dismantle the ball, and then remove the roots slowly and steadily. When we get ahead of Him, we tend to run forward while dragging old roots and cycles with us. He calls us back because He knows we cannot take this baggage to the next level.

Deliverance: Stepping Out the Healing

Supernatural counsel is often hard to explain in understandable terms. Often, however, such counsel is extremely necessary for our spiritual health. As I said earlier, we sometimes block out or fail to recognize the source of our pain. There are times when we cannot seem to find the epicenter. The Spirit has no such difficulty.

I found it helpful to seek a deeper level of guidance on this step. It had to be someone who had walked with the Spirit through the hurt and all the way down to the root. I needed someone who had treaded the depths of Heaven and hell and had been ordained by God to do His bidding. This had to be a person who could access the realms, guarding and guiding as the Spirit took me back to heal.

Go through this step carefully; you may discover unexpected pieces of your history. In my case, I did not even know that my first stepfather's presence and exodus from my life had caused so much pain. Looking back now, I have clarity. After gaining some experience in the healing steps, I realized that there was more work to do in some areas. I needed more godly guidance; this time I specifically needed the ministry of a prophet.

Deliverance—that is what this type of counsel is called, because it actually delivers people. The word *deliverance* should not seem strange. It is exactly what it says: delivery from root issues, iniquity, and generational curses to restore the soul. I do not want to weird anyone out with a title, but the title fits and there is no need to sugarcoat or call it something it is not.

So many times, we are afraid of the very thing that actually works because we cannot control it, explain it, or did not grow up with it. My husband and I definitely did not grow up with deliverance ministry, but it was exactly what we needed. We were open to believe and we had the faith. That fulfilled our part of the bargain, and we received.

Not Fooled by Rabbit Trails

On one occasion, my husband had just finished his session and I was on the way to mine. They liked to do them back to back, so that one of us would not get ahead of the other. I arrived at the church, stepped in, greeted my God-fearing counsel, sat down, and began to walk backwards through my life.

For the record, you do not always have to go to a special meeting for this. God just happened to call my husband and me to one. In fact, you can do this alone or with guidance at home. All you really need is to have cleared the steps thus far and know how to become vulnerable to God so the Holy Spirit can do the work.

At one of the deliverance sessions, I began to speak about a childhood occasion when I was around eight or nine. It was the first time I'd felt like I had a family. After my birth parents divorced, my mother remarried. I felt comfort in knowing we were not alone anymore. My stepdad had two children, a girl roughly my age and a younger boy. Jackpot! I even gained a sister and brother. Finally, I was normal and safe; no longer was I free-floating without a foundation.

After my parents' divorce, the loneliness and insecurity settled in like a flood of hopelessness. As a vulnerable child, I suddenly felt the need to protect and provide for myself. When children have to assume adult associations whether physical, spiritual, or mental, it cracks their foundation. The enemy is then free to drop in his seeds; roots push down and weeds spring up.

Most times, if we go back to the place we think caused the hurt, we will find a string of events like machine gun fire that occurred back, to back, to back. The devil loves to kick us while we are down, just to guarantee the root will take and tangle. Normally, the reason we identify as the cause of the pain proves to be nothing more than a distraction to keep us on a rabbit chase.

So often we do not see the actual issue or we ignore it; that is why we are still hurting. We, however, are prepared and will allow the Spirit to do the work.

My parental history was complex. I was happy to have a "real" family again. I felt God's love in allowing me a second chance and a live-in father. I also loved seeing my real father. I saw him on weekends, some Wednesdays, and in the summer months. He was a pilot, so we traveled a lot. I loved to travel with him. The trips made me feel loved and important. I never understood the transitions going back and forth from Mom to Dad. They were hurtful. It was a case of "never the two shall speak." That left me feeling like I had to pick a side.

During my deliverance session, I remembered all the neat things my stepfather used to build for me. Somehow, these moments and offerings triggered my recollection of the pain. There was a tree house, a doghouse, a solar system game for a school project that won first place, and the most perfect, beautiful dollhouse ever (it looked just like our home).

My stepfather was an alcoholic. Pretty soon, Mom began to feel insecure with him and so I lost my family again. They divorced by the time I was entering high school. Never thinking that this separation had caused more pain than my biological father's exodus, but sitting there in the presence of God decades later, I could see how the consistent losses had affected my life. At the time, I did not realize the impact. I also learned that, without God, we will assume incorrect sources for our pain and waste years focusing on wrong or even phantom roots.

Close the Gate

That session showed me how the lack of security and the breach of trust and stability had weakened my faith. I wept for the loss I had experienced at such a young age. Why was I not worthy to have security, a family, a sister, or a brother? For all those years, I had let other people's faulty decisions determine my worth.

These types of issues become embedded in the family because no one closes the gate on them. Generational pain is anything ungodly that a parent, blood relative, or grandparent passes on to future generations. What losses have you endured from generational sins or curses? Which of these surprised you when God revealed them? How are you forgiving and moving past them? Have you let God remove the iniquity and close the gate?

Grief over losses we have neglected to face is an important part of our journey. We need to make sure we do not just react to the removal of the roots. We need to give ourselves time to grieve the events and their effects. We need to allow God to help us to forgive and forget. We can allow the process to be sad. Matthew 5:4 says, *"Blessed are those who mourn, for they will be comforted."*

Our goal is to acknowledge and release the root in order that it no longer continues to manifest. We will allow God to comfort us and we will agree that it is OK to rest and lament. We will let the emotions run their God-ordained course: not too long, not too short, not too high, or too low, if you know what I mean. Ultimately, the grieving needs to stop; acceptance and forgiveness need to engulf the grief. What I did was to go backward and then forward throughout my childhood and all the way through my young adult years—even through the hallways of my early marriage and addictions.

The Spirit walked with me through deliverance. He took me to where the pain originated. He wiped my tears and helped to remove the roots causing the pain, hurt, and sadness. He then removed guilt, fear, and unbelief. Then He told me to forgive.

Forgiveness is a critical part of healing. Until forgiveness is given and received, the root remains. Forgiveness is a multilevel process and a difficult concept for us to understand. We need to allow God to help us along the path of forgiveness so that we know it is sincere and fruitful. True godly forgiveness is committing within your heart to forever forgo an offense and letting God remove the emotions attached.

Let go of what you can and only by God's direction. Release the shallow roots and the deep ones, too, if possible. Bind them in the name of Jesus. Loose them from your being and release them to the place where God will hold them captive. Then fill yourself with God's love, His Spirit and all of Isaiah 11:1-3. Stay far from entertaining them ever again. Be sensitive to allow the Spirit to walk with you back into your life to clean house, but never forget to fill it back up.

Luke 11:24-26 warns:

> When an evil spirit comes out of a man, it goes through arid places seeking rest and does not find it. Then it says, "I will return to the house I left." When it arrives, it finds the house swept clean and put in order. Then it goes and takes seven other spirits more wicked than itself, and they go in and live there. And the final condition of that man is worse than the first.

Isaiah 11:1-3 counterattacks:

> A shoot will come up from the stump of Jesse; from his roots a Branch will bear fruit. The Spirit of the LORD will rest on him—the Spirit of wisdom and of understanding, the Spirit of counsel and of power, the Spirit of knowledge and of the fear of the LORD—and he will delight in the fear of the LORD. He will not judge by what he sees with his eyes, or decide by what he hears with his ears.

A word to the wise: the step we are on can take hours or years. We need not rush it or get discouraged. God's great authority covers us. He has firmly planted us on His foundation. His ground is still, sound, powerful, without cracks, and never shifting or shaking. In this place of security, we can go back and relinquish any insecurity we have received from our earthly family. The pain was and is no more. God has grafted us into a much bigger family.

There are still places I am sure I did not have time or energy left to travel. I am certain He will help me with those, as I am ready. His timing is always perfect.

We are stepping up to steps that require us to use our authority in Christ. They take work but they also begin the harvest.

Resist Generational Fallout

There is a lot of truth to generational curses and sin, but not in the sour-grapes, blame-everybody-else kind of way. God even rebukes them in Ezekiel 18 for that mess. We need to break curses but we also have to take up authority and responsibility to not receive or walk in them. God places the sins of our fathers not in our hearts, but in our laps. When we grab hold, the habit activates and pain takes root in the soul (PP).

Jewel for the Journey

We will allow God to plant in the empty places left when we allowed old roots of pain to be pulled up.

Unless they are broken by us, generational curses can function in the lives of people who are affected lineally simply by being born into the family. They literally fall into our laps, and in our weakness or ignorance we pick them up, according to Jeremiah 32:17-19:

> *Ah, Sovereign LORD, You have made the heavens and the earth by Your great power and outstretched arm. Nothing is too hard for You. You show love to thousands but bring the punishment for the fathers' sins into the laps of their children after them. O great and powerful God, whose name is the LORD Almighty, great are Your purposes and mighty are Your deeds, Your eyes are open to all the ways of men; You reward everyone according to his conduct and as his deeds deserve.*

We are not defenseless, even where generational sin is concerned. The choice is ours: we can carry the curse forward or stand against it and walk away free. If your family raised you in alcoholism, you are more likely to pick up the sin and take it with you. But, through prayer, worship, and rest in God, you can arrest the progress of the curse.

Do you see yourself repeating the sins of your parents? Have you learned any sinful behaviors from either or both of your parents? Iniquity functions on two levels: there is the curse and there are learned behaviors. Unless you address both aspects, you will deal with the nuisance forever.

Usually, the poor choice to pick up such a habit is an attempt to combat some type of pain. That pain originates from a root issue. Removing that root issue will usually resolve the coping mechanism attached to it. Too often, we attack the issue the other way around. We see the drinking and want to eliminate the behavior. We assume that if the habit has ceased, the problem is solved. However, we are only halfway there. That is why addictions, disorders, depression, and pain resurface so often.

We need to cease the habit by allowing God to remove the root. Even then, resolution is not complete: we also need to resolve any bitterness we hold toward the ancestor who nursed the lovely habit long enough to hand it off to us. Here again, forgiveness is very important. I still struggle with disdain for those who are passionate about sinning continually. Most people would call this self-righteous judgment. I prefer to call it what it is: protection from infection.

As we get to the higher stairs, it becomes easy to spot blatant sin (especially other people's sin); at the same time some sins (our own) become harder to spot, easier to hide, or easier to deny. I see this as a factor of our new "altitude"; as oxygen levels decrease, reduced levels of cognition support the tendency to become self-righteous. The enemy gets more deceptive because our newfound wisdom threatens him.

Maybe we are not standing bellies up to the bar these days; but our bellies might still be parked in the back pew trying to cop a read of someone else's highlighted Bible in judgment. How does this affect our spiritual health differently than drinking does?

The Princess Palace

My mother obviously did not think my stepdad was as much fun as I thought he was, so she left him. After they divorced, we moved out of the big family home in the suburbs and into a condominium that sat just behind a gas station flanking the highway surrounding the city. My teen years up into my very early twenties, I lived in the roach room atop the condominium's castle tower. It is here that the future title, *The Roach Princess,* was formed.

My foundation had crumbled, and satan routinely nudged me. Every choice we make, whether we realize it or not, is a choice for God or for the devil. Each decision builds on the foundation of promise or of failure. There are no neutral choices. For a biblical example: read the account of Laodicea in Revelation 3:14-22. When God infills us with His Holy Spirit and removes the roots of our pain, we are able to choose success over failure (PP).

The weakness of the flesh is well documented throughout Scripture. Paul describes it powerfully:

> *I know that nothing good lives in me, that is, in my sinful nature.*
> *For I have the desire to do what is good, but I cannot carry it out.*
> *For what I do is not the good I want to do; no, the evil I do not want*
> *to do—this I keep on doing* (Romans 7:18-19).

Left unchecked, the weakness of the flesh feeds the roots of our pain. As you look back and walk through your life story, you will notice where each root issue began. You will see which roots have been addressed and which have been suppressed. You will be able to identify the stream of pain in your life. For me, much of the pain trafficked through insecurity and disobedience.

Living in a condominium with a single mother and very little discipline, I developed an unwarranted independence and defiance to authority. My mother provided as best she could, but was physically incapable of filling the role of the complete family unit I so craved. This lack birthed and nurtured bad roots in my life.

We lived on the outskirts of an affluent area—the kind of town where you carry the expensive purses and drive the shiniest cars, both smelling of true cowhide. I attended school in this well-heeled (but unfortunately, not necessarily healed) part of Atlanta. Eighth-graders attended the local high school. I was among the class of sub-freshman when we arrived.

We were not even a football field away from the Baptist Church that buffered us from the onslaught of interstate traffic Atlanta would produce hourly. It was not just a church but a megachurch. It was like having an enormous, flashing billboard in our yard that screamed, "Go to church, you fools. I have put one right next to your mailbox!"

God could not have made it more obvious. Yet, we never went, not even once.

The cool kids at this new high school accepted me. That spoke volumes; they were rich, spoiled, and had cliques dating back to their Pre-K days, and my purses smelled of plastic (there is a sad irony in that statement). They did not take well to newcomers. Satan made sure I fit in with the popular group; I made it into cheerleading and got so mixed up with the social order that I neglected to study and read. Take note of where satan has set you up for a fall. And know this: your purpose is often found in the very things the devil convinces you are purposeless.

The roots of appearance, idolatry, and social structure began to grow in me during this time. I allowed my identity to be based in what others thought of me. That root began to birth disappointment, jealousy, bitterness, perfectionism, and more insecurity. I had very little self-worth beyond their glowing opinions of me. As we have clearly seen, our identity is to be based in Christ.

There is healing in knowing that God did not intend for us to covet or compete with one another. This is so important that He mentioned it in His top-ten list of principles (see Exod. 20:17) and wrote it in stone twice.

During my stint in high school, I left the track team. Track was an area in which my abilities were strong. This gifting could have eventually paid for my college tuition. I ran a five-to six-minute mile with little effort and carried a 4.0 average. In fact, the high school coach in our old district had already integrated me into his team when I was in sixth grade.

When we moved to the condo, I replaced running with cheerleading. Friends and status replaced my studies; the world order replaced my childhood innocence. Society became my backbone. Evil seeds began to take root. I no longer ran, and my grades were Cs and Ds at best.

Look back, dig deep to find the talents you had as a young child. Remember the purpose God has for you. He never changes and His purposes never change; we just hinder them. The pain and hurt hide the promise and purpose. This concealment becomes an unhealthy protection mechanism.

My mom had that condominium, the one behind the church we never attended, decked to the hilt. She maxed every credit card to make the place and me look beautiful. I began to manifest a root that would sprout divorce, bankruptcy, eating disorders, severe depression and anxiety, and addiction.

Notice, I said that I *looked* beautiful. I did not feel beautiful. Roots of idolatry, covetousness, and greed can make us poor, not just financially but spiritually and emotionally. Thankfully, my future deliverance made me the proud recipient of God-ordained prosperity. He is not bound by earthly cash-driven commerce that is our ignorance and, sadly, our security many times. The devil wants us to live in financial defeat, but the Lord wants us to live in abundance. (For more on this kind of prosperity, see Malachi chapter three.)

By its very nature, godly prosperity is indescribable. God's profusion encompasses things like joy, peace, purity, truth, wisdom, health, and fruitfulness. I find it difficult to formulate words that are multifaceted enough to describe these miracles. I want to make sure that we do not misunderstand prosperity by placing it in an earthly context that is limited to material possessions.

Right next to my bedroom in the condominium, there was a tanning bed installed. I remember seeing the faint glow of purple oozing out from under the attic door daily. The tanning salon attic was where the roaches lived while we were awake. We weren't the only residents of the condo; we shared it with a colony of roaches. These were physical roaches; but looking back I realize there were many more on a spiritual level.

I would wake up in the middle of the night, knowing the bugs would scatter as soon as I turned on the light. The sight is enough to send you reeling. Roach movements are not predictable; they are fast and devious and have the ability to circumvent obstacles by sliding through tiny cracks.

Jewel for the Journey

Godly purpose, when acknowledged, furthers healing.

To this day, I have an aversion to the things. They say for every one you see, there are countless numbers in the walls and surrounding land. What a nasty thought—and another truth for Demon Training 101. Demons reflect the same behavior. Light makes them scatter; just because you cannot see them does not mean they are not in attendance.

One time, ticks covered the stairs leading up to my room. There were 20 or 30 of them, and they were all alive. I had to pick them up one at a time and flush them. Unlike the roaches, which are merely filthy and carry disease, these guys are parasitic and they feed off blood. Blood sucking is *not* a life-giving characteristic.

I learned at a young age that if anything was going get done, I had best do it myself. When it comes to healing, we need not look around for someone else to initiate. Healing with God and godly guidance is the surest and best way. God sends others to help, but we hold no expectation of our offenders sharing in the workload. Root issues are our issues, even if someone else caused them. If we wait for our perpetrators to release a root by apologizing to us, we postpone our healing.

The roaches had to be removed and I had to do it myself (for decades, sadly enough). I scraped together some change and got as many roach motels as I could afford. I remember they smelled like dog food when you had 16 of them together. I lined them up like soldiers, side by side in a row. They formed a protective barrier between my bed and the attic door.

Not only did they block out some of the purple glow; they allowed me to feel a little better about going to bed at night. The funny thing is that, when we try to solve things ourselves, our solutions rarely have any effect on the actual problem. The roach motels trapped lots of roaches, but never eliminated the source of the infestation. The solutions we conjure are masks; they afford temporary peace and subdue our negative feelings.

I should have also put a wet towel under the other door to stop the smoke from coming in from my mother's incessant puffing downstairs. It would not have helped for long; I soon picked the smoking curse from off my lap and gave it place in my life. I was the only 15-year-old, cigarette-smoking cheerleader with my own ashtray.

The smoke was not all that smelled at our house. We had an undisciplined dog as well; imagine that. He had some major root issues. The dog that bit my mother's lip clear off was as undisciplined as I was. He was a tick magnet, too, but he liked the roaches; he would actually eat them.

He was a beautiful buff-colored cocker spaniel named Buffington, Buffy for short. This dog used the dining room table and chairs as a restroom, saturating the carpet with urine below every chair and table leg. We could not afford new carpet, but the smell got so bad after years of urine that I finally convinced Mom of an alternate solution. I would pull up the soiled area of the carpet, clean whatever was underneath, and cover it with a floor rug. She agreed.

How often do we use this method to try to heal? We try to cut away the broken parts and fill them in with something that looks better. Yet, the problem remains unsolved. That was how life went in the Princess Palace. The cover-up and partial removal methods do not extract the root of the issue or solve the real problem (PP).

Divine Solutions Are the Answer

Here is the good news: The steps we are climbing lead to a place of divine and lasting healing. We need to address the root issues in our lives just as surely as my family needed to address our dog's lack of control. Our dog, Buffy, represents issues in our lives that we enable, embrace, and fail to restrain for comfort's sake. A lack of discipline is attached to many root issues in our lives.

Our condo story perfectly illustrates my point: Parasites and disease-carrying insects infested the house, yet no exterminator was called. Our dining room smelled of urine and was full of toxic smoke; we just lived with it. The attic contained a nuclear, neon light bed that addressed no legitimate need (and we had many). We had a vicious animal and tons of alcohol in the house; nothing changed. Strange men slipped in and out, but no father sat in the big chair where the remote control lay. There were drawers full of revealing clothes and even drugs; there were no church visits scheduled on our calendar full of shopping sprees. Now how many bad seeds were planted in our lives? Yet nothing of benefit or true value was allowed in.

Our next steps are so necessary for the endurance of our healed state. They will begin to add into the empty places left from the removal of all the pain. Obedience is a step God can bless abundantly. Pick your chin up, look around and start looking for blessings as you tread through this next chapter. It is the area where my deepest passion lies; it is also the place where so many people give up.

Please keep stepping upward, my beautiful princess friend. We are entering territory that will cement our healing. The next two chapters form a mini-transition; we empty out, fill up, and learn how to "sew into" God.

Are you staying in the Word and walking it out as James 1:22 tells us to do? The pastor cannot do it for you. You must step out in the truth of God's Word. You may not have stepped perfectly all the time, but you are coming to a place of adherence. Don't quit!

It is amazing when we look back from a healed and healing perspective. We begin to see where God ordained hope and where we finally chose Him. We see where we allowed Him to replace the old root with the root of the Word through faith-filled rest in Him. (See Ephesians 3:17-21; Colossians 2:6-7.)

This takes us up to our next step: *obedience.* It will ensure our healing and keep the pain away. *Authority, accountability, discipline, obedience*—these are all words people want to run from or falsely own. In reality, authentically achieved they are steps toward freedom. They are actions we need to take if we want to be healed.

THE PRINCESS PRINCIPLES PRACTICE

Step Into Root Excavation

- Be willing to go deep into your past, with God, so that He can heal you.

- Realize that your soul has been fragmented by pain.

- Face the hurts from your past and allow the Holy Spirit to heal, reveal, and restore.

🙌 Accept the fact that iniquity exists and that generational sin is only eradicated by God. It requires our compliance to His Word and ways.

🙌 Agree to rest in Him, allowing Him to pull your soul out of captivity and completely reestablish His design for your life.

Life Application Action

Resting

Come to Me, all you who are weary and burdened, and I will give you rest (Matthew 11:28).

Journal where your burdens are too heavy:
Pray for Him to give you rest and lighten those areas.

Summary of Princess Principles

 Some hurts are hard to face, but God will always cushion us and carry us to victory.

Consider it pure joy, my brothers, whenever you face trials of many kinds, because you know that the testing of your faith develops perseverance. Perseverance must finish its work so that you may be mature and complete, not lacking anything (James 1:2-4).

List your trials: Write the reason you must face the pain in order to persevere with faith:

God places the sins of our fathers not in our hearts, but in our laps. When we grab hold, the habit activates and pain takes root in the soul.

Ah, Sovereign LORD, You have made the heavens and the earth by Your great power and outstretched arm. Nothing is too hard for

You. You show love to thousands but bring the punishment for the fathers' sins into the laps of their children after them. O great and powerful God, whose name is the LORD Almighty, great are Your purposes and mighty are Your deeds, Your eyes are open to all the ways of men; You reward everyone according to his conduct and as his deeds deserve (Jeremiah 32:17-19).

List the sins of your fathers; We never know them all so be diligent to allow God to reveal and cleanse you of things unseen; give Him full access to your lineage. Journal a prayer of deliverance from the iniquity in your bloodline:

 When God infills us with His Holy Spirit and removes the roots of our pain, we are able to choose success over failure.

I know that nothing good lives in me, that is, in my sinful nature. For I have the desire to do what is good, but I cannot carry it out. For what I do is not the good I want to do; no, the evil I do not want to do—this I keep on doing (Romans 7:18-19).

Write a prayer containing this scripture to help you out of your sin:

 The cover-up and partial removal methods do not extract the root of the issue or solve the real problem.

I know your deeds, that you are neither cold nor hot. I wish you were either one or the other! So, because you are lukewarm—neither hot nor cold—I am about to spit you out of My mouth (Revelation 3:15-16).

List areas where you know you are half in and half out:

Congratulations! You have *released many bad roots* unto God. You have also added a new Life Application Action! You are *resting* in His arms. Do not grow weary in well doing, for this process, however long it takes, is blessed! Step up, dear friend.

Chapter Seven

Obedient as a Palace Guard

Step Seven: Step Into Obedience Through Fasting

Whatever you have learned or received or heard from me, or seen in me—put it into practice. And the God of peace will be with you (Philippians 4:9).

Drop and Give Me Ten

MANY women struggle with obedience. They are overwhelmed and believe that finding a quiet moment to do God's bidding is impossible. Obedience often feels like the fragment of a coal in your running shoe of life. It irritates your foot all the way to the bubble bath of peace. You see it as an obstacle and want to remove it. In truth, it will become a diamond of provision if you will leave it in place and subject it to the pressure of your endurance (see 2 Corinthians 12:7-10).

We will learn ways to embrace this step forever—and with joy. While we always need to allow Him to deal with our issues, we are now adding good habits and godly actions to support our endurance. Our healing and purpose depend on our fortitude in sticking with God's ways indefinitely (PP).

God's expectations are clear in the Old Testament. He called them His *law* and then exemplified them perfectly in His Son. So often, we excuse one another from obedience by casually saying we are in the dispensation of grace. While God has saved us by grace (everyone would be on a hot road to hell if He hadn't), we are not exempt from His decrees if we want power and blessing.

We are exempt from attaining salvation by adherence to rules, but it is not an excuse for sin. In Romans 6:1-2, Paul challenges the implications of free will by asking: *"What shall we say, then? Shall we go on sinning so that grace may increase? By no means! We died to sin; how can we live in it any longer?"*

God's rules in the New Testament are love, faith, brotherly love, the fruit, the Great Commission, evangelism, sanctification, praise, worship, prayer, fasting, giving, listening, resting, and turning from evil, among others. We will attain to them if we crucify our flesh and allow Him to give us His Spirit.

Christ came to fulfill the law, which He did. He did not abolish God's edicts. If you look closely at the behavior of those who are being sanctified by His Spirit, their conduct reflects adherence to none other than His law!

In the Garden, God's only requirement of Adam was that he not eat from one tree. With all the lures and ungodly options surrounding us today, I would love a simple list of commandments that said:

1. Do not eat from the tree in the middle of your front yard.

2. End of stone tablet.

Every inclination of our hearts is toward evil. To me, that means pain. God tells us this in the first book of the Bible (see Gen. 6:5). I think He wanted to make sure we did not start out in denial. He reiterates our deficiency of holiness often. We are sinful and need not only a page of commandments, but also a book full of pages of commandments (PP).

I realize that God commands us to love. That does not mean that you rip your Bible in two and commence grace period. Matthew 22:37-40 Jesus said:

> *"Love the LORD your God with all your heart and with all your soul and with all your mind." This is the first and greatest commandment. And the second is like it: "Love your neighbor as yourself."*

All the law and the prophets hang on these two commandments. This book cumulates in His love; to know the depths of His love, we must assume His Son's likeness into the very fabric of our actions.

The law consists of the entire Bible, precept upon precept, without excuse or exception. I am not advising strict regulation to a law that Christ fulfilled. Habitual nonsense is unnecessary and is a good way for satan to keep us busy. I am pointing to the respect that is due every word of God; I am talking about our accountability in allowing the Spirit to impose God's ways and Word on our lives, and even our trials.

Proverbs 30:5 stresses the perfection of God's Word: *"Every word of God is flawless; He is a shield to those who take refuge in Him."*

His commandments should be kept. While this is impossible in our flesh, it is possible with our infilling. I am not talking about all Levitical law. I am talking about forgiveness, mercy, grace, love for our enemies, communion, prayer, fasting, giving, consuming His Word—anything and everything that pleases Him.

I even feel a pull to honor His feasts (see Lev. 23:1-2). He says to keep them! The apostles and Jesus kept them, so why not us? We need to be on His calendar all the time. We ignore precious commands because we were never taught or are unwilling to undo our mindset. Lord, let us have the mind of Christ!

We love in grace and we obey through grace. Grace is the only way to true healing, but we must reside in that grace in due course by obeying His decrees. We allow His glory to pass through us to refine us to obey continually.

You could hear the crickets chirping as I sat alone night after night, day after day, hour after hour, week after week, immersed in God's Word. I would stop only to sleep. God's isolation will teach us how imperative discipline is to our success and well-being.

In my isolation from the world, I was not displacing addiction. I was captivated by God's love. This time I was not trying to fill a void. God was packing in what He needed me to have for my healing to stick.

There were so many empty places left by the removal of what the world had planted in me. My Vicki D would always say, "When you feel them, the empty spots, drink in the Spirit like water and feel it running in, filling up all the areas left open."

We will succeed, not by our might but by His Spirit (see Zech. 4:6). Once again we reference Zechariah because here discipline unto obedience becomes tolerable and accomplishable.

The Fast Track to Adherence

Now we will add fasting to our list of Life Application Actions. God calls us to difficult tasks and one of the hardest things to do is to stop eating. Nourishment sustains life and most of us enjoy not just eating, but gorging ourselves at times.

Jewel for the Journey

Obedience is difficult and fasting takes great obedience. They balance each other; fasting by its very nature teaches good discipline.

We can read the first chapter of Daniel as one of many good references to fasting. God gave Daniel, Shadrach, Meshach, and Abednego knowledge, wisdom, and insight because of their obedience to fasting (see Dan. 1:17).

We will ask Him for the things that matter to Him during our fast. Solomon just asked Him for His wisdom. He gave Solomon so much more because he asked for only what mattered to God.

He has already healed us and is healing us daily. We have the record of accomplishment to support our faith for the next request. God does not suggest that we give, pray, and fast. He tells us to do these things, saying *"When you give," "When you pray,"* and *"When you fast"* (Matt. 6:2,5,16).

When we fast, we do so healthfully and with professional advice, if necessary. (Seek your doctor's input, particularly if you have any health issues.) We seek God for His timing and process. We then commence prayer to get us through. We commit, start, and do not cheat or stop until our intended conclusion.

We fast for Christ, not for blessing. We fast because He gave us the knowledge of His expectation of this promise (PP). If you fast with a pure heart, you will experience a peace that is inexplicable and worth the trial. He even tells us in His Word that some issues can only be resolved through fasting (see Mark 9:29).

I remember once, I had just come off a three-day fast and was heating up wax to use for a project. I remember putting the wax in the microwave for a minute longer than usual. When I pulled it out, the steam was so aromatic I had to take it outside.

I was in a hurry and waited a moment for the steam to exhaust itself outdoors. Then I went back inside and began to work. When I finished, I closed the jar and realized that steam was still pouring out of the sides of the closed lid. I did not want to cause the jar to expand and break, so I decided to remove the cap. When I did, the jar tilted and slipped. The hot wax covered my hand. It looked like I was trying to cast a mold of my hand. The coverage of wax was thick and consistent.

I heard a sizzle and hiss as my skin became singed under the thick, waxy coating. The layer was stuck to me like glue. The burn and piercing sting began to travel up my fingers, hand, and arm. It was excruciating. My mind raced as I thought about a relative who had been in the hospital days earlier from a similar burn incident.

Quickly, my thoughts went to faith. My mouth opened and professed with belief for healing, "Jesus, heal my skin." God instantaneously healed me.

Now I still had to withstand the hours it took to remove half a jar of drying, sticky wax off my hand, arm, floor, and countertop. My fingers were the size of cucumbers, but there was no pain, no burnt skin, *nothing*. Because of my obedience to His ways and His Word, I knew exactly what to do. He heals through grace and mercy, with His love and our faith.

You have been methodically collecting life applications, too. You have learned to practice hope, faith, prayer, reading, worship, and rest. Now you are ready for fasting.

In this step, there are three devices that lead us into obedience and there are three warnings. Past steps have been hard, but in a different way. They were steps out of sickness and into healing; they were vulnerable and raw. Now that we have a little more strength, the next two stairs form a transition; while needed for our healing, they also begin to push us toward staying healed.

Marching up the Stair of Obedience

We have seen from our stepping so far that we can only obey through grace. Our own righteousness goes before Him as filthy rags (see Isa. 64:6); His righteousness empowers us (see 1 Cor. 1:30).

Between growing up with a military father and having an all-or-nothing personality, obedience is akin to breathing for me. In fact, this important truth is the very heart of this book. I have already told you that I am most passionate about this step. When we are passionate, we tend to have trouble conveying simple methods to those who see the topic or practice as unappealing or difficult. Knowing this, I called my mentor and asked her for help. Many times when I cannot see things, she can help me understand to better see.

I asked her to explain to me how she would describe victorious obedience. She told me that in her Spirit she saw three components to proper compliance: see, receive, and act. Her words literally turned the switch for me. I had been acting without needing to know why. When she articulated this concept, her terminology became the mini-steps I needed to convey.

Immediately, I prayed that God would show me this in His Word. He took me to Philippians 4:9: *"Whatever you have learned or received or heard from me, or seen in me—put it into practice. And the God of peace will be with you."*

I noticed that He asks us to put each action into practice. The three facets of obedience, as I see it are

See/hear.

Receive/learn.

Do.

When we just see or hear, we are still in operation mode and not yet what I call *flow mode*. We must do what we have seen or heard, even if it is difficult. Now our hearing is where the activation of the Word resides (see Rom. 10:17). It becomes two actions in one: seeing and then the activation that comes through hearing. Activation is when the Word comes alive in you and leads you into a changed behavior—the sign of reception and true learning.

The second mini-step is to receive and learn through the activation. This also involves two actions in one. We must receive first in order to learn. The Holy Spirit commences our understanding that lies within our heart. As we learn to crucify our flesh, it becomes natural to reside in the Spirit and obey. Then comes the third mini-step, doing or acting on what we know is true regardless of what we feel.

Job's righteousness was in direct relation to his obedience. My obedience to sobriety and discipline has made it easy to stay sober. My obedience to my marriage, my husband, and my covenant with Christ has blessed me beyond measure. My obedience to overcome fear and walk in faith has helped me to master my faith, which is the vessel for healing.

Your obedience is determining your path of healing right now.

Detoxification From the Poison of Emptiness

When pain is the central feature of our lives, we are toxic, spiritually and often physically. I have seen this in my own life.

Several of the first nights during my drug detox, I had to get up, peel off my pajamas, and change the sheets. There was a splash of water that hit the floor as I wrung out my hair; it unnerved me. I had sweat through the mattresses and my pajamas. The drugs had confused my entire system. I did not realize how sick they were making me until I allowed all the drugs to come out, and it took days. Watching the poison leave my natural body was bone chilling, almost unbearable, and desperately sad.

I felt like I was going to self-destruct. I knew obedience had arrived and I was unsure of how much I liked it, if at all. Have you felt the same disdain for adherence to your process? Can you see how your endurance has brought you out so far? How has your success added to your faith?

These were not the questions I immediately asked myself that morning. When we arrived at the hospital, my husband inquired as to my condition. He explained every detail and then waited patiently for a response.

"She could very easily have multiple seizures during this transition. You will have to make sure she does not swallow her tongue. If you plan to stay at home you have a lot to think about."

The nurse, rather nonchalantly, told my husband the frightening news. Her tone was shocking, considering the weight of the information she was presenting.

Swallow my *what?* I thought I needed a pill to keep *that* from happening. I was serious; gagging on my tongue did not sound like healing to me.

Because of how long and how much of the drug I had been ingesting, the nurse wanted to place me in the hospital to detoxify safely. I will never forget sitting in the waiting room and being asked to enter the admission room. The seriousness of my toxicity was plain.

Unfortunately, getting the drugs out of our system is not as easy as putting them in; detoxification was, for me, hell on earth. From my perspective, if I had not endured this period of hell on earth, I would have endured the real hell for all eternity. The drugs were blocking the Spirit in my life. This concept God proved true when, after six months of sobriety, the Spirit finally entered in His fullness. He needs a clean, willing vessel.

When your habit is 15 years in the making, detox is just the beginning of the end. The next step was to lock me up every day, away from my children in the circle of chairs room (outpatient rehab). God blessed me with the "out" part of outpatient; however, it required that I do the "up" part of stepping up. It was not easy. This step up is synonymous with obedience.

We looked for a facility that would work. We visited some of the nastiest places with some of the weirdest people in the world in attendance. I begged and pleaded; I did not need treatment. It went in one ear and out the other and I went straight in the facility.

I quickly learned not to judge in my deceived state. I fit the description of a weirdo myself, and my husband was not going to enable me any longer. I had to be obedient to him, God, and the process. Skipping steps was not going to cut it.

I was used to playing on a lopsided chessboard. My husband had suddenly set up all his rooks, his knights, his bishops, and his King. My husband was determined that God would heal his "queen." The Roach Princess was going to claim new ground. I was selling my real estate in hell while my husband's obedience was helping me understand that Christ had already purchased my castle in Heaven.

"Please Lord; I command the spirit of addiction out of my wife, by the blood of Jesus. I believe for her restoration, recovery, and healing."

That is how my Brett would pray over me. He would read warfare prayers right off the page. We would believe, not even sure what was happening. Our faith met God's faithfulness and our God answered.

Not only was I undisciplined, but I was, as you know, "The Princess of the Kingdom of Pain and Woe Is Me," the reigning Roach Princess who was now on her way to stepping through the gate and into the court of *doing*. I was about to become a princess of the Most High!

The far better place I was looking for was a way off yet. Psalms 84:2 says, *"My soul yearns, even faints, for the courts of the LORD...."* I yearned...and waited...and pressed.

God proved to me that our preparation, pressing, and positioning for healing are relative to how much or how little we allow God to work. Our obedience is inadequate without His Spirit, but His Spirit responds to our desiring Him above all else. *"As the body without the spirit is dead, so faith without deeds is dead"* (James 2:26). Works complete our faith and are a natural outgrowth of walking in faith. Works equal obedience by their very nature, yet still they cannot occur outside of God's grace. I consider discipline to be a work for and of God. As we account we can see where He requires us to attempt to attain to the impossible before the possible can divinely be imparted. Anything that takes crucifying our flesh unto God is unnatural to us. I surrendered with one eye closed and my fists clenched tightly. I finally allowed God to decide what I was doing for the day. I determined to obey Him on the highest and most reputable level I could humanly attain to. It was a new day and a new step; obedience had arrived.

Duty Delivers Us From Defiance

The Lord says in His Word that obedience is better than sacrifice.

> *But Samuel replied, "What is more pleasing to the LORD: your burnt offerings and sacrifices or your obedience to His voice? Listen! Obedience is better than sacrifice, and submission is better than offering the fat of rams"* (1 Samuel 15:22 NLT).

That is a powerful statement. He wants us to see and listen *"to His voice."* When we are fasting, we are able to better hear the voice of God.

The Old Testament tells about our need to bring sacrifices in order to commune with God. Jesus has fulfilled the sacrificial system. However, God did not dole out a list of rules merely to fill up a stone tablet. He did not do it just for the Old Testament folks. The law shows us our inability without His Spirit; the law teaches us about His ways, His preferences, and how he expects us to act. (See Galatians 3:24.)

When Christ returned to Heaven and Pentecost rolled around—*Bam!*—the infilling of His Spirit engraved His laws in men's hearts. As Second Corinthians 3:3 puts it:

> *You show that you are a letter from Christ, the result of our ministry, written not with ink but with the Spirit of the living God, not on tablets of stone but on tablets of human hearts.*

While we are always struggling with our nasty ways, His ways come more naturally to us as we change into His likeness.

Be patient; do not let the devil deceive you into giving up. Tripping is normal. Half the time I am looking down on each step checking my shoelaces. Everybody stumbles along the way. Every once in a while, we need to return to a previous step because if we do not see the beginnings of a trend toward Christ likeness, then we have missed a stair somewhere.

Keep doing your "duty." Do not get discouraged. If the trend seems to be going in reverse, pray and ask God to reveal the missing stair. He will show you which step you need to revisit. Obedience is not easy, but through your obedience, your faith grows.

Now, if healing is a staircase, relationship is the handrail. When we trust and obey God, we begin to build relationship with our Father. We step into the seeing and hearing we desperately need. When the relationship deepens, the ability to adhere to the step becomes easier. We move from seeing and hearing and enter the place of receiving and learning.

Time is essential to maturity. Obedience is just like hope; at first it feels manufactured, but as time and maturity develop, it becomes a part of our lives. The *doing* part starts to happen.

Three Slippery Steps

Before we continue, let me say this: While there are three steps to obedience there are also three things, in my experience, that make compliance difficult: a lack of discipline, ignorance to society's wrong methods (displacement), and genuine fear (which is the opposite of faith).

Discipline is a very important part of healing. We have talked about it before in more practical terms. I am not talking now about ten miles on the treadmill every day. I am talking about a love and genuine passion for wanting to please God. "Spare the rod and spoil the child," is true. The Shepherd has a rod for discipline, direction, guidance, and protection for His sheep. Keeping our healing takes discipline and obedience.

When I started writing *The Roach Princess,* I had filled the pages with streams of random thoughts; it was an unbalanced book of memoirs. My chronicle was lopsided because I was missing discipline to a plan, the glue that binds ideas together. This step allowed me to see and hear my pain and it taught me how I healed. Upon accepting the need for this discipline, I knew I needed advice for the how-to of writing a book. A book takes diligence and is a labor of love.

Healing takes obedience, slowing down, listening to trusted authority, and digging deep. Healing is just the training camp for your true purpose in life. How excited are you about your purpose? Are you glad to know that all you have to do is obey God and you are in training for your mighty purpose?

My prior discipline (in walking out the steps described in this book) taught me how to implement them to complete this project. The successful experience of traveling the path was necessary for the *doing* that was required to complete the book. I felt incapable and wanted to give up. What I was capable of was seeing my lack, listening to good counsel, hearing the voice of God, receiving criticism, learning the necessary techniques, and then doing them. I got the input I needed, wrote the book, and, to be honest, it was just as hard as healing from drugs only in a different way!

We have been through hell for a reason. Let us begin to switch our focus as we mount this step. We will be transformed as we receive and learn out of seeing and hearing and then turn it all into doing. We begin to start walking in our healed and healing state with power, knowing our abilities as we summon our divine purpose to come to the surface and compel us forward.

We can pray, read, fast, rest, listen, persevere, and above all else, obey. Hebrews 10:16 quotes the Holy Spirit:

> *This is the covenant I will make with them after that time, says the Lord. I will put My laws in their hearts, and I will write them on their minds.*

Then He adds: *"Their sins and lawless acts I will remember no more"* (Heb. 10:17). He makes us able. We receive the ability in our hearts and minds that enables us to *do* what we are called to do.

The three slick steps can catch you off guard. Be alert and examine your heart and life. What happens behind closed doors? How does your heart react to pain when no one is looking? We know that many of our problems are rooted in a lack of discipline. Where defiance reigns, ignorance and pain are flourishing. Uproot these lies and keep moving upward.

As always, God gives us a choice. Jeremiah 21:8 says: *"Furthermore, tell the people, 'This is what the LORD says: See, I am setting before you the way of life and the way of death."*

Obedience is a step consisting of multiple parts. Each mini-step can lead to life or death. Christ showed us discipline through His own humble love and obedience unto death. All of it is for our healing.

Now that we have covered the importance of discipline, let us examine how to combat society's wrong methods of healing and learn how displacement keeps us sick.

Societal Traps

The Lord impressed upon me a 3-S lesson to teach one month: social order, sorcery, and soul ties. The message was for women who loved the Lord and recognized that ignorance to society's methods of healing was keeping them sick. Many times, we obediently (by society's standards) ignore truth to make sure we stay comfortable and do not offend anyone.

Instead of dealing with our hurt and pain, we cover or hide it with worldly cures. An example is the overuse of antidepressants. Sometimes this is necessary; too often, they are used in obedience to the devil's sorcery.

Jewel for the Journey

Stay on the narrow path; go to the Word and not the world.

I included this discourse on society because it involves our daily environment; we cannot avoid exposure to society's sinful ways. We need to be aware of the pull society has on us. Awareness of the constant beckoning to society's discipline instead of God's will help us to protect our healing. The awareness of our weaknesses gives us strength.

Anxiety and mental disorders can be very real. While I suffered from these issues, the worldly cure was keeping me sick. Many times, medication puts a blanket on the cold. If you are obedient to things contrary to God, you will find yourself obedient to pain. We live in a medicated society; it has become as "normal" as O.J. in the A.M.

Is God not capable? I am not talking about warranted, necessary prescriptions. I am talking about using pills to escape and cope. When did we forget that God is *Almighty?*

Our society sells sex, drugs, and rock 'n' roll. It is full of fabricated values, false religions, and heresy. There is a sin-coddler on every corner ready to fulfill and accept every opinion and created flavor. Our world is full sin-affirming axioms like: *It is OK...Don't worry about it till tomorrow...What goes around comes around...As long as you're happy...and The only thing to fear is fear itself.* No, the only thing to fear is God and the rest of those are unfortunately not scripture references. If the media and the neighbors are going against Scripture, we must ignore their advice and pray for them.

We need to sincerely separate ourselves from the world's ways and many times a few "friends," extended family and neighbors. God tells us clearly in Matthew 10:34-39 that we need separation from the enemies even in our own camp. We need to let God remove the sorcery, soul ties, familiar spirits and familial spirits.

Just quitting something does not make us free from sin or from the refiner's fire. If it is bad for us, we need to quit completely and allow God to redirect the passion. If it is good for us and we quit, God will keep resurfacing the purpose until we conquer the fear.

An example of this would be my fear of heights. I thought I could hide from it. I did what I could to manage the fear and control the circumstances that triggered the fear. That did not satisfy God. He kept presenting the issue until I complied with His wishes and got free of the fear. Our society will usually tell us if something scares us to give up. God wants us to be delivered and set free of the fear not of the obstacle.

God will keep presenting His "good stuff" to us. The world has another opposite tendency: it tries to disguise the bad stuff by presenting it in new ways or through new actions, thinking God will not notice. Many times, we stop doing the wrong thing just to overindulge in something else that *looks* healthier. Unless it is God-ordained, we are mistaken to call it obedience (PP).

Our attempts to disguise the world's ways do not deliver us from sin and its pain. They serve only to displace one error and substitute with another one. Our list of things to obey must be whittled down to the things on God's list, not society's list.

We can say that drinking three Cokes a day is OK because "It is just Coke." We are still addicted—not to crack but to caffeine and sugar. It may be a slower-killing method, but it is just as offensive to God. Somehow we think that moving things around makes them better. It doesn't; junk is junk no matter what you call it and hiding is hiding no matter how camouflaged you are.

I used to change the furniture around in my house all the time. I would redecorate because I was trying to change the dynamic of my life. If things looked different, then they were different. Wrong. I merely shifted furniture around and destroyed my back in the process; which God has healed with my surrendering shifting armoires from room to room.

Moving weighty furniture around does a job on carpet tension, too. Our carpet looked like the beach when I finished; there were waves everywhere. I thought I was being obedient to something good because it took labor to accomplish it. Hard work equaled good work in my mind.

That is not the case. God's work equates to good work. We have to pray and allow Him to show us the difference.

Do Not Fear, Just *Do*

In our pain and sickness, the greatest culprit is our fear. My years of anxiety and panic disorder proved this fact. My biggest fear was *fear;* in point of truth, our biggest fear needs to be God.

The devil takes our weaknesses and trumps them. But God never intended us to fear. He intended for us to use feelings of anticipation, grounded by faith, to propel us into greatness. Find the opposite of your downfall and there your blessing will be.

In my life, Christ makes parallels to show me what is going on in the heavenly realm. We are fleshly beings and physical examples are very easy for us to grasp. I have mentioned how He used the house, the owl, and the double rainbow to show me in the physical realm what He was doing in the supernatural or spiritual in my life. When you are obedient to intercession, the natural will line up with God's intent for your life. He arranged it this way so that we would not miss Him, because all His work is done in the Spirit first.

God has positioned me to minister His Word publicly. At one point, public speaking was tough for me. In our flesh, exposure makes most want to run back down the stairs. I cannot; my life is to serve Christ so I serve in the capacity He intended. I walk the anticipation out in faith, by His love.

> *There is no fear in love; but perfect love casts out fear, because fear involves torment. But he who fears has not been made perfect in love* (1 John 4:18 NKJV).

He wants us to look fear in the face and remove our sword from its sheath without even contemplating the fears involved. This sword is the Word of God as described in Hebrews 4:12 and Ephesians 6:17. We are still journeying into the faith place; until we arrive in the heavenly Jerusalem, fear will come calling but by walking in His perfect love we will fear not.

My obedience to overcome fear on thrill rides paralleled His teaching me to overcome and rule out fear of all kinds when it came to Him. That drop in the stomach feeling, onstage or off, is something I wanted to be done with; I wanted to place it in the past. This may seem silly to you. God's dealing with me through frightening physical experiences may seem trivial, but fear was the manifestation of my largest root and all the subsequent roots.

My husband is a faith-walker. He rarely flinches when it comes to trusting. We zip-lined in Mexico. When our guide, Pepe, led us out onto the suspended wire, I gulped. We had a mesh platform jutting from the mountainside 300 feet above the jungle floor and only a repel line straight down to lead us out. I grabbed Pepe's shirt and hollered, "Get the donkey! I'm riding back!"

Pepe grinned and led me to what I felt sure was my death. I never looked into my husband's eyes; he wanted to tell me to find peace in Christ. He also wanted to know that I trusted him. I failed him because, in my fear, I never looked to him for comfort. All he wanted to do was to tell me to look up during my jungle terror. All Pepe wanted to do was argue with me about Jesus having never ridden a burro. The lesson in this exercise is this: Dropping hundreds of feet without dying will kill at least part of your fear.

I prayed for months that God would forgive me and give me another chance to overcome fear and prove to my husband and God that I believed. God still had to heal that trust and He did. Months later we were standing atop a Mayan Pyramid water drop called "Leap of Faith." My husband looked at me and in that instant, the devil taunted me. I froze in fear. I accepted the faulty information instead of casting it out and trusting who Christ gave me for protection and comfort.

I had climbed all the stairs praying, "God, thank You. I know this is Your will. Thank You for giving me a second chance."

I even saw the word *believe* tattooed on a woman's back at the top of the pyramid. I looked down. We were hundreds of feet above a shark pool. You had to leap off the side and fall hundreds of feet. The slide would then capture you and shoot you through the pool of sharks.

I froze. I took my eyes off my husband's eyes and off the cross. I turned around and went back down the stairs. As horrible as it sounds, that is what I did. I took the wide path—you know, the one where if you stumble you fall all the way down. I failed God and my husband in my fear. I repented and prayed, "Forgive me and please give me one last chance, Father."

He did not even wait a month. "Jesus!" I whispered as I looked away from the dark tube I was about to enter. I switched my fearful focus to the bright, beautiful sky. My stomach ached. The acid churned as the adrenaline stirred it. My vision was off and on from the lack of oxygen. The tunnel was tight and dark all the way to the bottom. I thought how difficult it would be to breathe once I entered. The air was already dense and thick even at its opening.

"Jesus, without You I am incapable, claustrophobic, and terrified. Help me, Lord. Calm me, I need Your strength. In my weakness, You are strong" (see 2 Cor. 12:9).

I repeated a Princess Principle as the fear arose in my throat. The tube was long and built into a mountainside. You could not even track the path prior to entering the buried passageway.

I sat at the pinnacle of a trinity of waterslides: "Nightfall," "Three Fall," and "Freefall." I sat there terrified. Fear is not an option in the Kingdom and God, however. He was making sure I trusted Him above all else.

I sat atop a mound of fear with not one challenge, but three: one for each failure and one for good faith. I felt like Peter, who was faced with three opportunities to deny Jesus. Nevertheless, my plan was to conquer "Nightfall" and do the rest much later.

Silly as this may seem to you, falling off things horrified me. Every step that I climbed caused me pain. My muscles would lock up. I felt like I was progressing, but I was not moving forward. The higher stairs were the hardest. This elevation was where the faith line would become hard to find and we would have to stop and rest. I would have to listen to the voices in my head. In the stillness, I would cast out the fearful ones and replace them with faith. This time I knew not to take my eyes off my husband's eyes. Every step closer tightened my chest and paralyzed my muscles.

Finally, I was at the top and it was my turn. I gave in to my weak knees and sat down. "Oh Lord, this is dark and I am scared, Jesus now!" I said as the lifeguard commanded that I go.

I did not even know where I was going but I had faith. I crossed my legs and arms and pushed myself into the black abyss. The dark, tight tube embraced me with thick air that was hard to take in and let out.

I panicked and began to spiral into anxiety. The war zone was in my mind. I was battling between Christlike thoughts of relaxing and allowing the ride to carry me and thoughts of "I am stuck...bound...closed in...cannot breathe...cannot escape...cannot get out...trapped."

The air became fresh, cool, and palpable instantaneously as I hit the light. "Thank You Jesus! Thank You for faith." I whispered.

I did not know how much my faith had grown. I hoped enough to conquer the remaining two rides. I decided for a moment to let it sink in before climbing again. I rested in God.

Again, we made our way up the stairs. Knowing my fate this time, I resided in Christ. I cast out bad thoughts and kept my eyes focused in the right direction. I made it through two of the three slides. I had "Freefall" left to conquer.

I had to ride through another dark tube for an undisclosed amount of time, which would eventually drop me hundreds of feet straight down into a pool. For the third time, I sat there looking into the pitch-black unknown. I looked to my right as my fear began to well up and saw the word *believe* on a girl's headband. The word was no less beautiful than a crown of jewels upon her head. At that instant, my husband and daughter hollered, "Leap of Faith!"

I leapt in faith. As I entered the darkness, the last thing I heard was my husband voice shouting, "The name above all names!" We were on the same page.

The slide was dark. The incline steepened. I used my last breath to pronounce, "Jesus!" I bellowed His name as my stomach muscles tightened. My breath left me as the slide catapulted me into midair. I was hundreds of feet above the pool now soaring in freefall, but finally in the light. Just as I felt a tinge of fear, the pool's water baptized me.

I began to weep for my lack of faith in my husband and heavenly Feather. Both of them forgave me. My honor was in their knowing that I honored them above any earthly fear. This time I obediently completed the steps instead of descending the stairs. As He always does, God kept me repeating the step until I obeyed His expectation of faith.

My fear had kept me bound for many years. Yet, God never gave up on me, even when I wrapped myself in defiance and avoidance. He is faithful!

This Scripture bears repeating: *"Such love has no fear, because perfect love expels all fear"* (1 John 4:18 NLT). The power in these words describes our healing; memorize and repeat this truth often.

Simple, Faithful Obedience

I had realized at this point in my life that faithful obedience is where most people struggle. I also realized that this step is neverending and a big part of healing.

This is where we finally step out of denial in regard to an issue. We surrender control at the beginning to heal; we allow ourselves to be vulnerable; we choose to accept godly guidance; we even rid ourselves of bad roots and cycles.

But then comes obedience. It is more than a step; it is a lifestyle. We must adhere to it forever. It is another place where failure can occur because the devil knows the power in our obedience to God. This was literally the area of his own terrible, eternal downfall.

Jewel for the Journey

Fear causes us to go the opposite way of God. When we think we are protecting ourselves, we are really hindering the fulfillment of our purpose.

Obedience has shifted the healing process in the direction of our ordained purpose in the land of *do*. We are allowing the Spirit to train our souls and to mold us according to God's ordination.

Let God infuse healthy, healing, loving roots into the empty places. Matthew 13:21 says, *"But since he has no root, he lasts only a short time. When trouble or persecution comes because of the word, he quickly falls away."*

If we see and hear Him and we learn and receive His ways, we can do His work. We can then see and ignore society's wrong methods and apply the hearing of truth to have faith for the right methods.

My princess, we are on a glorious journey together! I am so proud of you. You have been so faithful and so strong. Your reflection is becoming more Christlike.

These steps, principles, and actions begin to move us into His purpose for our lives, our part in His Kingdom work. If you do not feel quite ready to move into that yet, please rest in Him and review. We will move onto this exciting and powerful step only as He leads our growth in Him.

THE PRINCESS PRINCIPLES PRACTICE

Step Into Obedience:

❧ Accept His ways and walk in them.

❧ Reject your fleshly preferences, wants, and needs.

❧ Put into practice what you see, hear, learn, and receive from God.

❧ Fasting is the practical way to learn how to obey God.

Life Application Action

Fasting

The Lord is asking us to rend our hearts:

"Even now," declares the Lord, "return to Me with all your heart, with fasting and weeping and mourning. Rend your heart and not your garments" (Joel 2:12-13).

When you fast, do not look somber as the hypocrites do, for they disfigure their faces to show men they are fasting. I tell you the truth, they have received their reward in full (Matthew 6:16).

Fasting is the best way to put the flesh into submission! If you have never fasted here are a few scriptures to meditate and pray over: Joel 2:12, Matthew 4:2, 6:16-18, Daniel 9:3, Acts 13:2, Mark 9:29. Fasting is best taught in its personal discipline. In other words you have to do it and in the midst of it you will understand.

Summary of Princess Principles

 Our healing and purpose depend on our fortitude in sticking with God's ways indefinitely.

> *Whatever you have learned or received or heard from me, or seen in me—put it into practice. And the God of peace will be with you* (Philippians 4:9).

God honors obedience. Obedience to repent of sin is a way in which He can fill us and take us to deeper levels in Him. We can only go as far as our willingness to surrender to Him. If we cling to only what we know, we hinder our healing.

List what you have given up and pray about never going back to things that have entrapped you in the past. Be encouraged to know with faith that your obedience to God's ways will keep you free indefinitely from everything on your list:

 We are sinful and need not only a page of commandments, but also a book full of pages of commandments.

> [The grace of God] *teaches us to say "No" to ungodliness and worldly passions, and to live self-controlled, upright and godly lives in this present age...* (Titus 2:12).

We are always holding something back. List what you are holding back:

 We fast for Christ, not for blessing. We fast because He gave us the knowledge of His expectation of this promise.

> *Is not this the kind of fasting I have chosen: to loose the chains of injustice and untie the cords of the yoke, to set the oppressed free and break every yoke? Is it not to share your food with the hungry and to*

provide the poor wanderer with shelter—when you see the naked, to clothe him, and not to turn away from your own flesh and blood? Then your light will break forth like the dawn, and your healing will quickly appear; then your righteousness will go before you, and the glory of the LORD will be your rear guard (Isaiah 58:6-8).

Study all of Isaiah 58 and allow God to show you the true meaning of fasting and how it heals and delivers us from our pain. Journal about your fasts and what God *teaches you about* through them:

 Many times, we stop doing the wrong thing just to overindulge in something else that *looks* healthier. Unless it is God-ordained, we are mistaken to call it obedience.

For the wisdom of this world is foolishness in God's sight. As it is written: "He catches the wise in their craftiness" (1 Corinthians 3:19).

List any areas that may be a diversion, unhealthy replacement or excuse to your healing:

Congratulations! You have successfully made it up one more step and are *stepping in obedience* to God. You have also added another Life Application Action to your day *fasting*! You are healing and doing a great job.

Step, step, step up...up...up!

Chapter Eight

Hear What the Spirit Says

Step Eight: Listening in Isolation With God

I pray that out of His glorious riches He may strengthen you with power through His Spirit in your inner being, so that Christ may dwell in your hearts through faith. And I pray that you, being rooted and established in love, may have power, together with all the saints, to grasp how wide and long and high and deep is the love of Christ (Ephesians 3:16-18).

KNOWING how much He loves you allows His power in you to be widened, heightened, and deepened in exact proportion *"to the measure of all the fullness of God"* (Eph. 3:19). Paul wants us to grasp this concept. God needs our time and absolute attention in order to grant us revelation on this truth. If we allow Him, He will isolate us to deepen His love in us. This is a big step and represents the last step of healing. It leads us into our section on staying healed.

Consistent time alone with God, allowing His impartation, and His Holy Spirit to touch us, is the crescendo of a healthy life. On this step, we are going to let God seal and transfer all the knowledge on the infilling into a reality in our hearts and lives. We know how to let Him restore our soul. Now He can teach us how to increase our spirit. So grab hold of the horns of the altar and let's go!

Listen for Your Healing

God has dedicated this step to making sure we understand the principles, Scriptures, and concept of being filled to fullness or baptized in the Holy Spirit.

Making it up the prior steps successfully brings us to a place of purity and humility where we can begin to ascend the hill of the Lord (see Ps. 24:3-5). I have purposely placed this step after obedience. In my walk, sin was so rampant and my ignorance was so deep that until I became obedient to God's ways and not my own, I was incapable of understanding this beautiful lifeline.

God wants to fill us to a degree previously unknown to us. This fullness changes us and transforms our lives. It requires one-on-one interaction away from the distractions of life. It will require us to adjust our habits and even our schedules. He wants you to consecrate your day, your time, and your attention unto Him only for healing (PP). The benefits far outweigh the sacrifices, but *we* have to give Him access to our soul to receive them.

To accept His gift, we must be vulnerable, surrendered, clean, pure, and free from bias. We are healing and need to allow Him to infill all the open places with truth and power. Be pure before Him. If it is not simply from Him, clear out your "religious" training. Do this in part by applying our Life Application Action: *listening.* Allow intimate isolation with God; keep it free from anticipation or supposition on your part. Embrace His expectations and reject yours (PP).

His voice is so worthy of our discussion. Only His voice can create worlds. His voice will heal us.

My mother once tilted her head to the side and asked, "How do you hear God's voice?"

I explained to her that we hear Him by having faith in His Word, receiving His blood covering, receiving the infilling of His Spirit, and lying prostrate on our faces and listening in prayer. We hear Him by worshiping, praising, fasting, studying, allowing sanctification, resting, listening, stepping into His folds, being obedient, allowing isolation, refusing to deny the reality of His voice, giving Him control of our ears and tongues, and living for Him. I gave her just a few suggestions to chew on.

When people always ask you, "How do you hear God?" answer them in one word: *listen.* I found that my mother merely turned her head to the opposite side and looked more confused than ever after I finished my catalog of suggestions. I have since summed up my list into one neat word and a silent prayer for the inquisitive.

The command to listen is listed repeatedly in the Bible. Here it is in James 1:19: *"Understand this, my dear brothers and sisters: You must all be quick to listen, slow to speak, and slow to get angry"* (NLT). We hear God when we slow down and stop ourselves.

Our list of actions now consists of hope, faith, praying, reading, worshiping, resting, fasting, and now listening. These we need to honor and trust during our healing, because they are medicine for our sickness. To listen to God means slowing down and trusting that He will speak to you.

The Smallest Room Ever

The church that housed our women's Bible study had moved to another location. It had been roughly six months from my miraculous in-filling and we had one last meeting in the old building. I was battling fear—yes again, I know big sticky gatekeeper, in the process of healing and knew the Lord was working on me. I followed my mentor into the elevator after class. We arrived at the first floor and the doors opened one inch and stopped.

The elevator doors did not stop for a moment. They stopped for good. This was the exact opposite of the straight down trip in the dark tube. In fact, it was like standing still in a light box and may have been even more terrifying than the tube was.

The doors did not move; not knowing when they would move again nauseated me. My blood pressure shot through the roof. Well not literally, or we would have crawled out. If an elevator has never trapped you, it is confining, hot and not fun.

I kept thanking God for the one-inch crack. The air was so thick inside that I felt like I was exercising just to breathe. The crack allowed us fresh air and a sense of freedom from the little box that was now our home. To be honest, it allowed *me* fresh air and a sense of freedom. I kept my nose pressed between the doors and was not about to move; therefore, I was the only one who could partake. We were not only at the mercy of the broken door; we were at the mercy of my selfishness.

The funny part is that my mentor was behind me as I monopolized the fresh air crack. I tried to suck all the air out of the building in a nervous fury. She stood in the back corner on the elevator phone chit-chatting with the emergency representative in California. We were in Mississippi. The location of the tech did not encourage me. I foresaw an unknown number of hours between us and a walk in the lobby.

I pictured my mentor with her feet propped up, a pineapple drink in hand, and palm trees surrounding her. She was relaxed. She was my reference point—the "after" photo of healing. I was clearly the "before" shot; my eyeballs bulged out of the sockets trying to see through the inch-wide crack. All the while I crammed a crinkling Bible through the slot to ensure the crack would not close and cut off our air supply.

I was debating whether to lie down, which would eliminate the fall when I passed out in fear. In a panic, I began trying to do stuff. There is not a lot to do in a four-by-six-foot space except panic and push buttons. My mentor said, "Jnifer, you have to quit praying for alone time with me. This is getting ridiculous."

While what she said was funny and true, my unbelief, fear, and control were sad. The minute the elevator doors stuck, she grabbed hold of the lifeline, listened, and did not get off it until the trial was over. I never once grabbed onto the line. I just frantically and sporadically babbled in fear. When we are running our mouths and have no conduit, faith, or clarity, we have no connection and no ability to hear.

In that little box, God allowed me to understand that, while I also possessed the very thing that I kept trying to obtain from her, I never tapped into the power for myself. I had to slow down and listen to Him to receive the power that would transition me out of constant neediness and into being healed and healing.

So often, we expect others to do stuff for us or teach us. However, God allows in us an ability to grasp and do the very thing we are waiting to receive from someone else. Although He chooses to use true prophets and the gifts of the Spirit to convey information to us, the biggest part of our learning must come from listening for ourselves.

First John 2:27 says as much:

> *As for you, the anointing you received from Him remains in you, and you do not need anyone to teach you. But as His anointing*

teaches you about all things and as that anointing is real, not counterfeit—just as it has taught you, remain in Him.

We will take with us the authority to hear God for ourselves.

The Sweet Voice of Heaven

If we pray for alone time with God, He will meet us. It is glorious what happens in the aftermath. My daughter asked me in the sweetest voice, "Do you ever go on dates with God?" We always talk about intimacy with Christ and our Father in Heaven. She knows her daddy takes her on special outings; she figured mine does the same.

Jewel for the Journey

Time alone with God allows the fullness of the Spirit; that is when power begins to seep down from Heaven and into your being.

"I do, precious girl, all the time," I said, waiting for her response.

"Where do you go with Him?" She really wanted to know. I could tell because she replied so fast I could hardly make out her words.

"Well, I meet Him at church when I sing and worship; at home when I praise and pray; He is with me in the prayer room and while I am reading Scripture and studying; sometimes He shows up unexpectedly during the day when I need Him; He is with me when I run, write, work, and even when I sleep. Whenever I seek Him He is there. He speaks to me and I listen," I said, waiting to see a gesture of understanding.

If we do not isolate and listen to God, we will not have anything to pass on and God wants us to pass on His love. He tells us He has set us apart and this is good. God has segregated us out from among the world and we need to let Him teach us how and why. What we learn during our time alone with God is provision necessary for a healthy life. I have learned the importance of listening more than I speak especially when I get angry. If we are quick to listen in our weakness, we may hear others' needs over our own and respond in love instead of hate (PP).

I have spent countless hours isolated, reading and studying Scripture; listening to sermons; reading Christian authors; dissecting testimonies, books and passages (many times just still listening to His voice); hours in prayer and praise; days, at times weeks, in fasting; months in waiting for Him to build my faith. He builds, tweaks, and mends; but not without our attention set upon Him, our minds free of distractions, and our ear tuned to the sweet voice of Heaven. It is all worth it every moment with Him. Add glory to your life by isolating with the great I AM.

Matthew described Jesus' focus on fellowship with God in the midst of His ministry: *"After He had dismissed* [the crowds], *He went up on a mountainside by Himself to pray. When evening came, He was there alone..."* (Matthew 14:23).

Jesus spent time alone to get renewed and restored. He was in between glories. He went from feeding the 5,000 with five loaves to walking on water. In between, he needed time alone with God. After we spend time alone with God, we can step into the glory. God is the substance we need in order to perform the blessing and withstand life in a healed state.

John 6:15 highlights the same truth: *"Jesus, knowing that they intended to come and make Him king by force, withdrew again to a mountain by Himself."*

John's was the most mysterious of the four Gospels. He denotes that Jesus actually retreated from the people for protection as well as restoration. If we let them, the world will try to take our purpose by force and drain us. We need to allow God to infill us to fullness; we must stay there persistently. Jesus spent a lot of time alone in prayer. We are to mimic Him:

> But when you pray, go into your room, close the door and pray to your Father, who is unseen. Then your Father, who sees what is done in secret, will reward you (Matthew 6:6).

We do not forsake the assembly of the saints (see Heb. 10:25), but the assembly is not our sole link to God. If we are covered in the blood and full of His Spirit, we *are* the Church and we should be the Church every day.

This takes discipline. Many times, discipline and isolation go hand in hand; it takes discipline to stay still enough to study or pray. I found undeniable intimacy with God when I released everything I thought I had heard from Him for all that

I knew He would yet speak. The infilling of the Holy Spirit takes listening to God. When you have intimacy and isolation with God, you need no human conduit.

Healing With the Holy Spirit

Here is the crescendo of this entire book! You have reached the pinnacle in our healing process. It is your "I have crossed the Jordan and I am transformed" moment.

The first eight chapters have led us into God's healing and up toward His Son's likeness. The last two chapters have taught us imperative truths that readied us for this amazing moment. Now we are going to understand scripturally the truth behind *the healing and healed*. Then, in the last five chapters, we are going to learn and receive the glue that will bind our healing in Jesus indefinitely.

Let us return to the baptism, or infilling, of the Holy Spirit Jesus foretold in Acts 1:5. Now that we are practiced in spending quiet time with God and have an intimate relationship from listening to Him, we need to make sure we are walking in His fullness.

I am not saying that God did not fill you to overflowing upon salvation. I am not saying that He didn't fill you up three chapters back. I dare not say that you have not received already. What I am saying is that we need to be very sensitive to the breadth of power available to us and to ask God to fill us to maximum capacity daily. We have talked about this, but we have not listened to God's Word on it yet.

There are many schools of thought on this. The terms alone can provoke much controversy. I have found that I do best when I stick directly to His Word to prove my testimony. According to His Word, the blood comes first.

There are other areas, areas that He chose to leave as gray areas, in which I do not choose to have an opinion. This is not one of those. Nor do I presume that anyone needs to follow the order that I do or did. All I know is, He took me in to know Him deeper.

God made us all beautifully different, and He deals with us all perfectly. I have been walking around in His circles long enough to have an understanding of many doctrinal positions on the baptism of the Holy Spirit or infilling. I have even heard of their being many fillings. The only thing I will teach is what

Scripture proves true. I will leave the rest to you; you choose the vocabulary and doctrinal position as He leads you. It really doesn't matter to me what you call it as long as you get it or have it! Amen and Amen.

Sometimes this baptism comes after salvation; it did for me. My mentor, on the other hand, received it at the point of salvation, and it grew to overflowing as she walked in her fullness. My aim is to make sure you do not live without any of the precious power God has allowed for us all.

After my salvation, I could feel the Spirit's work in my life, and at times, I allowed its strength. I did not know there was any more of anything. So I moved into all I knew, which was not much. Yes, I could feel amazing moments of peace and joy, but I could never quite seem to "get there." When God infilled me, I still was not aware scripturally of what had occurred in my life.

Do not think that if wind and fire have never appeared in your living room, they never will. We have to remain humble and broken forever, regardless of how much time goes by as we await His fullness. Mine took close to two decades. As long as you are saved, and even if you are hurting, the fullness is available to you. If you have not obtained it, your fear may be blocking the flow.

Do not stop seeking and asking for it (see Luke 11:9). Remain and He will fulfill His promise to you. His promise is written in His Word (see Luke 24:49). He never changes, and neither do His promises. Hebrews 13:8 says, *"Jesus Christ is the same yesterday and today and forever."* Sometimes the fullness comes 20 years after salvation. The fulfillment of the promise is related to our surrender and God's order.

Here are three examples of the baptism of the Holy Spirit from the Book of Acts (there are many examples throughout the New Testament):

> *Peter replied, "Repent and be baptized, every one of you, in the name of Jesus Christ for the forgiveness of your sins. And you will receive the gift of the Holy Spirit. The promise is for you and your children and for all who are far off—for all whom the Lord our God will call"* (Acts 2:38-39).

When [Peter and John] *arrived, they prayed for* [the Samaritan believers] *that they might receive the Holy Spirit, because the Holy Spirit had not yet come upon any of them; they had simply been baptized into the name of the Lord Jesus. Then Peter and John placed their hands on them, and they received the Holy Spirit* (Acts 8:15-17).

In Acts 10:46-47 we see that *"...Peter said, 'Can anyone keep these people from being baptized with water? They have received the Holy Spirit just as we have.'"* These examples teach us not to presume that everyone must follow a certain order to receive the fullness. The point is that God poured out His Spirit for all. We need the fullness of His Spirit at some point during our journey to stay healthy and walk in freedom.

Hearing God comes naturally when you allow His control in your life. You notice a new understanding of Scripture. Prayer will become like breathing; isolation with God is a requirement. Bless you, my sweet princess friends. Be filled with all the fullness of the Lord!

Montezuma's Revenge

The hours with Pepe my trail guide were not my only time of obedience and isolation during my trip to Mexico. It seemed that every time I placed a foot down in that country, God was there to meet me with a challenge. He gave me tests I could not walk through without dependence on Him alone.

I went to Mexico right after my infilling and got really sick. Two years later, after walking in the fullness, listening to God, isolating in His Word, fasting, praying, and studying, I went to Mexico again and got just as sick. However, the difference was like night and day.

The first time, we arrived at our resort and realized they were trying to contain a virus. About

Jewel for the Journey

You know you are walking in His fullness and are infilled when you begin to change. The things of this world become less appealing and the things of God become your necessities.

150 of the 200 guests within the establishment were forced into quarantine and required to receive medical attention. I had the power to tap into, but he had just baptized me with His Holy Spirit, I had no revelatory experience in His Word or isolation with Him to prepare me.

We awoke at midnight and had to call a physician. Mind you, we were in another country; it was not the same medical system the States have. The doctor arrived, what felt like hours later, with an orange tackle box. He began drawing what I wanted to call potions from already-opened vials into one syringe that I did not see him open in front of me.

The doctor's box resembled something an 11-year-old boy would use to play doctor on his dog. Sterilization may not have even been a term in this country. The doctor strapped up my husband's arm and put the serum into his vein. My husband passed out immediately. I was left wide-eyed, hyperventilating, and alone with a handful of colored pills and some chicken scratch instruction as to how to administer them.

I was panic-stricken and dizzy. I was no help to anyone. No faith, no prayer, all fear. I did not know to make a declaration of healing. I had the power, but had not had enough time listening intimately to God's voice to know how to operate in the anointing.

The next thing I remember is waking up sweating and then turning to my husband to confirm there was breath in him. He was alive and getting better. Whatever the illness, the doctor administered an antidote along with several other potions of unknown chemistry. My fear lingered, however. I still felt ill, and it took almost a month to recuperate at home in the States.

God allowed two solid years of isolation with Him in between trials; the difference in the outcomes was amazing. The training, filling, knowledge, and wisdom were life-support. I did not think I was ready when it hit, but looking back, it is miraculous what time spent alone with God does for our healing.

My husband and I awoke simultaneously at 3 A.M. Sitting in silence, neither one of us wanted to acknowledge a repeat of the trial from two years before. It was same location and the same symptoms, but this time we were spiritually prepared. Within 30 minutes, the illness set in. We were very sick. My sickness mimicked my biggest enemy, trepidation. Physically, I was extremely sick, but the worst part was the fear; its power gripped me.

We were revisiting hell in our Mexican virus-ridden resort. I felt like I could not breathe. I shook slowly, my muscles paralyzed in terror. Now, for anyone who has not experienced this type of fear, understand that it does not need a valid reason to show up. Anxiety visits us sometimes for no logical reason. Fear is awful and is the opposite of faith; it is the enemy's bitter candy.

From the previous test, I learned why I was so pathetically unable to stand against the enemy. The last trial was awful and my flesh was not willing to endure it again. As Matthew 26:41 tells us, *"The spirit is willing, but the body is weak."* Yet, I had determined that my flesh would not win this time.

My isolation in His Word had paid off. God had trained me so well that I stood, opened the Bible, and began to walk the room with authority, casting out fear with His words. Faith has to initiate the healing. Whatever this may represent in your life, speak it out of existence through the blood of Christ, even if it takes hours or days. Trust it will work.

I do not know about you but when I get physically sick, I add in worry, fret, anxiety, fear, sadness, and a splash of "woe is me." Having successfully traveled up the stairs, we know that we can implement the blood immediately, at the first sign of sickness. God heals and gives a peace that surpasses all understanding to guard our hearts and minds (see Phil. 4:7).

Well, here we were again, two years later. We knew full well how sick we could get, but we had joy, peace, and God's power in the midst. I had stepped this out already. I knew exactly what to do spiritually, and that was all I needed. This did not mean that the manifestation did not reoccur. The fear arrived. However, this time it met opposition.

Remember, satan likes to use the same old cycle repeatedly; do not beat yourself up if you fall for it more than once (PP). Thoughts of the toolbox doctor and a brutal, fevered, eight-hour journey home haunted us with every trip to the restroom. Nevertheless, we knew truth and we used truth. We believed that *"...with God all things are possible"* (Matt. 19:26).

I began to pray Heaven down. I laid hands on my sick husband. I allowed God to transcend my fear of the panic and illness. I spoke to the sickness directly.

I commanded the virus to leave according to Isaiah 53 and the fear to leave in the name of Jesus. My husband could not believe the strength I had. I knew the joy of the Lord was my strength and I was counting on Him alone.

Faith was the only option. I knew not to fear. God's peace came down from Heaven like a thick blanket. While being sick was still a struggle; we were blessed through it all. We witnessed the undeniable effects of Christ's covering; this reinforced our faith. It was the kind of fight you weep through because you know it would be humanly impossible to step through it. However, with God and only because of God's love, we can walk it out.

It was a battle, but I could not allow my anxiety to distract me from my tunnel vision of prayer. I was barely able to get my husband, who had to stay for business, situated before I had to make my way to the States alone with many, many thousands of miles to travel. My airplane seat felt like a coffin. Therefore, I focused on the cross, the blood, and all the healing God had provided thus far in my life. I just kept saying, "Thank You, Jesus You are making me stronger through this. I am going to trust and obey You." I kept thinking of Him, asking God to relinquish Him of His cup. I wept. My cup did not hold a candle to His cup.

Jewel for the Journey

Your testimony is born in your weakness.

My trial was tough, but the test made me that much stronger. People would come up to me after flights, after luggage carousels, in the custom line, and even in bathroom stalls and say, "How are you still going? You are so sick!" I would just smile as I clutched my black Bible. They saw, they knew, and I did not have to say a word aloud. The Word of God spoke for me, just as David had spoken to encourage his son, Solomon:

> *Be strong and courageous, and do the work. Don't be afraid or discouraged* [by the size of the task], *for the LORD God, my God, is with you. He will not fail you or forsake you* (1 Chronicles 28:20 NLT).

Just as He did with the waterslides, God continued to refine me until I got it. If you do not like your situation and believe it is God-ordained, make sure you are prepared and ready to repeat it. It would have been easy for me to have chalked up the second Mexican illness debacle to a fluke; but having it occur twice with just enough time in between to allow much spiritual growth changed my view. It was obvious that God wanted us to gain awareness of what His isolation can accomplish.

Amazing Grace

God's greatest moments are seen in our weakness. That is where God's power works best. This was a truth the apostle Paul knew well:

> ...[Jesus] *said, "My grace is all you need. My power works best in weakness." So now I* [Paul] *am glad to boast about my weaknesses, so that the power of Christ can work through me. That's why I take pleasure in my weaknesses, and in the insults, hardships, persecutions, and troubles that I suffer for Christ. For when I am weak, then I am strong* (2 Corinthians 12:9-10 NLT).

We sometimes want to give up right before the trumpet blasts. If we will press a little further, He will heal us. Listen. Listen. Listen to His voice and in the stillness, receive.

Let us praise Him, saying, "Thank You, precious God, for speaking to us and for granting us the ability to hear You. Thank You for infilling us with the fullness of your Holy Spirit. Thank you for isolating us and giving us second and third chances to get it right!"

Are you ready to receive the glue that will bind your healthy life to Christ's for endurance in your healed and healing state? God created you for a mighty purpose, a hope, and a future. You can look at fear, quote Scripture, and reside in faith because you, my friend, are walking into power on the next step.

These remaining steps are less about our actions and more about allowing God to impart His power and transform us into His Son's image. We are stepping into a new section where we will learn how to stay healthy for life. These steps are imperative. You are transitioning into what I call "the stamina stairs."

Congratulations!

THE PRINCESS PRINCIPLES PRACTICE

Step Into God's Isolation

❧ Leave your to-do list undone; stop and listen for God's list instead.

❧ Release your expectations and wait for God's direction.

❧ Learn to ask God before you step forward.

❧ Allow the transformation of your mind by tuning to His voice.

Life Application Action

Listening

The way of a fool seems right to him, but a wise man listens to advice (Proverbs 12:15).

Journal how you can refrain from speaking and be a better listener:

Find Scripture on listening and write it in your journal:

Summary of Princess Principles

He wants you to consecrate your day, your time, and your attention unto Him only for healing.

Then Jesus said to His disciples, "If anyone would come after me, he must deny himself and take up his cross and follow Me. For whoever wants to save his life will lose it, but whoever loses his life for Me will find it" (Matthew 16:24-25).

List things you need to give up so that you can set aside quiet time to hear Jesus:

Allow intimate isolation with God; keep it free from anticipation or supposition on your part. Embrace His expectations and reject yours.

Every word of God is flawless; He is a shield to those who take refuge in Him. Do not add to His words, or He will rebuke you and prove you a liar (Proverbs 30:5-6).

Journal about how casting out your opinions and "ungodly training" while in isolation with Him and His Word has helped you grow and shield you:

If we are quick to listen in our weakness we may hear others' needs over our own and respond in love instead of hate.

My dear brothers, take note of this: Everyone should be quick to listen, slow to speak and slow to become angry, for man's anger does not bring about the righteous life that God desires. Therefore, get rid of all moral filth and the evil that is so prevalent and humbly accept the word planted in you, which can save you (James 1:19-21).

Write down the truth above regarding what we need to be quick to and slow to. Know that the Word has been planted in you and through the humility of a closed mouth and open ears we will receive all that God has for us.

PP Remember, satan likes to use the same old cycle (Chapter 6) repeatedly; do not beat yourself up if you fall for it more than once (or even again as we are climbing up).

> *for though a righteous man falls seven times, he rises again, but the wicked are brought down by calamity* (Proverbs 24:16).

We are constantly learning so write about recent falls and how you got up or are getting up and receive hope:

When we are pure, humble, broken, and surrendered, He can then baptize us into the fullness of His Holy Spirit. You have successfully made it into *isolation with the Father* and up another step and added a new Life Application Action: *listening!* Before we go on to the next step, let's do an important study.

The Baptism (Infilling) of the Holy Spirit (Acts 1:5)

Again, we do not presume that everyone's experience with the infilling must follow a certain order or experience. God poured His Spirit out for all. We need the fullness of His Spirit; He will give it to us at some point during our journey to walk in freedom.

Meditate on the Scriptures below that we touched on previously. This time underline the order of water baptism versus Spirit baptism. Jot down the orders and how they differentiate. Then journal what a broken Spirit and a contrite heart mean to you (see Psalm 51:17).

> *Peter replied, "Repent and be baptized, every one of you, in the name of Jesus Christ for the forgiveness of your sins. And you will receive the gift of the Holy Spirit. The promise is for you and your children and for all who are far off—for all whom the Lord our God will call"* (Acts 2:38-39).

> *When* [Peter and John] *arrived, they prayed for* [the Samaritan believers] *that they might receive the Holy Spirit, because the Holy Spirit had not yet come upon any of them; they had simply been*

baptized into the name of the Lord Jesus. Then Peter and John placed their hands on them, and they received the Holy Spirit (Acts 8:15-17).

...Then Peter said, "Can anyone keep these people from being baptized with water? They have received the Holy Spirit just as we have" (Acts 10:46-47).

Just a few things the Holy Spirit does in our life:

- Convicts the world of sin, righteousness and judgment (see John 16:8-11)

- Guides us into all truth (see John 16:13)

- Glorifies Christ (see John 16:14)

- Marks us and seals us (see Ephesians 1:13-14;)

- Is Christ in us (see John 16:14-15)

- Gives us the mind of Christ (see 1 Corinthians 2)

- Leads and teaches us (see 1 John 2:20 and 27)

- Sanctifies, restores, regenerates, renews us (see Romans 8)

- Empowers us (see Acts 1:8; 1 Corinthians 4:20)

- Fills us (see Ephesians 5:18)

- Teaches us to pray (see Romans 8:26-27; 1 Corinthians 14:15)

- Tells us that we are children of God and that we share in His glory (see Romans 8:16-17)

- Produces the fruit of the Spirit in us (see Galatians 5:22-23)

- Gives us special supernatural gifts (see 1 Corinthians 12:8-10)

Take a look at these scriptures and pray for revelation:

*And I will ask the Father, and He will give you another Counselor to be with you forever—the Spirit of truth. The world cannot accept Him, because it neither sees Him nor knows Him. But you know Him, for He lives with you **and will be in you*** (John 14:16-17, emphasis added).

*I am going to send you what My Father has promised; but stay in the city until you have been **clothed with power** from on high* (Luke 24:49, emphasis added).

When the day of Pentecost came, they were all together in one place. Suddenly a sound like the blowing of a violent wind came from heaven and filled the whole house where they were sitting. They saw what seemed to be tongues of fire that separated and came to rest on each of them. All of them were filled with the Holy Spirit and began to speak in other tongues as the Spirit enabled them (Acts 2:1-4).

There is also a prayer language that accompanies this truth. I did n*ot know this when I was baptized,* and my controlling type A nature did not allow my tongue to relax enough. *Therefore,* I had *to tarry for it* or ask for my gift. It is the ability to talk to God unhindered by the enemy, and it goes directly to the throne of *grace. It builds up your Spirit.* A few Scripture references are: Romans 8:26-27; 1 Corinthians 2:13 and 14:15, Mark 16:17, Acts 2:4.

For this reason I kneel before the Father, from whom His whole family in heaven and on earth derives its name. I pray that out of His glorious riches He may strengthen you with power through His Spirit in your inner being, so that Christ may dwell in your hearts through faith. And I pray that you, being rooted and established in love, may have power, together with all the saints, to grasp how wide and long and high and deep is the love of Christ, and to know this love that surpasses knowledge—that you may be filled to the measure of all the fullness of God. Now to Him who is able to do immeasurably more than all we ask or imagine, according to His power that is at work within us, to Him be glory in the church and in Christ Jesus throughout all generations, forever and ever! Amen (Ephesians 3:14-21).

Before you step on please ask for this mighty power and know that I have prayed and believe for you already.

Step Into God's Fullness

ॐ Repent for all sins of omission and commission.

ॐ Ask God to baptize you in His Holy Spirit to fullness.

ॐ Request a special measure of faith for your request.

ॐ Remain in His will for your life with faith.

ॐ Believe in His promise with all your heart, mind, soul, and strength.

Congratulations! You are now headed into *balance* for your steps and are about to step into *God's fruit*. We have studied on the infilling and we are stepping in or at least toward authority and freedom, so step up!

Section II

Chapter Nine

Wielding Your Scepter With Balance

Step Nine: God's Balance Through Giving

*Be well balanced (temperate, sober of mind), be vigilant and cautious
at all times; for that enemy of yours, the devil, roams around like a lion
roaring [in fierce hunger], seeking someone to seize upon and devour*
(1 Peter 5:8 AMP)

The Rat of Imbalance

WE are the ones who limit God because we do not believe His abundance and fullness. We are going to step up into God's measure and allow His completeness to balance us. God will counterbalance our chemically imbalanced pain with His steadying hand. His love is the antidote for our unnecessary reactions to adversity.

It was one of those moments. Awakened by the sound, I glanced toward the clock. The neon numbers read "3:00." The scratching that awakened me was coming from inside our bedroom.

"Brett, do you hear that?" I was not comfortable sleeping with a rodent in the same room. Not to mention our three-month-old baby was nestled in between us.

"Brett?"

He rolled over and said, "I'll kill it in the morning."

"OK, great! I'm sure it heard you and will stand real still till you are done with your coffee and paper. Perfect," I said.

I froze in fear. This reaction always happened. When fear came, the muscles locked up. I would not move. I just kept thinking, "If I touch my foot to the floor, that thing is going to come into contact with me."

Chills and an itchy tingle made me twitch. The scratching did not cease. Even the addition of our voices to the quiet of the room did not hinder the thing. I lay awake all night listening to gauge its whereabouts. The thing was under the bed at one point. The clock ticked rather slowly.

Finally, the window's silhouette showed up out of the darkness. The sun came up and with it the revelation of what the scratching had produced: a hole in the wall with droppings all around it. I began to investigate. I found the signs of an infestation. I saw droppings all over the house: in the cupboards, bathrooms, couch cushions, even the baby's room. In my mind, the problem could not possibly be just one rodent.

My husband had to leave town for several weeks and left me alone with the pack of rats. I was desperate and dramatic. This was not OK with me, not OK at all. The rodents were like big fuzzy roaches to me; they were just as fast and just as nasty. I was already writing *The Rat Princess* in my mind.

My imagination had them reproducing for months and I had just slept through it all. They are nocturnal. Therefore, their schedule had not crossed my schedule, until now. I was oblivious and had convinced myself that one little rodent could not have done this much damage. We are so easily deceived.

From my reign as The Roach Princess, I knew exactly what to do: traps! I bought glue traps, snap traps, poison traps, employed a pest trapper, called in relatives to trap the rodents, and invited some trapping friends to help. I lined the room with the mechanisms. I surrounded the bed, pantry, and attic with them. My house was filled with them. Everywhere I saw a dropping, I stationed a solution.

My mom flew in with panther urine, a supposed cure. That would be logical in some countries; if a rodent thought a panther was nearby, it probably would not want to stick around too long. But, do American rodents innately know this? If panthers are not indigenous to, say, a subdivision in Mississippi, would the rodent know enough to run?

Not only were we doused in exotic animal urine; I had already made contact with the health department. I had a bad cold, but I was sure it was from exposure to bacteria from the unknown number of rats surrounding me as I slept. I will not even bore you with the steel wool and duct tape episode. Suffice to say, I am still pulling it out of crevices.

Weeks passed. One night, before leaving for church to head up a ministry called Lifehouse, I pulled the decorative pillows off the back of our bed to wash them. What do you think I found? Right above the place where my sweet baby slept there were droppings! I went into freak-out mode, an imbalanced approach to fixing anything.

I stripped the bed. I called the ministry folk and told them I had a war to fight and would not be joining them. I said, "Please pray for us."

My plight was not entirely uncommon. I know almost everyone has had the odd rodent drop in. But it flipped me out. I wanted to pop a tent up on the roof to sleep at night; thankfully things never quite got that insane.

Balance Wins the Day

The battle was over when I finally told God I trusted Him for the outcome. That night I slept instead of playing night watchman. His hand was seen. The next morning, one tiny, spotted mouse sat wiggling on a glue trap. That is it! I realized that I had likely imagined my home to be the site of Armageddon—all because of one little mouse.

My measure had been way off. I had traps *everywhere*. Until I allowed God to reveal His measure, I was a mess and extremely out of balance. You can imagine me getting the paper in the morning in a beekeeper's suit with mousetraps dangling from a tool belt and a broom in my hand. I was worn out from sleep deprivation. The slightest wind would send me jumping. I had allowed one small mouse to imbalance my whole life for two weeks.

This example is silly, I know. But I am not kidding when I say that I was not right those two weeks. I could not function. My reactions were out of balance from the fear of one tiny mouse. He was ruling my life.

Our heightened, imbalanced reactions to pain are the fleshly responses the devil loves. We must step toward God in prayer and worship to stay steady. God never intended us to allow our circumstance to control and throw us out of balance. He is, after all, the One who controls even the wind.

In our weakness and sickness, our gasping for breath and allowing things to overwhelm us is expected. Once we have proper coping mechanisms and God in our lives to buffer the fear, such reactions are senseless. We are merely letting one tiny demon rule us.

When we view issues through the eyes of faith, knowing that God is in total control, we are measuring life's situations using God's ruler. That keeps us balanced.

God's measure is vast. Paul tells us in Ephesians 3:8 that His power at work within us is immeasurable. He also talks about our being filled to the measure of all the fullness of God. In Ephesians 4:13, he talks about the full measure of Christ in regard to our unity and our service to the Body of Christ.

When God fills us with His Spirit, the measure of power we can tap into becomes limitless. When we tap that measure, He balances us. That measure is a measure of faith, peace, and joy during times of infestation or solo varmint issues. This measure is beyond sufficient to produce serenity in the midst of chaos. We rely on God engaging His fruit and balance in our lives in order that we stand when all else is falling. In fact, His balance is so stabilizing and so abundant, we can even step up when all else is declining.

In our prior step, as we reveled in God's isolation, we were made ready for this bountiful stair. We will never feel totally prepared, but we are ready. We know that we are not capable without His Spirit in us. With His Spirit in us, we might fall (as I did) but we get right back up, dust ourselves off, and keep stepping (see Proverbs 24:16). We do not allow the enemy to hinder our healing.

More Blessed to Give

We are stepping up into giving that will add to our healing. We needed to heal before we could help. Once we have committed to healing, we can begin to pour into others. When we pour out, we feel God pouring more in and we realize that we are healing even more. God's measure of healing will increase as we allow it to flow outward.

When I get down and feel like I am sad, my husband always says, "Get your blood covering on, pray, invite the Spirit back in, and go help someone. Go minister, give and serve. Get out of yourself."

I was almost two years into healing when my pastor's wife asked me to start a healing ministry in our church. I stared at her for an undisclosed length of time and then took a breath. I realized I had not breathed for quite a while. I did not want to startle her by turning blue.

When God speaks to her, she fulfills His requests. Leadership had asked me a year earlier to head up a similar group. That leadership left when the church split and the group was never established. God did not stop asking. Once everything was reestablished, His request was declared again.

I, however, did not want to be responsible for a group. The Lord took me to Second Corinthians 8:10-11:

> *Here is my advice: It would be good for you to finish what you started a year ago. Last year you were the first who wanted to give, and you were the first to begin doing it. Now you should finish what you started. Let the eagerness you showed in the beginning be matched now by your giving. Give in proportion to what you have* (NLT).

Lifehouse was born. It was a healing ministry for sin issues. I had been the princess of pain that overcame, but being asked to help others was foreign to me. My heart was selflessly in love with Christ, so His passion became my passion. I got involved as a way of giving back; what I realized a year later was that what I had put in had come back to me beyond measure.

Because I knew my sin nature was to serve myself, I had to serve others. This allowed God to train my ways to serve Him. My sacrifice to service allowed God to create balance in my life.

> *God the Father comforts us in all our troubles, so that we can comfort those in any trouble with the comfort we ourselves have received from God. For just as the sufferings of Christ flow over into our lives, so also through Christ our comfort overflows* (2 Corinthians 1:4-5).

He had pressed down blessing and healing, shaken them together, and poured them running over into our laps. God used that beautiful ministry and all of its precious leaders to heal us. We were willing, humble, and open. We all received beyond measure. Luke 6:38 explains:

> *Give, and it will be given to you. A good measure, pressed down, shaken together and running over, will be poured into your lap. For with the measure you use, it will be measured to you.*

We are finding understanding about the balance in our lives by allowing God to impose His standards of measurement. Job 31:5-6 says, *"If I have walked with vanity, or if my foot hath hasted to deceit; let me be weighed in an even balance that God may know mine integrity"* (KJV). His measure teaches us proper balance and function within the boundaries of grace.

Left Brain, Right Brain

Most of us are being ruled either by the right brain or the left. Right-brainers are spontaneous, creative people. They are purpose-oriented, poetic visionaries who work best with others. Left-brainers are logical, task-oriented, goal-oriented, technical people who work best alone.

In order to flow freely in God's will, we must allow Him to merge the left and right sides of our minds. We can allow God to transform our minds and create the mind of Christ in us (PP). We can pray for Him to enlarge the territory we use in our minds and give us more of a capacity to understand Him, His ways, and His Word.

In our fleshly state, we are allergic to God's balance. God attributes balance to integrity in Job 31:5-6:

> *If I have walked in falsehood or my foot has hurried after deceit— let God weigh me in honest scales and He will know that I am blameless...*

God honors those who honor Him. Unfortunately, most of us are unbalanced. You often hear people complaining about balancing the checkbook, the scale, their opinions with others, or their schedules. The Lord holds the power of balance. We can only attain it through the cross of Christ. Without salvation and the infilling of the Holy Spirit, godly balance is a rabbit we can never catch.

Jewel for the Journey

We do not want to be something we are not; we just tend to be too much of what we choose and not enough of what God created us to be.

The imbalance produced in our sickness literally tilted us. I like to think our struggle with equilibrium results from having a foot on one step with the other attempting to step too soon or step in the opposite direction. We just cannot seem to commit. Even our churches seem to be out of balance. We have heavy "Word" churches or "too spiritual" churches. Revelation 2 depicts the absence of balance. Without His Spirit and His truth, we are imbalanced (PP). We are crooked at best; without Christ, our feet walk a crooked path toward destruction.

The cross represents perfect balance, physically speaking, from east to west. In the cross, God perfectly balanced justice and mercy; both are satisfied and fulfilled. Extreme emotional turmoil is the opposite of God's plumb line. His line rests in righteousness between calm and peace. James even tells us in 3:18 that *peacemakers who sow in peace raise a harvest of righteousness.*

Balance is important as we step up. We realize this is where the permanence in our healing is found. Balance will keep us away from the extremes that pull us back into sickness. When we realize that balance is God's, we begin to appropriate it for our lives. The first place I felt it was in my emotions. God balanced my feelings into a peaceful state.

Before He blessed me with the fullness of the Holy Spirit, I was up and down on an emotional roller coaster. I allowed satan to jerk and manipulate me at the slightest provocation. The enemy uses our emotions to control us. Even after I came out of some healing, I became too legalistic in my left-brained ways. I had to let Him guide my thoughts away from the left side and over to the right a little.

The "Albino" Came to Kill Me

I did not know he was watching me. My friends and I were careless in the last years of high school. The sidewalks we trod led through some dark alleys and turnstiles most people would avoid. I was chemically imbalanced from alcohol and depression. My unstable emotions caused me to make life-threatening decisions. Sometimes in our pain, we think we want to die.

I was about to, had the angels not intervened. My friend and I wandered the streets of the city, in and out of all the bars. Our last stop on a particular night was a shady, back-alley pool hall where a predator was hanging out. Whether satan had assigned him specifically to me or not, my sickness and addiction had tilted me enough to fall prey to his attack. I was intoxicated, unaware, and unguarded.

The rain came down in sheets as we left the smoke-filled bar. Thunder cracked and lightning lit up the street periodically, allowing us to see in front of the car. What was behind us went unnoticed. The predator was there following us, not too close and not too far.

The methodical beat of the alternative music from the dash was haunting. My friend turned the steering wheel and maneuvered the station wagon down the long, winding driveway. It curved around a ravine and up into the thick woods. The house was dark; no one was home. The thunder rumbled; it sounded as if God was not pleased. I was dizzy from the alcohol and beginning to get sleepy. I stepped out of the car and shivered as the cold rain hit my skin and sobered me a little.

"See you later. Be careful driving home," I hollered as I ran for the protection of my parents' carport. The predator was watching from the protection of the woods as my friend pulled away. Alone, I entered the house. I noticed the lightning had turned off the alarm; it was an old system that would shut down when storms affected the electricity. The green light was all that I could see in the darkness. I entered my house, locked the door, and reset the alarm.

The house was so dark that I tripped upon entering. I flipped a switch to navigate and headed for my bed. I was dizzy from drinking all evening and almost sick. I remember sitting on my bed listening to the storm and worrying. Worry was one of the operating habits I had formed from the lifestyle that I was using to escape my pain.

I did not even know a predator was standing at the back door waiting for the right moment. The power failed again, disengaging the alarm. Instead of waiting for the alarm to come back on, I felt my way into my father's room and reached into the top drawer. My fingers welcomed the hard cold metal buried in the soft socks. I gripped the gun properly and pulled it out. As I turned, I heard breaking glass hit the hardwood floor in another part of the house.

The back French doors were in the living room, just one room over. They creaked open. I could hear the thunder and rain as though it were inside the house. The movement I heard was not the storm. Someone was in the house with me. My stomach felt like it had crawled up into my chest. Breath was hard to draw in.

I went into fight-or-flight mode, but realized that I would have to reside in fight if I wanted to make it to flight. I began to make my way down the narrow hallway to the living room. Everything became surreal. I calculated my steps in the darkness. My goal was safety. When death came knocking, I suddenly wanted to live.

As I turned the corner, the moonlight illuminated a man entering the living room. I could feel evil. I lifted the gun and cocked it. I will never forget the pressure of the trigger against my fingertip. I had the power to pull his very life out of his body with one motion.

My mind could not even conceptualize the magnitude of the moment. Seeing the pistol and realizing his fate, he lunged toward me. I faced a life-and-death choice. I like to think since God knew I was incapable of making such a weighty decision, He pardoned me.

My ears rang as the gun fired. The rain and thunder went unheard. I believe in that moment God changed my hearing forever; I know my life was altered. The intruder could have raped me and then killed me.

I was blessed enough not to have killed him. I do not even know where he went in that moment or whether God took him away. I made it to my car and to my mother's home. She then called law enforcement. The police took care of the predator's whereabouts from there. A week later, our cat and dog ended up dead on our lawn, but I went unscathed. We knew it was him, but he was never caught.

I didn't think that I led the predator there; I did not realize that I had until years later. My friends and I ran around the back alleys of a big city. We never expected foul play around us. Our imbalances put us in jeopardy of making bad choices.

But now, you and I have a new ability to let God balance our minds. He will give us the capability to make sound choices that will protect our lives and healing.

If most cats have nine lives, I have ten. In all truth, I did have ten of God's fingers wrapped around me at all times. An act of God on behalf of an unworthy sinner—how often it occurs. The bullet struck also ten feet from the doorframe where the man stood. No one could have heard the shot. Because the bullet did not hit him and because I was temporarily deafened by the blast (and shocked overall), the predator could have finished me off. He had free rein to do so; but God's reign is freer still.

Prognosis of Pain

If you feel like you are chemically imbalanced and are not involved with substance abuse, it could part of satan's plan. Sometimes terms like depression, anxiety, bipolar disorder, ADD, ADHD, and agoraphobia can be defeating. We feel we must label everything. Sometimes in our fervor, we mislabel things. Once we name them, we take ownership of them. Why do we want to own this stuff? Do you want to own these labels or defeat them?

I was not depressed. I was oppressed and had been allowing it for years. I was not fearful and anxious. I was lacking faith and truth. I was spouting injustice from a mouth unprotected by the third chapter of James. I was implementing no justifiable means by which to produce godly fruit. I was not wandering in pain; I had the map of the desert in my back pocket.Occasionally our issues are a combination of our personalities mixed with the devil's promises of sickness and confusion. Some issues are legitimate and physical, but the devil takes our weaknesses and intensifies them. When issues are legitimate, we need to accept them and ask God what He wants us to learn through the trial. "Impossible," you say to some issues; but nothing is impossible with God!

We need "preScriptures" to rid us of our prescriptions. Named disorders are warranted at times. But we must be sensitive to our society's overuse of titles and medications that blanket the pain. Why are we making covenants and agreements with the enemy without any wisdom? Stop agreeing with your pain and issues and agree to believe God is able.

If we trust, God He will allow us to understand exactly what we need in order to get out from under the pain. We can label the issue "nullified in the name of Jesus" and step out of denial, but then we must step out of considering ourselves broken as well. We are no longer broken; we are complete and becoming completely balanced.

Trusting God to heal the imbalance will bring balance to iron out the wrinkles and kinks of emotionalism in our lives. When the Holy Ghost came into my life, I began to sleep eight hours a day, eat healthy, and exercise regularly. The extremes leveled out and my life came into balance.

His intention is for you to be complete in His image. If you let Him, He will balance you as He is balanced (PP). God's perfect balance for our lives lays the foundation for purpose. We are well rested, well versed, well fed and getting ready to give back. Are you finding this in your life also? It is proof that you are healing and allowing God to balance your life.

I remember the days when balance was the farthest thing from my mind and labeled ailments were piling up in my medical file.

"You have a typical case of agoraphobia. This pill will help. There are side effects and they will subside in a few months." As the doctor handed me a prescription, those words tumbled out of his mouth without a shred of empathy. He did not have to endure the few months, the uncertainty, or the expectation of having all the not-so-pleasant symptoms. I did and I was determined to have them all, and so I did.

Improper prognoses often happen when we are sick inside. We become hypochondriacs who feed off disorders. The more ailments we have, the more attention and medication we receive and the more explanations we have for our pain. Sometimes it is all too defeating; it feels as though, if we are going to be labeled sick, then we might as well do it with gusto. At least, I was going to be the best at something, even though it was absurd.

I began to feel like everything around me was surreal. I felt like reality had left me somewhere along the line. I could not seem to relocate it. I was dizzy and at odds all day long. My breathing was shallow. My stomach was turned. Shaking, breathing in paper sacks, and taking pink oval pills was the sum total of my life. I longed for the feeling of reality. I cried. I missed stability and balance. I had lost them. In fact, the devil had them so well hidden I was like a five-year-old child on a hunt for the Holy Grail.

"Your brain is imbalanced. Your serotonin and GABA (a neurotransmitter) are not right," the doctor said in a deep tone. He did not even look at my blood to determine this. In five minutes and from two sentences, he determined my destiny and brokenness. I was wrecked and could not be fixed by this guy. All he could do was try to regulate my symptoms with chemicals that tasted like battery acid.

I spent many days crying and feeling labeled and segregated. I felt like the ugly duckling. I had my own pond, but with no lily pads, cattails, flies, frogs, or fish. I was the only one floating around trying to hide the bottles of regulation under my feathers and mask the injustice. I was hoping my insanity would go unnoticed.

My brain chemicals were not imbalanced; my spiritual life was imbalanced. I was professing truths with my mouth, but the devil had closed up my heart with an orange bottle of medicine for an empty soul. Had you asked me about my plight back then, I would have convinced you of my brokenness and my desperate need for chemical assistance, all while calling myself a Christian. Where was the power behind my proclamation, because satan had me believing the sickness?

I was not purposefully turning away from God. I was imbalanced in my approach to finding Him. My path was my left-brained way of logic and not His complete-brained way of grace. Looking back, I feel like I was in the ranks of those foolish virgins in Matthew 25 or the guys described as saying, "Lord, Lord," in Matthew 7:21-23:

> *Not everyone who says to me, "Lord, Lord," will enter the kingdom of heaven, but only he who does the will of My Father who is in heaven. Many will say to Me on that day, "Lord, Lord, did we not prophesy in Your name, and in Your name drive out demons and perform many miracles?" Then I will tell them plainly, "I never knew you. Away from Me, you evildoers!"*

I do not think in my fear of imbalance I was doing His will. I needed to buy my oil and gold (see Matt. 25:9, Revelation 3:18) with the broken parts of my life. I was not understanding that all I had to do was release the pain up to Him to receive.

Benevolence Balances Your Brain

The devil usually has an evil counterbalance for things. My scale weighed so heavy on the wrong side for most of my life, I can immediately recognize wrong stuff and have to be very careful not to judge. My severe demand of total adherence to God's ways must also be smothered in grace and love and be free of judgment.

Our Life Application Action for this step is *giving*. When we give instead of take, we are balancing the need to exalt ourselves. If you have been badly hurt through some of the same issues as me, you have probably developed some street smarts. They cannot be taught; they have to be ingrained by tough living. They are real handy for protection and even handier for self-preservation. This type of training, however, makes many unsympathetic to other's needs.

To stay healthy, we need the balance of give and take in our lives. At first, doing the right things did not come naturally to me. I had to figure out ways to make good actions happen. Thankfully, it does become natural if you keep stepping up.

For example, if you are experiencing frustration, you have a sense that it is a response of the flesh (which means it comes naturally to us). The antonym of *frustration* is *satisfaction*. The two words are miles apart; it is not difficult to decide which you would rather be. Frustration is a common issue; we are prone to it, and many of us are experiencing it right now.

The callousness attached to being street smart stems from anger and frustration that reside within us. Although from the outside we may seem pleasant enough, the street-smart individual erects walls against even those whose intentions are innocent, believing it is better to guard against being wounded than to trust. Do we have ourselves so protected by merciless resentment that we create our own issues?

We need to relax, trusting and relating to others with a balanced approach. With every correct reaction, we allow God to bring more balance into our emotions. He is slowly training us to act and react like His Son—to step out of selfishness and into servanthood.

Our current step is about giving as much as we feel we can. As we release our selfish nature, we realize the balance that giving brings to our hearts and minds. This is the process of becoming a servant.

Over and over again, His Word tells us to give (our current Life Application Action). Here are just two Scriptures, one from the Old Testament and one from the New:

One man gives freely, yet gains even more; another withholds unduly, but comes to poverty (Proverbs 11:24).

Give, and it will be given to you. A good measure, pressed down, shaken together and running over, will be poured into your lap. For with the measure you use, it will be measured to you (Luke 6:38).

Jewel for the Journey

Selfishness leads
us downstairs;
servanthood leads us
upward to God's glory.

Opposite Actions

Before I discovered my antonym theory, I began to pray that God would reveal specific ways to improve my responses to stress. When I became frustrated I would ask, "God what word or action can turn this feeling away before it leads into anger?"

He told me to go find a treasure in His Word to combat the flesh response. He knew my personality; He knew I was a treasure hunter that would use the jewels I stumbled upon and give them to others.

That is when I really began to understand how to use His Word as a weapon. When you find wisdom and realize it counterbalances weak behavior, you have found a cure. I meditated on Proverbs 19:11: *"A man's wisdom gives him patience; it is to his glory to overlook an offense."*

I realized the antonym to frustration is satisfaction. The minute the first syllable left my tongue, I knew that was my issue. I was not struggling with frustration. I was struggling with an imbalance; my expectations were skewed between wanting to serve and be served.

Often, the answer to healing is found in the counterbalanced sides of an issue. We must search for the remedy in the Bible (PP). We need to be satisfied that we have breath. If we are serving with an expectation of servanthood we are safe from frustration.

I do not know why, but I am always flabbergasted when a rocky road ends in a cool, calm lake of simplicity. I love intricate revelations of wisdom; I enjoy figuring out complex issues. In the final analysis, however, the most profound and life-changing things are simple. True satisfaction is an impossible feat without godly balance, giving to counterbalance self and God's wisdom.

We are never hopeless with Christ. We may feel that way at times, but He loves us and remembers us. Our trials are for His glory. Step for Him in and out of your pain, even if it seems impossible. We are stepping higher, but we are still human. We need to keep our physical and spiritual expectations balanced.

That is where we are heading to—balance. We are obedient, full, and allowing God to balance everything. We need to grab hold of our Vine, Jesus Christ; the Vine will impart balance and sturdiness in our lives. We also reach for the handrail of godly relationships to steady us and lead us forward.

God's fruit produces life—in our lives and in others as we give and serve others (*serving* is our next Life Application Action). Godly fruit brings healing in our lives and through our lives to others.

In a powerful passage from the Gospel of John, Jesus teaches us how godly fruit is borne:

> *I am the true vine, and My Father is the gardener. He cuts off every branch in Me that bears no fruit, while every branch that does bear fruit He prunes so that it will be even more fruitful. You are already clean because of the word I have spoken to you. Remain in me, and*

I will remain in you. No branch can bear fruit by itself; it must remain in the vine. Neither can you bear fruit unless you remain in Me. I am the vine; you are the branches. If a man remains in Me and I in him, he will bear much fruit; apart from Me you can do nothing (John 15:1-5).

We must *remain*. He says this word more than a dozen times in John 15. He tells us that we can do nothing apart from Him. We cannot balance our emotionalism without Him.

If you notice, God's fruit are opposite of our emotions. Antonyms reveal the dichotomy: The opposite of peace is worry. The reverse of self-control is rudeness. The opposite of gentleness is brutality. The opposite of hate is love. We can step up knowing that God's fruit is the remedy for our chemical imbalance.

God's fruit brings spiritual satisfaction, just as physical fruit pleases the physical body and senses. My stomach growled at the nauseous feeling. A lack of food had plunged me into a sugar imbalance, making it difficult to do my work. Dizzy from hunger, I made my way over to the fruit bowl and lifted out a white peach. I rinsed it and took a bite. The juice and sweetness was satisfying.

In that instant, I could relate to God's spiritual fruit. It was the "medicine" my out-of-balance soul needed. The sense of satisfaction to be gained from serving others was becoming evident. The connection was settling into my mind. It is time to step up with our newfound balance. Our fruit baskets are about to become full; we don't want them to tip over and spill God's precious remedy.

I told you this step would be less about our actions and more about allowing God's impartation of power to transform us into the image of Christ—balanced and willing to give, makes us healthy for life. This step and the coming steps of impartation are critical to your staying healed.

THE PRINCESS PRINCIPLES PRACTICE

Step Into Godly Balance:

- Desire to crucify excessive emotions and to birth a calm reverence for God.

- Acknowledge your strengths and weaknesses. Ask God to transform your weak areas so they rise to the same level as your strongest characteristics.

- Pray and wait instead of reacting hastily.

- Be willing to give even in times of need, knowing that this action brings balance and blessing.

- Deal with your feelings, but do not embrace the ones that are contrary to God's Word.

- Practice acting and reacting like Jesus.

Life Application Actions

Giving

In everything I did, I showed you that by this kind of hard work we must help the weak, remembering the words the Lord Jesus Himself said: "It is more blessed to give than to receive" (Acts 20:35).

If you are still timid, give by praying in private for others. Let God order your steps into giving. Journal about interesting ways you can give:

Summary of Princess Principles

 We can allow God to transform our minds and create the mind of Christ in us.

> *The spiritual man makes judgments about all things, but he himself is not subject to any man's judgment:"For who has known the mind of the Lord that he may instruct Him?" But we have the mind of Christ* (1 Corinthians 2:15-16).

Journal about your mind: do you tend to be more *right-brained* or more *left-brained*. Write how your actions and thoughts *are* coming into balance as you allow God to tend you in your healed and healing state.

 Without His Spirit and His truth, we are imbalanced.

> *Yet a time is coming and has now come when the true worshipers will worship the Father in spirit and truth, for they are the kind of worshipers the Father seeks. God is spirit, and His worshipers must worship in spirit and in truth* (John 4:23-24).

Read all of John 4 and study the woman at the well, then list and meditate on the meaning of this Scripture to you:

 His intention is for you to be complete in His image. If you let Him, He will balance you as He is balanced.

> *So God created man in His own image, in the image of God He created him; male and female He created them* (Genesis 1:27).

How amazing that we were made to be like Him! Pray for godly balance in your life. List the areas you need to persevere unto completion:

PP **Often, the answer to healing is found in the counterbalanced sides of an issue. We must search for the remedy in the Bible.**

The Spirit of the LORD will rest on Him—the Spirit of wisdom and of understanding, the Spirit of counsel and of power, the Spirit of knowledge and of the fear of the LORD—and He will delight in the fear of the LORD. He will not judge by what He sees with His eyes, or decide by what He hears with His ears (Isaiah 11:2-3).

You will hear people preach on Luke 11:24-26 and Matt 12:45. I like to believe the seven spirits listed in this passage above will counterbalance the attempts of the enemy to come back seven times stronger. Ask God to reveal and share with you the seven areas in this Scripture:

Congratulations! You are *balanced*! You have also added the Life Application Action of *giving*. Keep stepping princess; step up into *His fruit*.

Chapter Ten

Vineyard by the Castle Court

Step Ten: God's Fruit Gives Us a Servant's Heart

But the fruit of the Spirit is love, joy, peace, patience, kindness, goodness, faithfulness, gentleness and self-control... (Galatians 5:22-23).

Produce Aisle of His Love

W E are not naturally of noble character. In fact, we often label our-selves "Christian" without giving enough thought to what it means. We think the label alone will cover our actions. Grace makes healing available; our choices makes healing possible. Stepping in His will dictates our blessings and will keep us healthy. Living for God and being healed is not about outward appearances.

A healthy life is about what God has done on the inside through the blood of His Son and His Spirit. People will know He lives in us when they see His love and His fruit operating in our life. According to Matthew 7:17, fruit is either good or bad; it cannot be both.

Galatians 5 talks at about the fruit of the Spirit. These fruit are not mani-fested through our natural physical efforts. Galatians 5:25 makes that clear: *"Since we live by the Spirit, let us keep in step with the Spirit."*

As we step up in spirit and in truth, we heal. The temple stairs that we are climbing trail beneath the torn curtain and into the Holy of Holies as we manifest

God's functioning fruit to provide stability for our healing journey. We are to be "fruitful trees," blessed and producing the fruit of God's choosing.

Jewel for the Journey

We will produce God's fruit when we are ready to serve Him and others first.

Fruitlessness is contrary to God's ways, as Jesus demonstrated:

In the morning, as Jesus was returning to Jerusalem, He was hungry, and He noticed a fig tree beside the road. He went over to see if there were any figs, but there were only leaves. Then He said to it, "May you never bear fruit again!" And immediately the fig tree withered up (Matthew 21:18-19 NLT).

We need blossoms on our fig tree and grapes on our vine. John the Baptist said in Matthew 3:8, to *"produce fruit in keeping with repentance."* Our godly sorrow in repentance keeps us in His grace our fruit keeps us moving forward.

We so often connect man's morality and performance with God's fruitfulness. However, man's principles often produce bondage and perfectionism. The plan of satan is to keep us feeling like we need to *achieve* salvation. We know better: we know that salvation is received because of grace, not performance but then we confuse ourselves thinking the rest will be just as easy.

We have thrown off the hindrances to healing, including performance mentality. Now we must take on those things that will assist us in staying healthy. We do not need to perform a song and dance in order to feel like we are of noble enough character to call ourselves *Christians*. God sees our hearts. He wants full access, not a front row seat to a fake fruit extravaganza. If we are seeking Him in obedience and allowing Him to access our hearts, our fruit will blossom in His time. Just as is true with balance, the fruit will come from Him only.

Now that we are successfully stepping up into this divine promise, we must understand that we are not miraculously going to produce superior character at once. It is not ours to manufacture, but to receive through intimacy with God.

Just as was true with obedience, we become what we see, hear, learn, accept as truth, and do. This infiltration and initiation becomes how we live and eventually who we are. We know enough to protect our children from the world, yet we allow society to infiltrate our hearts with death every day. We must arrest this process, as our ingestion will eventually affect our children and the world around us.

I operated in the opposite of the fruit for so long that when God began to change me, my new character was suddenly foreign to me. We cannot expect God to heal others through us if we are constantly trying to be something we feel we are not. We have to allow God to genuinely make us these things and accept His ways. Fake fruit will not change hearts.

We look for the fruit, but we cannot assume that because kindness looks good at church, it is God's fruit. My Grandma used to have plastic grapes on her kitchen table: they looked like real grapes; they even felt like real grapes; but they were just rubber. Our true fruit surfaces behind closed doors, where no one is watching. Fruit does not need an audience or applause. True fruit comes from a seed that goes into the ground and then dies before it becomes what God intended. All the glory, honor, and praise to Him.

Fruit Before Gifts

As we regain spiritual health and balance, we realize we are sensitive to those who are still hurting. We will love them enough to descend to the base of the temple stairs for their sakes. We help them by gently nudging them upward and not judging them for their weakness. Let us remember: it was in our weakness that God met and healed us.

On this tenth step, we begin to realize that we are healing and healthy enough to begin serving. To obtain a true servant's heart, we must serve from the place of purity rather than capacity.

That is why we are accepting this Life Application Action before we know our spiritual gifts. Please sweet friend, never allow anyone to make you feel like you are not worthy to serve the King of kings and Lord of lords. Serving helps establish fruit in our lives; the fruit of the Spirit must be established before we exhibit the gifts. At every stage of the process, we pray for faith, fruit, and wisdom.

So many want the blessings, but so few want to do the work. So few are willing to climb upward to find what we are seeking. Healing unto serving is not a quick fix; this action takes ridding ourselves of self. Selflessness is blessed, and every step in servanthood to Christ brings us closer to Heaven, where God's truths and love reside (see Rom. 12).

The Service of Our Life

As we ascend, we feel the reverberation of the angels dancing about the throne of God singing *"Holy, holy, holy is the* LORD *Almighty; the whole earth is full of His glory"* (Isa. 6:3). Revelation 4:8 describes the Lord God Almighty as the One *"who was, and is, and is to come."* As we get closer to Him, we truly can feel His love, joy, and peace.

Too often, we are motivated by the desire to see the blessing. I always try to keep my mind focused on eternity. We cannot have worldly expectations and live a healthy godly life. Our expectations need to be focused on servanthood (PP). I am repeating this truth because our flesh wants to do the exact opposite, and pure humble servanthood in its essence heals, delivers, and sets us free.

Jesus did not seek recognition. He did not flaunt His power or draw attention to Himself as a means of stroking His ego. He was focused on the reality of eternity and the needs of people:

> *When He saw the crowds, He had compassion on them because they were confused and helpless, like sheep without a shepherd. He said to His disciples, "The harvest is great, but the workers are few. So pray to the Lord who is in charge of the harvest; ask Him to send more workers into His fields"* (Matthew 9:36-38 NLT).

Several years after my transformation I was asked to speak at an outdoor worship service. I went to the location prior to pray and, looking out on the most glorious field, I noticed that the wheat glowed as if the sun was shining out from within. A blanket of mist hovered above the luminous harvest. I wept and prayed. I prayed for all the people's hearts to soften; I prayed that they would arrive that evening to join as a community unified to worship Christ.

God impressed upon me just how plentiful His harvest was to be and how few were in place to bring the harvest into the Kingdom. Therefore, I took my cue from Matthew 9, praying for one more worker with every step I took. I must have walked a mile that morning. The mantle of fog was His Holy Spirit hovering about His wheat. That evening I asked the crowd to work for Him in power without holding back.

We are to produce fruit in increasing measure. We cannot fill a need unless seed is planted. If the only place we are professing Christ is in our church pews, we may not be working the totality of our harvest. The unsaved are hurting, as we once were. Do you remember your life without Christ? Does your heart ache for the harvest? Fruit abounds when healing takes root and God's love becomes our ultimate motivation.

Months prior to this experience, God deposited the vision of a community-wide woman's **K**ingdom **A**ccountability **G**roup into mine and my husband's heart— the template for KAG. He showed me a group of women from all different churches and denominations who would strengthen one another and would vow to go out and work the harvest from a kingdom perspective with power from on high. *"As iron sharpens iron, so a friend sharpens a friend"* (Prov. 27:17 NLT).

Our first year, we read the Word straight through (Appendix C) and studied the deep foundational truths from Genesis to Revelation. We met regardless of the weather, schedules, and pleasures. We stayed on the narrow path and we have seen God's glory for it. The group is actually a seed bed for a much larger structure that I hope will spread across the nation—one whose agenda is purely to seek after the Father's heart.

That group has been going strong for several years now and is producing lots of fruit. Women are moving in their purposes for the Kingdom and working to bring in the harvest. I have seen even some shy ones standing in purposes so mighty, proving only God can receive the glory. The power of the sovereign Lord is drawing us to awaken His bride to His plan, His Kingdom and His harvest for His glory.

My prayers are that God will lead me to publish the template for KAG so that if you feel led you can begin one in your community. This particular service helped me further my healing. Service to assist our sisters and guide those around us to fashion their lives for the cause of Christ will keep us healthy. Keep stepping and know there is always more glorious riches in His Kingdom for us to attain to.

We are gaining understanding of the fruit and we are learning to distinguish them from their opposites. When we stroll down the rotten produce aisle of satan's grocery store, we will accurately identify the ailments we see. Let us move with fresh oil toward the lamp that lights the path to God's produce aisle. Jesus wants to use us to save a part of His harvest.

Fruit Is Our Protection

As we heal and learn, we become fruitful and accept the call to servanthood. We begin to flow upward in more of a glide than a pulse, moving seamlessly by the Holy Spirit. Our stepping up is becoming more fluid, almost like an elevator in motion. Love, joy, and peace are coming down from Heaven into and through our lives.

> *For the Kingdom of God is not a matter of what we eat or drink,*
> *but of living a life of goodness and peace and joy in the Holy Spirit*
> (Romans 14:17 NLT).

God is honing our character; we are becoming more Christlike with each day. This equipping for service helps us to produce fruit in keeping with His desire.

> *For this very reason, make every effort to add to your faith goodness;*
> *and to goodness, knowledge; and to knowledge, self-control; and to*
> *self-control, perseverance; and to perseverance, godliness; and to*
> *godliness, brotherly kindness; and to brotherly kindness, love. For if*
> *you possess these qualities in increasing measure, they will keep you*
> *from being ineffective and unproductive in your knowledge of our*
> *Lord Jesus Christ* (2 Peter 1:5-8).

When these things begin to increase, they will help us to be more productive in our service. In the above passage, Peter names some of the fruit of the Spirit. Self-control is a quality only the Spirit knows in its perfection. Here, the Spirit presents it in relation to knowledge and perseverance, showing us how these qualities work together in us.

Many times, Christ's kindness doesn't look kind (in our terms), but tough. We need to be careful not to use human kindness to enable others to sin. We need to pray and allow God to give us His actions and reactions. Now that we are healthy, we need to practice restraining our flesh by crucifying our desires or bad fruit.

Sometimes, godly kindness means refraining from doing the things we think will help. Kindness and gentleness remind me of a soft-spoken, sweet old lady. Godly kindness does not always look that way. Our opinions about what kindness looks like are not important. We must judge kindness and any other trait or fruit by godly standards. The nature of secular kindness often lies in emotionalism; often our kindness is gauged by the level of personal satisfaction the doling out of kindness brings to us. It is of no use to look and act "kind" while we ignore God's promptings, refuse to read His Word, and fail to call on Him as He asks us to do.

Jewel for the Journey

Biblical fruit is always, under every circumstance, beneficial.

Satan was the leader of worship in God's Kingdom. He was a good and beautiful angel in Heaven. He fell because he allowed himself to be reduced to evil. He was tossed out of Heaven and landed among us. Goodness, kindness, and every other godly quality are easily counterfeited on this earth.

In order to deceive, a counterfeit must look, to the naked eye, exactly like the original (PP). We must be keen to discern! Worldly goodness has implications of a degree of excellence. What is important is resurrecting our goodness to that which is in Christ Jesus.

When we are sick and hurting, our godly fruit remains unexpressed and hidden in our hearts. This is true of goodness. We settle for the secular version of goodness that is easily accepted, but not pleasing to God, because it is not based in truth. We should not and do not accept any concept that runs contrary to the biblical model—*period!*

Apart from the biblical context, the word *good* means different things to different people and cultures. To some, *good* means making sure your kids have a designated driver when they go out drinking. To God, abstinence from drinking is *good*. He does not want anyone to stumble or to be required to accept unwarranted responsibility (see 1 Cor. 10:31-32; 2 Cor. 6:3).

God describes Himself as *"abounding in goodness"* (see Exod. 34:6 NKJV). The idea that we must be good in order to approach the throne is satan's devious scheme. His words seem just "good" enough to keep us from the very place of healing. Make sure your "good" is God's "good." Choose your words carefully: if they are not based in God's Word and do not reflect His fruit, the enemy will use them to hinder souls.

Our society has mutilated good words. They have dumbed them down and stripped them of their power and godly purpose. Scripture tells us that words have extraordinary power. When we speak, our words are either fruitful or unfruitful; they produce either life or death (PP) (see Prov. 18:21). James also stresses the power of our words to create or destroy (see James 3:3-12).

If we do not know and accept the full power of our words, we cannot use them to their full power. God's fruit is power. We are going to attempt to understand the fruit in His full measure. When we are healed, we can quit coddling sin with worldly "fruit." Instead, we correct one another with godly authority and love, thereby enacting true change.

Romans 15:14 says, *"I myself am convinced, my brothers, that you yourselves are full of goodness, complete in knowledge and competent to instruct one another."* Paul binds fruitfulness with full knowledge and a warning to serve each other. This gives us insight into what he knew and expected from Christians in Rome.

When we are hurting, it is most times a byproduct of evil done to us or by us. We can protect ourselves from evil with goodness. We can let God heal our evil hearts and allow forgiveness and goodness to master the pain. What unwanted consequences have come from the world's idea of goodness in your life?

Be aware that we are stepping into authority on this step. This is a bold step, because God's authority will set things in alignment with His will. If we truly want to see others healed, we will use God's fruit to witness to others. We must empty ourselves out and allow God's love to flow in and through us. God calls us to hold others accountable at times, but most of the time He does that silently as

He works directly in their hearts. Our fruit, whether shown in righteous fervor, gentle admonition, or biblical authority, must first reside in love.

Bad Apples and Pomegranates

Many consequences come from satan's versions of God's fruit of the Spirit. We have seen much pain through the deception of worldly concepts of fruit. Let us look at the exact opposite of godly fruit and see what manifests from "bad apples." In our flesh, we exhibit bad fruit at times and we just flat-out need to stop. Bad spiritual fruit is poisonous to the soul; its effects are more damaging to the soul than salmonella is to the body.

It may seem elementary and silly but how often do you find yourself reacting in an ungodly manner? Well then, we need this little lesson on bad versus good. We are revisiting the antonym theory: the opposite of love is hate; the opposite of joy is rage; the opposite of peace is chaos; the opposite of patience is impatience; the opposite of kindness is meanness; the opposite of goodness is badness; the opposite of faithfulness is fearfulness; the opposite of gentleness is roughness; the opposite of self-control is self-indulgence.

When we are busy, rushing, and quick-tempered, when we justify our actions with excuses about having "too much to do," we are walking on the staircase without God.

The bad-apple mentality encourages us to retaliate. If we are attacked, we want to attack back. If we follow the devil's ways, we justify our retaliation. If God's fruit guides us, we keep our peace even when our flesh is screaming for us to slam someone verbally. Not only will the situation end on a better note, but every time we choose to react in peace, we gain ground in the fruit aisle of His love.

Guided by God's fruit, we attain a new sense of things. We are empowered to focus from our new, higher perspective in life. The fruit of God's Spirit resides inwardly in your every thought, word, and action (PP).

We have an endless supply of resources and tools in Him. God fills our lives with love. This is the place where we gain ground and gather fruit. We are both healed and healing—all at once.

God abounds in fruitfulness and greatly desires to give us His fruit. We have degrees of faith as measured against this absolute standard. In the person who is converted, but not healed, we see a pale reflection of this fruit. In the surrendered, vulnerable, healing, obedient person we see a more vivid reflection. When we look in the mirror, we want to see a virtual cornucopia of fruit pouring out all over the place!

I remember when I bought my first pomegranate. I was well into my adult years and had gained some wisdom in Christ. I bought the pomegranate because I knew it was one of the seven foods listed in Deuteronomy 8:8. It is a beautiful fruit and it adorned the priestly garments. When I realized that it was full of flesh-covered seeds, I put three pomegranates in my shopping cart.

To my delight when I cut into the fruit, a treasure trove of jewels poured out. The seeds were like beautiful prismatic rubies. The fruit was broken into chambers just like our hearts and full of red juice. I asked God to make my witness like that of a pomegranate. I asked for every seed that I put forth to be as beautiful as pomegranate seeds. I asked to pour out as much love as would fit. I asked that the red, red blood of Jesus would cover everyone who came near me.

Be a pomegranate for the Kingdom. If you still feel like a bad apple, ask God to anoint you with the harvest of a pomegranate. (Some even say that pomegranate was the fruit on the Tree of the Knowledge of Good and Evil in the Garden of Eden.)

We will make stepping up about something bigger now. We can position our lives to revolve around God as we move for the Kingdom, focusing on stretching our minds and spirits daily in a wholehearted task to understand, learn, and grow up in His Word. Now we spend all our time in the courts of the temple, praising our Lord. We step up into fruit and a blessed and blessing life as we become consistent in our walk for Him.

Psalms 27:13-14 says:

> I am confident I will see the LORD's goodness while I am here in the land of the living. Wait patiently for the LORD. Be brave and courageous. Yes, wait patiently for the LORD (NLT).

Our steps gently trailed from sickness and hurt into healing. Our lives shifted as we grabbed hold of an intimate relationship with Him; now we are allowing God to fill us up and bind us to Himself.

We placed our feet on the stair of His expectation to bear much fruit. We journey now with balance as we are changing into His likeness. We are traveling with abundance and love. Our baskets are full. We will learn how to reside with these attributes, consistently making a place for God's wisdom.

Hallelujah, my beautiful climber, you are harvesting! You are giving, serving, and living for Christ so that He can return for His unblemished Bride.

That is you!

THE PRINCESS PRINCIPLES PRACTICE

Stepping With God's Fruit:

- Acknowledge the opposite of godly behavior and choose not to partake of it.

- Come into compliance to guard what comes out of your mouth.

- Be willing to practice God's fruit even when you are being treated unfairly.

- Crucify your flesh and serve willingly.

ᘒ Study to understand how Jesus acted so you can emulate Him.

ᘒ Choose peace, regardless of the situation.

Life Application Action

Serving

...the Son of Man did not come to be served, but to serve, and to give His life as a ransom for many (Matthew 20:28).

List areas where you want to serve and areas where you should serve: Try to merge them and pray about where God wants you to serve.

Summary of Princess Principles

Our expectations need to be focused on servanthood.

Obey them not only to win their favor when their eye is on you, but like slaves of Christ, doing the will of God from your heart. Serve wholeheartedly, as if you were serving the Lord, not men... (Ephesians 6:6-8).

Journal about how much of your heart wants to serve out of purity versus obligation or even kudos.

In order to deceive, a counterfeit must look, to the naked eye, exactly like the original.

And no wonder, for Satan himself masquerades as an angel of light. It is not surprising, then, if his servants masquerade as servants of righteousness. Their end will be what their actions deserve. (2 Corinthians 11:14-15).

Read Matthew 7:15-23 and meditate on it. Keep a journal for all the times satan has come to you dressed in sheep's clothing:

 When we speak, our words are either fruitful or unfruitful; they produce either life or death.

With the tongue we praise our Lord and Father, and with it we curse men, who have been made in God's likeness. Out of the same mouth come praise and cursing. My brothers, this should not be (James 3:9-10).

Write down the power of a fruitful tongue in regards to your healing and giving others healing power:

 The fruit of God's Spirit resides inwardly in your every thought, word, and action.

The wisdom that comes from heaven is first of all pure; then peace-loving, considerate, submissive, full of mercy and good fruit, impartial and sincere. Peacemakers who sow in peace raise a harvest of righteousness (James 3:17-18).

Choosing peace during trials and attacks is the best and quickest route to healing! Break down the items James listed and describe on paper how you have exhibited each recently:

Congratulations! You have done it again! You have successfully made it up another step: You have *godly fruit* for the journey! You have also added a new Life Application Action to your day: you are *serving*.

Keep stepping. Step up into studying His Word.

Chapter Eleven

The Crown of Consistency

Step Eleven: God's Word Produces His Consistency

"Appreciate your pastoral leaders who gave you the Word of God. Take a good look at the way they live, and let their faithfulness instruct you, as well as their truthfulness. There should be a consistency that runs through us all. For Jesus doesn't change—yesterday, today, tomorrow, He's always totally Himself" (Hebrews 13:7 MSG).

WHEN we are persistent in our approach to biblical standards, it is a sign that we have overcome our fleshly nature of inconsistency. While each step makes us godly in an area whether *"...in word, in conversation, in charity, in spirit, in faith, in purity"* (1 Tim. 4:12 KJV), it is the cohesion that provides consecration into godliness. When we naturally live in His ways, we have stepped into His wisdom and become steady in His love.

When we feel tired and empty, let us go to His Word. To get to where He wants us to be, we will search for truth consistently, not just on the bad days.

When I was writing this book there were days when all I felt like I was doing, aside from cleaning a toilet or two and tending to the family, was typing. I needed a break and I needed some prayer, rejuvenation, and confirmation. But I had to be consistent regardless of my feelings; I had to finish the assignment.

We cannot remain constant in our fleshly state. In that condition, we most often repeat our bad choices and give up on the good ones. Godly consistency should run like a stream throughout our entire lives. Our plan is to mimic Christ with truthfulness and purity—and He is consistent, as we notice from our chapter verse the Bible states: *"Jesus Christ is the same yesterday, and today, and forever"* (Heb. 13:8).

We want to be consistent. We want to read, fast, listen, and pray consistently. We want to make sure what we do is not methodical, but genuine, from pure motives. God says that those with a clean heart will actually see Him (see Matt. 5:8).

Jewel for the Journey

We cannot build strong faith on weak understanding.

We know by now that our flesh will try to take over and tell us that this isn't a good time to read, seek Him, or fast. Excuses will pop up without effort. That is why we need the mind of Christ to rise up in us as a counterbalance to the lies. We want to be consistent to the cross.

The Bungalow and the Roach

I pulled up to visit with some friends at their cottage, dizzy in God's embrace from praising and worshiping Christ while driving there in the glow of the moonlight. The bungalow was precious, but the two saintly women who inhabited the place were much more precious. They were the type of women whose eyes sparkled like gates that could not keep the Lord's Spirit from bursting out of them. I imagined the possibility that after I left, they transported themselves right back up to the third level of Heaven. Whether they did or not, God had blessed me beyond measure with guidance during my visit.

I had a handful of real friends, but guidance was spilling over in my life. I knew this was a rare commodity. I felt more blessed than ever. In that abundance, I knew God's plan for me to learn His ways, stand in His purpose, and then share with others. He would not have covered me with so much wise counsel if I hadn't had a true heart for His wisdom. God knows the heart and He saw mine crying out for Him and all He was willing to give.

It was late as I stepped out of my car, but the air was still thick from the summer day. The darkness had a hard time pushing out the scorching Mississippi heat. The oak trees were swaying with the wind and the moon was almost full. A kitten ran between my legs and onto the first step of the porch. I flinched and laughed; I was as excited as he was to get inside. In fact, I need not even knock to enter; I just pressed on in.

A great group of saints had formed in the living room and had already begun to talk about Jesus' resurrection and the resurrections of the dead. I smiled and hugged my precious friends, making note of the twinkle of the Spirit within each of them, and took a seat. These types of encounters with godly friends and mentors in the faith are the very reason why I understand the phrases *balance each other, equally yoked, and as iron sharpens iron.*

I joined in the conversation. Hours passed without notice. My eyes got red. I got tired and my body needed sleep. Everyone felt the dawn approaching and we decided to pray out. As we gathered, with every heart hungry, pure, and humble, He met us. The saints bathed this book, *The Roach Princess,* in prayer.

I drove home to the house God restored; the one from Chapter 2 that we had occupied for well over five years at this point. I crawled into bed. We had seen maybe three roaches total over the period of those years. When I woke up the next morning after our prayer meeting, there was a dead roach right next to my computer. I love the physical manifestation of what is occurring in the spiritual. When you get tired and weary, He will send you a sign that He is well pleased; He will express His desire for you to keep stepping.

Because I studied consistently, God blessed and surrounded me with others who lived to know more of Him. When this is the case, the sharpening of iron lends itself to prayer meetings that shift the atmosphere and allow for a deeper communion with God. He puts us with like-minded saints; therefore, be like the saints you want God to surround you with daily. He will bless you with mighty warriors for Him. That is a powerful truth.

Jewel for the Journey

Three chapters a day will keep the devil away.

We are going to step up into consistent study of God's Word. His Word gives freely. He tells us to pray, seek and ask for wisdom, and He will give it to us. We are going to implement a Life Application Action of consistent reading, and we will call it studying or seeking.

Appendix C in the back of this book steps you consistently through a one-year reading of the Bible from Genesis to Revelation. This action involves digging deep in study—consistently. I may sound like a drill sergeant, but receiving blessings and keeping a healthy life in Christ takes work. It is not all work; where there is diligence, He graces us with ability, strength, and time.

He wants to see effort on our part. When we know that we are capable of understanding and navigating His Word, it solidifies our authority in our healing. By owning what God has put within us, and activating the blessing, we feel more comfortable asking for the gift.

Consistent Godly Stepping

Consistency is a major player on the stairs to healing. It is the upward rhythm or motion that we keep. Steadfastness is so intricate a part of the duration and endurance of our success that, without its influence, we will fail. We see excellence when we see godly consistency in our behavior (PP).

We are consistent when we are obeying the Spirit and the Word. I have realized walking through the temple that, more than anything, my consistency to God's ways is what ensures the longevity of my healed state. All the steps prior are important and necessary. This step is the center step of the impartation stairs it is the glue that binds them all. We have to step out all our principles and actions consistently day by day, hour by hour, minute by minute, unto perfection. We cannot deviate or let up.

Just like our Life Application Actions of hope, faith, praying, reading, worshiping, resting, fasting, listening, giving, and serving, studying has got to be done consistently to be of use. It is His *daily* bread. We are a give-up society. We stick with things until we get bored, tired, or until something new comes along.

Do not let the enemy determine your outcomes by allowing him to feed you lies.

> *...He was a murderer from the beginning. He has always hated the truth, because there is no truth in him. When he lies, it is consistent with his character; for he is a liar and the father of lies* (John 8:44 NLT).

When I read this Scripture, it makes me want to never turn and walk back down. By nature, we are flighty and shifty. We do not need anybody's help to quit. What we need is to stand on the Rock consistently. Jesus stays the same always; all else is sinking sand.

Remain consistent, even when the road gets tougher. Do you ever wonder why some people seem to get the easy road? Does your road seem to be always on the edge of a ridge of falling rocks? Do your stairs seem steeper than other people's?

When I go for a run, I pick a starting point and a stopping point. Then I choose consistency with no option of stopping. I want to remain victorious. But the route is often grueling and I ask Him why.

One day, I cried out, "Why Jesus?" He answered me at the very end of a long and trying path.

"You would not appreciate it otherwise. You would not be satisfied if your work was not grueling." His answer was ironic, because I thought I was trying to combat frustration (the opposite of satisfaction) with my run. He told me not to question His techniques in my life because I am the one who determines them.

As I puzzled through His words, He asked me to look back over my life and tell Him what I loved the most and what mattered most to me. As I glanced back into my past, I began to weep. The things that hurt the most meant the most to me. He told me some of His saints were completely content with the simple, easy road. He told me I was the exact opposite; therefore, I have to have a challenge.

He said that even in the physical I expressed this. When I ran I made sure I was sick at the end. When I loved, I loved unto death—my passions were extreme and my obedience was insane. My trials were not middle of the road but hanging off a cliff. He was making me adhere to how He had made me and how He sees pleasure in me.

He asked me why I would question Him, when it was He who created me. He wanted to know why everything had to be right *now,* when all He wanted to do was give me the ability to handle the blessings first.

I did not stop running as I wept screamed at the top of my lungs, "I love You, Jesus with everything in me! I thank You for making me so extreme, because while the bad may be really bad, the good is downright glory in You. Your will for me is amazing. And, yes, You know me and love me."

I screamed these words as I sweated in the noonday sun. I refused to stop running regardless of exhaustion until I came to the predetermined stopping point. Now you can take this story and begin running or you can realize that your consistency determines your destiny. When we have faith that God is in control, all we have to do is walk out His plan.

God's plan for you is perfect and in perfect order. If something is not part of His plan, we should reject it, too. God knows you better than you can ever know yourself. Trusting consistently that He has your life taken care is enough. He has not left a single detail to chance (PP). As long as you have breath breathe for Him, He is listening, and guiding your steps. They will be good steps.

Twenty-Six Point Two

Godly consistency only comes through the cross of Christ. We can attain productive, purpose-driven, consistency only through diligence toward God's call.

Jewel for the Journey

To know the power of victory, you must cross the finish line. First, however, you must train your body, mind, and heart to run the race with a victorious mindset.

Speaking of running, I ran the Chicago Marathon. Running 26.2 miles is tough. It takes never giving up and never stopping to turn around to look back. It may sound like a diversion, but running is a gift the Lord has given me. I feel God's pleasure when I run. What are the talents God has blessed in you? How consistently do you use them? What have they taught you?

Running gets you places fast, but you must be careful not to get ahead of God. When I am injured, I see how He gently slows me down and sometimes stops me to rest in Him and heal. My running has taught me a lot about endurance in trials and obedience in finishing the things I start.

More than anything, it has taught me about consistency. Without steady training, you lose your endurance and capability. Without consistent pacing, you lose your time and placement. Both are imperative to fulfillment of our God-ordained purpose, preparation, and position. Without a consistent mindset of finishing the race, you will lose— *period.*

Running has taught me to trust Him when I feel like running back down all the steps that I have fought so hard to climb. It has taught me to push forward when I feel pain and want to give up more than anything. It has taught me that without consistent and proper training there is no way to succeed. All these lessons are very important on this step.

We are winning the greatest victory when we feel the most opposition and are the most tempted to turn around or stop. We cannot always see the blessing, but we will be prepared and have faith that God has greatness in store for us. If we could see it, there would be no need for faith. When the race gets the best of you, stand still if that is all you can do. But my advice is, be consistent in the promise of His Word and pray. Do not give up, stay in the blood. Fight the good fight of faith. We do not like to be uncomfortable; however, that is the very place we must visit right before we reach the place of peace, blessing, and glory.

Throughout the Chicago Marathon, I said Jesus' name, through sweat and breathlessness. I prayed through the entire last half of that race. I had no big plans. In fact, my only plan was to track with the eight-minute mile marker sign. I whispered the name of Jesus in order to stay consistent with my pace up the hills. I said it when I felt like there was nothing more in me. I allowed Him to move for me when the marker sign got too far ahead in the distance. When I hurt, I gave Him the pain.

I finished that race in three hours and 40 minutes flat, chip time. That was the cut-off for qualifying for the Boston Marathon. I am not telling you this for your kudos. I am sharing this because I did not even know I could qualify or really, what qualifying was all about. Sound familiar to my room in "Damascus?" However, God saw my heart and my persistence and He blessed me. All glory and honor goes to Him in our undertakings.

I had accomplished two things with my Savior, one of which I had not the sense to even plan for. My husband always says, "If we are merely faithful, Jesus trumps our every request."

Are you making glorious plans with your talents? Make sure you are not selling yourself short. Do you know that with God anything is possible?

Majestic Trailer Park

Growing up, as you know, I had a general lack of godly consistency. However, there was hope for me through both sets of grandparents, especially my father's parents because of their proximity. I spent a lot of time with them. The time was so precious that it was magnified in my thinking. Their steadiness to each other and to me resides at the top of my memory bank.

Nonnie would always tell me, "Little girls are supposed to be made of sugar, spice, and everything nice."

When I was a little girl, I did not feel like that. I thought sugar and spice was an endearing way of describing my personality, but the "everything nice" part bothered me. I felt lonely and broken and did not feel like everything of *anything*, especially something nice.

My Nonnie and Grandpa loved to give me little sayings and sing to me. Nonnie would play the piano with her graceful fingers; she would play "Maria" from *The Sound of Music* and we would sing it together. Then Nonnie and Grandpa would tell me that they loved me. We sang all the time in my grandparent's trailer in south Texas, near the border of Mexico. They could not have had a mansion that would have made me happier.

The trailer park was like an adventure park. It had shuffleboard, a pool, and cool things in everyone's front yard. The streets resembled a flea market. There were things spinning, sparkling, and waving. There were gnomes, flamingos, fountains, and flags. Some trailers were even decorated for Christmas all year long. They either forgot or were practical and left the stuff up for the next year. What I remember most in the midst of all of this was that Grandpa loved Nonnie, Nonnie loved Grandpa, and they provided a pure, safe, stable place in my life.

We would wake up at the same time every morning and eat a big, nourishing breakfast. Later we had lunch, followed by dinner. In between, we had yard work, backgammon, and lots of love. Consistency and calm were the hallmarks of that majestic trailer park. The glue in my grandparents' relationship would be the thing I looked for when Jesus came calling, and when I had to fight for my own marriage. It gave me something to attain to. What good can you mimic from life (even if it only happened once)?

Nonnie's name was Vera, so I always thought it was neat that she had an aloe vera plant out behind the trailer. When I would fall off my bike, she would walk out back, hack off a huge chunk of the plant, and rub the green ooze on my injury, regardless of the size of the wound. Nonnie was always loving, kind, sober, vigilant, and working—as was Grandpa.

Out by the aloe vera plant was Nonnie's fountain with a statue of a little girl in the middle. Nonnie used to say, "That is you."

She had three boys. I think I blessed her as much as she blessed me. Finally, in her old age, and with much wisdom and time to share, God allowed her a little girl. I loved her and my grandpa so much. I felt safe and knew love when I was with them.

I remember when I was eight, how I loved wearing Nonnie's square dancing costumes. My favorite quest was to rifle through her jewelry box. Then I would load myself up with big, sparkly rhinestones that conveniently clipped to almost anything, including my ears. This dress-up was practice for my reign as The Roach Princess. As an innocent child, I felt just like a princess, with the King and the Queen in the trailer in south Texas.

Nonnie knew of my passion for royalty. She needed her square dancing clothes, but did not want to send me home without proper princess protocol. Therefore, she would spend hours sewing formal, ruffled dresses. My favorite attire for every occasion was a royal garment.

I wore these long dresses the way other kids wore shorts and T-shirts. My bicycle spokes always seemed to grab the lace and ring the bell sewn into the hem. I sported ankle-length gowns whether playing in the woods, riding my bike, or strolling down the street. I insisted the bells be sewn into the hems with velvet bows. I could not just look like a princess; I wanted to be accompanied by a princess chime—a royal jingle, so to speak. I knew all the way back then that it was not enough just to look the part; you had to smell the part, be the part, and sound the part as well. When I wanted something, I wanted it engrained in me; every fiber counted.

Nonnie and Grandpa, *a.k.a.,* Birdie and the Colonel, were beacons of consistency that I would remember all my life. Looking back, I can see that the little things...the hidden things...matter most. The way we act day in and day out is what adds up to significance (see Zechariah 4:10).

"Maria," the song Nonnie used to sing with me, was no accident. I noticed, even at such a young age and unchurched as I was, the line: "her penitence was real." The words stuck with me. I came back to them years later. God sees your heart. He knows its condition. Let us not forget that daily humility and penitence take us before the throne of God (PP).

Symbols of the Supernatural

As I have mentioned before, God often shows us in the natural realm what He is performing in the supernatural. He is faithfully consistent in this. We are like little girls standing on their fathers' feet; He sees our smiles as we dance with Him. He takes pleasure in the consistency He sees developing in us. We are His princesses.

I attempted to capture a certain feeling with the title of this book—not with the roach part, but with the princess part. Think back to when you first saw God stop everything and move the wind just for you. That moment reveals what being a princess of the Most High means. He will stop everything for you and replace your old with new.

I remember when I met Him that moment that I finally decided to die out. I could feel the velvet silkiness of the royal garment as He placed it over my weak shoulders. He had adorned the edges with pomegranates, jewels, and tassels. The garment produced sounds, like the gowns Nonnie used to make me, but instead of the peal of a small bell, it was the shimmering harmony of chimes. My ears heard deep and high pitches. The resonance produced the same melody that the angels hummed. My nose drew in the aromatic smell of raw silk and linen all in one breath; it was a deep, earthy, living scent that traveled straight into the soul.

My new mantle was not heavy, hot, or scratchy; the adornment was perfect. I was finally clothed like a proper princess in the cloak of freedom, joy, and peace. I looked down and my sash read, "Forgiven, for her penitence is real." The salt from my tears ran into my mouth as I spoke, "Jesus, King of kings and Lord of lords, there is nothing that You do not control and my heart is yours forever."

Let Him place a new mantle on you. If you feel like your consistency in healing has been difficult, allow Him to give you His burden and yoke (see Matt. 11:28). This time it will not just be a costume to hide the pain.

Our Lord desires to adorn us in His best changing every fiber, opening our eyes and ears to hear and encasing us with the scent of heaven. He stands waiting to amend our garments, crown us in beauty, and restore our joy.

> [He has sent Me to]...*provide for those who grieve in Zion—to bestow on them a crown of beauty instead of ashes, the oil of gladness instead of mourning, and a garment of praise instead of a spirit of despair...* (Isaiah 61:3).

Jewel for the Journey

Your new freedom in Christ will be authority to reign over your pain.

The Rhythm of His Word

When we are consistent in our studies, we allow wisdom to settle in on us and we discover the blessing of purpose uncovered by our healing.

Studying is the Life Application Action we are going to add on this stair. We must not only read the Word of God, but also study it diligently. It is not just for pastors or clergy. Learning God's Word is for us. Study should be our daily bread for life. When we truly study, we assimilate God's methods and take up His power for ourselves (PP).

Finding the meaning in each word that God has linked together in rhythm and synchronicity produces life. I told the women in my accountability group one night that I would not be the least bit shocked if my Bible began to beat or pulse just like a heart. His Word is alive and every word has unending depth; every page pumps life into our being.

When we study, we rightly divide the Word and join the Word together. When God leads you to a particular verse, connect it to the one above and the one below. See how the message fits in contextually within the chapter and book. Find out who wrote it, to whom it was written, and learn where, when, and why it was written. Then prayerfully take the Scripture and see where else in the Bible you see the same theme, the same meaning, or the same choice of words.

God's Word is not like any other book; it is alive. Did you hear me? The Bible is alive. The actual words are full of life-giving power. They heal, deliver, warn, rebuke, guide, protect, comfort, love...I promise this is truth. All you need to experience this truth is faith and salvation. Then the baptism of the Spirit helps the deeper revelation.

> *For the word of God is living and active. Sharper than any double-edged sword, it penetrates even to dividing soul and spirit, joints and marrow; it judges the thoughts and attitudes of the heart* (Hebrews 4:12).

Lesson of the Bees

I came home to a bee swarm in our backyard. The swarm was literally the size of a watermelon. We lived in a neighborhood with tons of trees and tons of houses. Our backyard had only one remaining tree. The other one had fallen down several weeks earlier. The bees were not on any one of the 30 trees in my neighbors' yards; the bees were on the solitary tree in my yard!

I started my research. I kept the kids inside and called a bee specialist. He told me to stay away—that they were migrating. He agreed there were probably over 30,000 of them and we did not need to be outside when they decided to move on. I was more interested in what God was telling me than I was in their migratory plans, so I began to study. What I learned would help me to understand a situation that was ahead. For now however, I was waiting for the bees to leave. When they did, they looked like a fog rolling out. The beekeeper used the word *tornado* to describe their formation in the sky.

Little did I know how God would use my bee study. The pastor of our church had to leave, which scattered the sheep. We sought God and gathered as many as we could, offering our home as a safe cleft in the rock in which to meet until the

Lord made a way for us. We had a consistent group that met on Sunday evenings. It was a church so to speak, like in Acts when the Church met in the home.

My research of the honeybee revealed that it is a symbol of consistent work and obedience. The honey it produces is a symbol of wisdom, rebirth, and positive changes in spiritual or moral direction and temperament. The bee's ceaseless activity surrounding the production of honey is comparable to the consistent action of the Spirit of Christ hovering about His Church.

He was letting us know that He recognized our plight and would reestablish His people and bring us back into His temple. We each, on our own, felt led to attend a small church down the road. That small church bought the building our church had assembled in prior to the pastor's departure. God put His sheep right back where He intended them to bee (pun intended) to begin with. We stood, stepped, studied, and He restored.

Had we not sought God consistently and studied His Word to know exactly what He wanted us to do, we would have missed the glory. Glory is what happens when you stay right where God would have you, even when your flesh tells you to hurry up and find a church. Wisdom that is consistently sought, regardless of emotion, leads directly to glory.

Are you getting this? I believe you are! You are doing so well that we are going to press further with God by asking Him to impart wisdom into our healing life. Wisdom is what will further bind us to His hem, the only royal garment we need. He is waiting for you to ask for His gifts, His wisdom and more faith to assist you in your healthy life.

THE PRINCESS PRINCIPLES PRACTICE

Stepping Into Consistency to God's Ways:

- Comprehend this truth: Consistency to God's ways is the path to staying healthy.

- Know His Word in order to live His Word daily.

- Allow His desires to become yours.

- Form habits to practice His truths.

- Reject all the old you in order to constantly step in the Spirit.

Life Application Action

Studying His Word

Do your best to present yourself to God as one approved, a workman who does not need to be ashamed and who correctly handles the word of truth (2 Timothy 2:15).

Journal how you rightly divide, join together, and handle God's Word: Jot down some recent revelation:

Summary of Princess Principles

 We see excellence when we see godly consistency in our behavior.

Blessed is the man who perseveres under trial, because when he has stood the test, he will receive the crown of life that God has promised to those who love Him (James 1:12).

List what you are surprisingly consistent to now and be edified that if you endure you will receive a crown: (Find all the crowns, in Scripture, that God offers us and why; it is a blessed study!)

 God knows you better than you can ever know yourself. Trusting consistently that He has your life taken care is enough. He has not left a single detail to chance.

But seek first His kingdom and His righteousness, and all these things will be given to you as well. Therefore do not worry about tomorrow, for tomorrow will worry about itself. Each day has enough trouble of its own (Matthew 6:33-34).

Read Matthew 6:25-34 and list specifically the things that used to make you worry:

Now list why they do not:

 Let us not forget that daily humility and penitence take us before the throne of God.

And when the Chief Shepherd appears, you will receive the crown of glory that will never fade away. Young men, in the same way be submissive to those who are older. All of you, clothe yourselves with humility toward one another, because, "God opposes the proud but gives grace to the humble." Humble yourselves, therefore, under God's mighty hand, that He may lift you up in due time (1 Peter 5:4-6).

(I helped you find one more crown!) List specific areas where you see pride in the ways of the world and how you have chosen daily humility:

When we truly study, we assimilate God's methods and take up His power for ourselves.

Instruct a wise man and he will be wiser still; teach a righteous man and he will add to his learning." The fear of the LORD is the beginning of wisdom, and knowledge of the Holy One is understanding (Proverbs 9:9-10).

Journal about what the fullness in regards to His Word has brought to you specifically:

Congratulations—you have successfully made it up another step: You are *consistent in godly stepping*. You have also added a Life Application Action: You are *studying God's Word* on your journey. We only have two more stairs to climb. Keep stepping!

Chapter Twelve

Wisdom:
The Moat Surrounding Your Fortress

Step Twelve: Functioning in Your Purpose Is Wise

Get wisdom, get understanding; do not forget my words or swerve from them. Do not forsake wisdom, and she will protect you; love her, and she will watch over you. Wisdom is supreme; therefore get wisdom. Though it cost all you have, get understanding. Esteem her, and she will exalt you; embrace her, and she will honor you. She will set a garland of grace on your head and present you with a crown of splendor (Proverbs 4:5-9).

From Mind to Heart

WISDOM is what occurs when we fearfully/reverentially allow God to transform our minds as He intends, broaden the understanding of our heart, and widen our capacity to contain His glory. Wisdom is the seed of revelation and the blossom of healing. Wise steps are peaceful, joyful, steps. Wisdom is represented as a woman in Scripture; she is beautiful and we are becoming her. She is also *"proved right by her actions"* (Matt. 11:19). So let's prove her right in our healing.

I see wisdom when I see someone covered in peace and letting God fight for them in a time of trial. Wisdom is love and stillness when the flesh says to struggle. Wisdom resides inside of faith, love, peace, joy, goodness, faithfulness, patience, kindness, gentleness, and self-control. Wisdom is joy in the midst of pain and loving forgiveness when we want to hate. The wisest people are willing to give their wealth away in exchange for wisdom.

Knowledge is fact, information, data. It is what you gain from education. Wisdom is the key to purpose. It unlocks knowledge and helps us to utilize it effectively. If consistency causes us to ascend the steps in a fluid motion; wisdom enables us to discern the perfect pace and flow in the current of love that keeps the motion going. True wisdom, godly wisdom, can only be grasped through access to the Spirit of God and His Word.

First Corinthians 2:9-10 says:

> However, as it is written: "No eye has seen, no ear has heard, no mind has conceived what God has prepared for those who love Him"—but God has revealed it to us by his Spirit. The Spirit searches all things, even the deep things of God.

We have taken this passage out of a chapter on spiritual wisdom. Paul concludes the chapter by telling us that, *"We have the mind of Christ"* (1 Cor. 2:16).

Are you allowing God to change your mind with His wisdom? Are you allowing Him to transfer all of His love into your heart? If you are willing, ask Him; He is more than willing to fulfill your request.

I remember the exact moment I realized God had fulfilled my request for some of His wisdom. It was a precious moment when I had the means to help someone in need and felt the flow of God working through me. All of my studying finally made sense as the release of wisdom came—from my heart rather than knowledge from my head. The activation of freedom unto glory occurs when, by faith, you allow Him to transform you into His image (PP).

When He transforms us, we can better walk in purity and humility. Remember that our initial steps into healing were meant to clean us out. These latter steps are meant to keep us healthy; they change us by teaching us to rely and receive from Him. We, in turn, are filled with His glory.

I am currently in seminary. God put me there for more than just knowledge. I love studying Scripture. Knowing all of Paul's missionary journeys, all the dates, all the prophets from Genesis up and all the history gives me more information.

Knowing all the power behind those journeys, understanding the symbolism in the dates, and hearing the hearts of the prophets for then and today, gives me wisdom about the Scriptures.

I was full of knowledge well into my healing even revelation, but it was not until I sat under a prophet that God transferred His wisdom to me in the form of active power coming out from the understanding of my heart. It was another level of His healing for His glory.

This encounter activated all of that knowledge into authority. I became a healing and healed vessel to heal for God. Such supernatural occurrences cannot be explained with words; you have to experience them with faith through life.

God's Fivefold Plan

Now that I have your trust, I want to tell you that the fivefold ministry, as well as the gifts, miracles, signs, dreams, visions, and wonders are for *today*. We are about to cover some of these in this chapter and I pray that you glean true wisdom from our study. Let me share my encounter with a true prophet; not one that just has the gift of prophecy (which we are about to study) but an ordained officer.

First, let me briefly explain prophecy. Revelation 19:10 tells us to *"Worship God! For the testimony of Jesus is the spirit of prophecy."* Jesus' testimony is life and life abundant. It is the actual healing we have experienced. We make things too complicated. Prophecy is God's love for us manifested in His power through His saints.

Once again, I was not sure what I was about to experience, but like a little girl I walked eyes wide open, and heart too, into God's arms through the prophet. Boxing God up in our thinking by deciding to cease or ignore things we cannot rationalize or have not yet experienced in His Word holds us in bondage. Prophets are here, and they are very real.

> *Anyone who receives a prophet because he is a prophet will receive a prophet's reward, and anyone who receives a righteous man because he is a righteous man will receive a righteous man's reward* (Matthew 10:41).

I stepped into the prayer room with a prophet whose ordination and mantle fell straight out of the throne room and I received the prophet! After we had spent some time in the presence of God allowing Him to flow into the depths of my soul, further healing me for purity in my purpose, blood came gushing out of my nose. When it finally stopped, I walked out of that room a changed vessel for God.

Remember that God uses physical signs to disclose and represent spiritual events. My spiritual blood transfusion activated the natural gifts and call on my life with supernatural power infused with the love of God to glorify His Kingdom.

This gift is proven true in Scripture and in my life experience. I want these encounters to be commonplace among you; they are healing, gift and call activating opportunities. I did not just walk in, fall out, and bleed. I worked hard. I let a lot of my flesh die out and stood with only faith at times for the reward.

I studied under her. In fact, you can thank her for being the vessel that assisted my awareness of the fragmented soul, initiated how our iniquity plays into our bondage, and birthed me into the true understanding of prophecy. I never missed a meeting, and I hope I never will—at least not one God intends that I attend. I was suddenly captivated by a larger dose of His love and this time a new level of His glory.

This advancement into His ways allowed for more deep revelation in my life, and a true prophet will for you, too. When I was barely out of treatment years earlier, I had a dream, but it wasn't until wisdom arrived at this step that it was interpreted: *My husband and I were at the beach in a contemporary house with a convertible car parked in the garage, which is not our taste. This showed me that this is His ministry, not mine. My husband was jogging, telling me he was healthy in our old age. I was on the balcony looking out over a strangely calm, yet raging sea. I felt peace as the moon filled the sky, although it was daytime and the moon was covered in blood.*

I did not even know that there was a Scripture describing this scene until this period of my life almost four years later (see Luke 21:25 and Acts 2:20). Signs and wonders are here and coming in abundance for us and the next generation. We need to be healthy enough to raise them up in the Word. Study, find wisdom, and stand in your purpose in order to impart power to our children and grandchildren knowing how to walk them into their call.

Some of the most intelligent Bible scholars will never advance in the ability to instruct in power if they refuse to walk the stairs, stepping out of their head knowledge and into His wisdom. We will now pass the step of knowledge and begin to study wisdom to flow in our purpose for His Kingdom to come.

Jewel for the Journey

Willingness to
understanding the
Kingdom of God from
a humble and pure
perspective is
an initiation point
of wisdom.

Explanations regarding wisdom can be perplexing; wisdom is one of those things we understand after it is established in our lives. Just as hope transforms into faith, obedience and knowledge flow into wisdom (when we let the Holy Spirit lead us).

You will know wisdom's power the minute God's perception is born in you. Wisdom is God's, and only God can impart the power to see beyond our limited minds, in our spirit. He said it is with wisdom that He formed the earth (see Jeremiah 10:12).

The Purpose of Wisdom

First, we need to recognize what pulls wisdom in and what lets wisdom out. Proverbs 2:10 tells us it is our heart that is the entry of wisdom. When we make the shift to accept and release only God's truth's from our heart, we are flowing in His wisdom. *The whole world sought audience with Solomon to hear the wisdom God had put in his heart* (1 Kings 10:24).

You are aware by now that I write and study a lot. Right before God's prophet took me in, I had to release all ownership of my intellect. Let me explain. I had filled my computer with exegesis papers, notes, Bible studies, this book, a guided journal, and so on. I would spend hours reading, writing Bible studies, and then saving them to protect my "important" knowledge. I would take days out to prepare notes for speaking engagements, all while God was waiting on me to let Him be my source.

I came home one day excited to begin another deep Bible study. When I turned on my computer, there was nothing but a blue screen. I guess it was better than having my hip out of joint. I left my knowledge and information at the foot of the cross while kicking, screaming, and trying to resurrect my hard drive in government "clean rooms" with men in beekeeper suits.

There I was, crying on the floor, surrounded in the refuse of my lost identity. I did not realize that, in the midst of my broken crowns and ripped sashes, He could best use me. He lovingly whispered about how Solomon's temple was glorious to Him, but because even a speck of evil had entered, He had to take it down. He told me He only destroys to restore unto glory; He said that if I would trust Him, He would put wisdom in my heart that no person could teach me and no person or event could take from me.

When I submitted to His love above all else and walked humbly through that prayer room, bloody nose and all, I became His hard drive, and the hard drive of my flesh was gone. He activated and deepened my spirit to contain more of Him and His love. Now I spend only what He requires preparing to speak, because I only want it to be Him speaking through me forever.

Most of us have devoted much time to study, and I thank the Lord for it. It has paved the way for amazing advancements and all kinds of wonderful stuff. However, as far as saving souls and bringing healing, our soul knowledge is useless if not coupled with His Spirit's wisdom.

The minute I digested the Books of First and Second Kings and learned about David's life, I realized that as long as our hearts are truly repentant and we realize our need for Him, our faith stream continues and God hears us. However, do we hear Him back? This is how faith enters, so we need to be careful to listen. Even in sin, David was in the lineage of the King of wisdom. David's son, Solomon, would crave the very heart of God's wise counsel. God saw Solomon's heart and answered his plea. The humility and purity of letting nothing come between us and God keeps us healthy. Even Solomon fell away toward the end. We do not want to heal and then step back.

Wisdom comes from one source: God. You obtain wisdom when you ask for the entire revelation of Christ and the Word of God—precept upon precept, nothing added, nothing taken away—to be sewn into your heart (PP). Problems arise when we seek wisdom in the wrong places and fall prey to false doctrine.

The Fear of the Lord

We are all in search of something God quietly tucked away in the Book of Job. It is beautiful, descriptive, and it takes you on a journey into the depths of the earth and through the secret trails that we know not. He sums it up saying, *"The fear of the Lord—that is wisdom, and to shun evil is understanding"* (Job 28:28).

People often live in the shelter of their own might, never to feel the torrent of wind from an eagle's wing (see Isa. 40:31). For instance, we need to teach and allow the gifts that the churches are to operate in and let them flow. God is not always tangible. He is amazing. Our imposition of practicality on spirituality is satan's way of making sure revival does not break out. Let us allow God to clothe us in the majestic royalty He intended so that countless generations can be blessed.

We are going to learn about our giftings, so that we can function in our purpose. Our life application for the step of wisdom is *functioning in our purpose*, or knowing and operating in our purpose in Christ. I am going to address the administration gifts only by title, for they are self-explanatory. I will give examples and some explanation of the spiritual gifts because they are the exact thing I am talking about here. We will also cover the importance of the fivefold ministry.

The very fact that so many avoid the spiritual gifts, entirely or in part, is the exact proof of their power. People do not flinch when it comes to accepting the administrative gifting, but the intangible, spiritual gifts—that is another story.

When I began receiving wisdom, I found that God impressed the knowledge of His spiritual gifts on me steadily by actual examples in my ministry. I feel like they were a part of the heart of wisdom. Our faith grows when we conceive and believe a prophecy and then actually see it birthed. God's spiritual gifts are this exact thing conceptually. They are a belief in the supernatural and, when they touch the natural, our faith grows. Wisdom's seed is first in faith.

God's purpose for us is to faithfully find and then function in our purpose in Him with wisdom (PP). God has healed you. He has brought you out of the mire and into His temple. He has given you His Spirit and His Word for your journey. First Corinthians 1:7-8 says:

> *Therefore you do not lack any spiritual gift as you eagerly wait for our Lord Jesus Christ to be revealed. He will keep you strong to the end, so that you will be blameless on the day of our Lord Jesus Christ.*

We can operate at times in all of the gifts, but we will have certain gifts that are stronger. This helps to reveal our function to strengthen the Body and affirms our call. This study will be brief because you need to begin to experience these things to fully understand them. We will gain knowledge on the gifts and then you can go to God to ask for the activation of them unto wisdom.

God tells us to pursue the gifts. Have you asked for specific gifts for your life? Our godly actions done in the humility that stems from wisdom will guide us to our gifts (PP). The first gifts we will briefly cover are the gifts of administration (no irony that the first gift listed is a spiritual gift). First, let's touch on what I call "a big lump of gifts in Romans" for the fact that many seem randomly pressed together here. They are found in Romans 12:6-8.

> *We have different gifts, according to the grace given us. If a man's gift is prophesying, let him use it in proportion to his faith. If it is serving, let him serve; if it is teaching, let him teach; if it is encouraging, let him encourage; if it is contributing to the needs of others, let him give generously; if it is leadership, let him govern diligently; if it is showing mercy, let him do it cheerfully.*

By the way, the next chapter, Romans 13, describes our debt to love others (see Rom. 13:8). Unless gifts operate from the heart of love, they will be ineffective at best and dangerous at worst.

Leadership ministry gifts are described in Ephesians 4:11: *"It was He who gave some to be apostles, some to be prophets, some to be evangelists, and some to be pastors and teachers...."* You can use your five fingers to remember these. This is the five-fold ministry and is the backbone of the Church with Christ as its Head. The foundation is the prophets and apostles (see Eph. 2:20-22). Many churches today are hurting because they do not accept this foundation

First Corinthians 12 is a great chapter to study. This letter describes the spiritual gifts and breaks down some administration gifts as well. Once again, love is the chapter that follows this dissertation. In fact, this book ends its last step in love.

I want to touch on the gifts of the Spirit because they are exactly that: gifts. They are beautiful and we need to pursue them. They admonish, bring revelation, edify, strengthen, encourage and teach us. The nine spiritual gifts divide into three sections, each housing three gifts.

During my studies, I learned that the nine could be neatly broken down in these three categories each with three subcategories. They are: the revelation gifts (word of wisdom, word of knowledge, discerning of spirits); the power gifts (gift of faith, gift of healing, working of miracles); and the gifts of inspiration (prophecy, tongues, the interpretation of tongues). (See First Corinthians 12.)

We must first have the Spirit in us in order to tap into His spiritual gifts. The Bible states that we are all eligible until the end (see 1 Cor. 13:10) and the end has not arrived yet. Several gifts that are alive and active today are merged into the following scriptures: Matt. 28:18-20 and Mark 16:15-18. They are sandwiched in with The Great Commission, which we can handle. The things we cannot explain in the natural some seemingly want to omit or cease them. Why, I do not know—it is power for our dying lives.

In addition to not denying any part of Scripture, we need to be cautious of blind guides who will try to squelch our gifts. God talks about them in the seven woes to the church in Matthew 23. People have been denying, abusing, and falsifying the gifts. In turn, this has done a great disservice to people's faith.

If you are confused about the gifts, ask God to show you. Remember, He is no respecter of persons. Why would He extend the gifts to me and not to

Jewel for the Journey

Encourage one another with the authenticity that comes only through God's Holy Spirit. Remember that the very purpose of the gifts is to heal, edify, warn, and reveal.

you? You are the Church; if you allow Him, God will keep you clean of man's ideologies so that His power is not stagnated by misguided resistance. He can keep us Kingdom-minded, opinion free, producing fruit, healing, healing others and saving souls.

When we like to reside in God's Spirit and prefer His Spirit to reside in us, we are wise. This is glory. My witness today of His Spirit performing real-life miracles, healings, and infillings (with all the gifts in operation) leads me to a definitive conclusion: There has been no cessation of God's gifts, nor does He intend one.

Let us look at an example from my life of the gifts in action. When God filled me with the Holy Spirit, my mentor spoke in an unknown prayer language. When she spoke in English during the revelation, she said things that only God and I knew about. The word of knowledge was in operation.

My healing and the transforming of my knowledge into wisdom were manifestations of the power gifts that were given to me through a vessel or directly from the Holy Spirit. Many may mock, but I say, "Do not grieve the Holy Spirit. Do not deride that which is truth. He holds the lightening and the thunder."

I have evidence of tongues from my infilling (see Acts 2:4; 19:6). This is different from the gifts of inspiration for the Church. This private prayer language allows me to go unhindered to the throne room.

> *In the same way, the Spirit helps us in our weakness. We do not know what we ought to pray for, but the Spirit Himself intercedes for us with groans that words cannot express* (Romans 8:26).

If you are infilled with God's Holy Spirit, you have access to this also. If it did not overcome you upon transformation, ask for it. I had to. Acts 1:8 (KJV) says, *"Ye shall receive power, after that the Holy Ghost is come upon you."*

If you really want to stay healed and want to see God, than seek God on every level. If we oppress these gifts or say they have ceased, we subject ourselves to lesser blessings. Why would God cease healings of any kind? We must not ignore or fear the obvious. We must let God speak to us and let Him anoint us with His gifts.

We read Acts; we study Acts; we *live* Acts. If satan can keep us fearful or ignorant, then he succeeds against us; if he can accomplish all of this inside the Church, he can enforce endless cycles of sickness.

The Most Beautiful Baptism

My husband had always felt a pull of the Spirit to be water baptized. I had been sprinkled at 18. Once God infilled me with the Spirit, I felt no need to do it again. However, out of a submissive acknowledgment of my husband's authority I agreed to it.

Therefore, we sought counsel from our pastor to understand water baptism scripturally. He led us gracefully through the Book of Acts. He showed us wisdom in three distinct instances.

Acts 10:47 said it all: *"Then Peter asked, 'Can anyone object to their being baptized, now that they have received the Holy Spirit just as we did?'"* (NLT). So Peter gave orders for them to be baptized in the name of Jesus Christ (see Acts 10:48).

The Friday before our planned baptism, I met with my mentor. Not knowing the specifics of the event, we did not even discuss them that day. She prayed over me and during the prayer, she received a picture from the Lord. It was a gift I did not yet understand—the gift of seeing something that is yet to occur.

"Jennifer, I see you on a high place with the sun in your face and the wind in your hair. You will be in a very good place spiritually."

That next Tuesday morning, five of us set out for the lake. My husband, our pastor, his wife, my mentor, and I met on the hill atop the sandy banks along the still waters. We shared the Lord's Supper and I was the only one in the circle with my face illuminated by the sun. The wind was whipping through my hair. My mentor had spoken a word of wisdom over me the week before and it quickly came to fruition.

The lake was still, but dark and murky. I fell back into the cold September waters and suddenly could not breathe or see; my baptism (as all baptisms) was a beautiful symbol of death. As I went into the watery grave, I thought of Christ's last words: *"When Jesus therefore had received the vinegar, He said, **It is finished**: and He bowed His head, and gave up the ghost"* (John 19:30 KJV, emphasis added). He gave up His life for me.

When pastor pulled me up into life, the light and air rushed in. I began to weep and speak in tongues, and so did he. Water baptism may seem just a symbol, but the act was powerful. A great move of God in our lives made this gift very real to us. While I do not know what is going on in the spiritual most of the time, I do know that the spiritual and the natural met for me that day. Heaven touched earth, not because we had planned it, but because we were diligent to follow God's plan.

Not only did the baptism confirm my husband's guidance, but God allowed me to see once again the connection between obedience and a physical manifestation of His truths and gifts in my life. We were in God's grace and presence during that beautiful baptism. We all felt the thickness of the Spirit and the peace of the Lord. I step in that thickness daily, not because I have an ounce of worthiness, but because He freely gives tons of grace.

Psalms 138:8 says: *"The Lord will fulfill His purpose for me; Your love, O Lord, endures forever—do not abandon the works of Your hands."*

His love, mercy, and grace are without end. Do you remember the fateful exchange between Peter and Jesus the night before He died? *"Jesus answered, 'Die for Me? I tell you the truth, Peter—before the rooster crows tomorrow morning, you will deny three times that you even know Me"* (John 13:38 NLT).

Peter did, in fact, deny Jesus three times. Yet, Jesus went on to give him not only the keys of the Kingdom (see Matt. 16:19), but asked him to shepherd and feed His flock (see John 21:15-17). Jesus gave Peter purpose after his sin and asked him to combat his denial with love. In asking Peter three times whether he loved Jesus, the Lord requested one life-giving statement for each act of denial.

God shows us here that there is no sin too big for Him to cover in love. He gives us a purpose once we shed the walls of the devil's masquerade of denial. He gives us a ministry so that we will stand up and say, *"Thou art the Christ"* as Peter did in Mark 8:29 (KJV).

A wise saint once told me to pray that God would increase my capacity in order to hold more of His wisdom. His knowledge is without end. His wisdom

Jewel for the Journey

You are grafted into that new fruit-bearing branch. You have allowed the Spirit of power to remain in you and you are healthy because of Him.

is infinite. His understanding cannot be fully captured and cannot be exhausted. Just as we are praying for wisdom, we will pray for our godly purpose to surface. We will pray for God to reveal our giftings and bestow His spiritual gifts on us.

Isaiah 11:1-2 made an irrevocable promise, one that I have mentioned in a different light previously, showing the beautiful depth and multitude of ways Scripture can be used:

> *Out of the stump of David's family will grow a shoot—yes, a new Branch bearing fruit from the old root. And the Spirit of the LORD will rest on Him—the Spirit of wisdom and understanding, the Spirit of counsel and might, the Spirit of knowledge and the fear of the LORD* (NLT).

We need to ask for more of Him and for more room to contain all of Him. Just as our fruit basket is overflowing and we need to balance it as we step up, we also need wisdom and the current of love to be so strong and full that upward is the only possible direction we can take. Our gifts and our studies provide proof of our healing, just as our giving and serving take us into the flow of our God-ordained purpose.

We have hope and faith for every step. We are praying, reading, worshiping, resting, fasting, listening, giving, serving, and studying—all with a purpose in Christ. In our pursuit of God, love trumps all. Everything ends in love. We pray that He shows us and gives us His love to live in and to give out. Our healing is in direct proportion to the amount of God's love we will allow to flow through us.

THE PRINCESS PRINCIPLES PRACTICE

Stepping Into God's Wisdom:

- Accept God's Word as the absolute truth in every facet of your life, with no exceptions.

- Ask for your wisdom to increase, as Solomon did, daily.

- Desire His fruit and gifts above worldly prosperity.

- Function in His love regardless of your circumstances.

- Prefer death over life without Christ.

- Know that you are nothing without Him, and He is everything.

Life Application Action

Functioning in Our Purpose

Then make my joy complete by being like-minded, having the same love, being one in spirit and purpose (Philippians 2:2).

Begin to journal about your gifts. List how they can help you stay healed and help heal others:

Define His joy and how it relates to single-mindedness in Christ:

Summary of Princess Principles

 The activation of freedom unto glory occurs when, by faith, you allow Him to transform you into His image.

Now the Lord is the Spirit, and where the Spirit of the Lord is, there is freedom. And we, who with unveiled faces all reflect the Lord's glory, are being transformed into His likeness with ever-increasing glory, which comes from the Lord, who is the Spirit (2 Corinthians 3:17-18).

I think you have hit wisdom when your daily goal is to reflect only His glory! Explain your transformation (unveiling), the freedom you have received, and how you reflect His glory from it all:

 You obtain wisdom when you ask for the entire revelation of Christ and the Word of God—precept upon precept, nothing added, nothing taken away—to be sewn into your heart.

Get wisdom, get understanding; do not forget my words or swerve from them. Do not forsake wisdom, and she will protect you; love her, and she will watch over you. Wisdom is supreme; therefore get wisdom (Proverbs 4:5-7).

Define wisdom. Realize how forgetting or swerving from God's truths can cause "accidents." Journal about the areas of your life where you need to be watched and protected:

 God's purpose for us is to faithfully find and then function in our purpose in Him with wisdom.

If any of you lacks wisdom, he should ask God, who gives generously to all without finding fault, and it will be given to him. But when he asks, he must believe and not doubt... (James 1:5-6).

Define doubt and write about any areas of your life where you see a lack of faith. Then journal how those areas are holding you back from flowing in your God ordained purpose:

 Our godly actions done in the humility that stems from wisdom will guide us to our gifts.

Who is wise and understanding among you? Let him show it by his good life, by deeds done in the humility that comes from wisdom (James 3:13).

List what you have done today. Now categorize the list under the headings, wise and unwise. Journal about your understanding of how your giftings will surface from godly behavior:

Congratulations! You have *stepped into wisdom*. You understand *His purpose and gifts* for your journey. There is only one more stair left to climb. The last one is the best one yet! Beautiful sister, keep stepping. Step up into His love!

Chapter Thirteen

The Topography of God's Love

Step Thirteen: God's Love in Everything

"The most important one," answered Jesus, "is this: 'Hear, O Israel, the Lord our God, the Lord is one. Love the Lord your God with all your heart and with all your soul and with all your mind and with all your strength.' The second is this: 'Love your neighbor as yourself.' There is no commandment greater than these" (Mark 12:29-31).

Back to the Masquerade

WHEN we allow the love of God, through the acceptance of Christ and the fullness of His Holy Spirit, to permeate every cell of our unworthy being, we begin to emit His love to others. We are now not only healed and healing vessels; we are healers as well. God's love in us is the all-encompassing reason for our consistent upward motion and an important determining factor in the direction that those around us take.

As we trust our experience with the steps, let us grasp the handrail, turn and look back just for a moment, and see how far we have come. We can see the tiny door far, far away at the base of the steps. Looking back, we will always remember our pain in order to operate with humility, grace, and mercy, but we will not reside in the pain of our dark days in the masquerade. Your pain is now your testimony!

It is not by our might that we stand this far up; our triumph is only by His Spirit (see Zech. 4:6). This is God's stairway built by His grace. There is nothing we did, no obedience so great or prayer so profound as to deserve even the deadbolt to have been unlatched. *"He draws us and we choose Him"* (John 6:44). We step up firmly into God's love with a surrendered heart filled with only purity and humility.

Jewel for the Journey

To share His unceasing love is the mightiest purpose of all.

I am so proud of you for persevering. I am so thankful that you are yet another precious person added to the ranks of the healed and healing. We are a Kingdom of mighty princesses vying for a cause much greater than our sickness. We now have a testimony to share, a history of stepping in power and love with Christ. Philemon 1:6 describes our goal: *"I pray that you may be active in sharing your faith, so that you will have a full understanding of every good thing we have in Christ."*

Looking back on the tiny, now insignificant door of sickness and shame, I realize that the very moment I knew I wanted out of the darkness was the moment that I let go of everything. I released everything I thought I loved and everything I did love. Look back for a moment. Do you see the same response? The devil no longer has you trapped!

God tells us that everything comes down to love. I released not only my pain, but I also released my husband, daughters, son, mother, father, family, hopes, dreams, freedom, friends, choices, gifts, purpose, life, everything—even my hard drive. We give up all we love. We give it all to Him. We do not know for sure whether we will get any of it back. That is the hardest part.

When we gave it up, He took what was not love and removed it like a vapor. He showed us the difference between love and lust, pain and healing, fear and faith, death and life. He then began to reestablish those things that were of His love back into our lives. We see Him adding love where we never expected to find it. We see the impossible becoming possible, only by His love.

The famous thirteenth chapter of First Corinthians has real meaning to us now:

> *Love is patient, love is kind. It does not envy, it does not boast,*
> *it is not proud. It is not rude, it is not self-seeking, it is not easily*

angered, it keeps no record of wrongs. Love does not delight in evil but rejoices with the truth. It always protects, always trusts, always hopes, always perseveres.

Love never fails. But where there are prophecies, they will cease; where there are tongues, they will be stilled; where there is knowledge, it will pass away (1 Corinthians 13:4-8).

As we walk together, He teaches us how love takes time and how His time is infinite more than our finite minds can even conceive. God shows us how His love is kind. He shows us people steeped in worldly riches and gently nudges our hearts to release envy because envy is not love.

He shares unimaginable gifts with us and says, "Do not boast. It is by My Spirit, with My love. Be not proud for it is by My stripes that you are healed." His love comes in the minute you concede to it and you cannot conceive of all the glorious riches it will bring to you (PP).

When we misstep and judge others, He softly reminds us that His love is not rude. When we huddle up in the corner with our Bibles and read the day away, He quietly says, "Now go use My Word to save a soul. My love is not self-seeking."

When frustration turns to anger and we want to yell, He helps us to see that His love is not easily angered. He tells us that love keeps no record of wrong and reminds us that our own trespasses have been forgiven.

"Love does not delight in evil but rejoices with the truth" (1 Cor. 13:6). This verse is very real to me. My husband fought for me. I weep over the endurance of his faith. God tells us His love, *"always protects, always trusts, always hopes, always perseveres"* (1 Cor. 13:7). When I think of all God and my husband have done for me, I understand that His *"Love never fails"* (1 Cor. 13:8).

Let us adhere to the exact methods and habits we need to stay healthy forever. If we protect the hard-fought healing we have received, we can do our part to help heal everyone that crosses our path on our stairway to Heaven. The true purpose of God's healing is for us to forgive and love one another guiding each other in unity toward Christ likeness (PP).

We may stumble occasionally, but His love keeps us treading upward, not tripping downward. We flow in His love as we grow into His likeness. Our healing is to reside on the peaks of His love during the valleys of our lives.

> *He restores my soul. He guides me in paths of righteousness for His name's sake. Even though I walk through the valley of the shadow of death, I will fear no evil, for You are with me; Your rod and Your staff, they comfort me. You prepare a table before me in the presence of my enemies. You anoint my head with oil; my cup overflows* (Psalms 23:3-5).

A New Look Back

More than a decade after we moved away from Atlanta, we went back to visit and happened upon The Masquerade. My eyes flew open as we passed the club that serves as a metaphor for the message of this book.

"Brett! No way! How can that place still be standing? And, look! The marquee says something about the devil. Please turn the car around I have to go and look. Maybe the albino is still there."

I gasped with anticipation. The parking lot was as dusty as ever. The building was just as eerie and dark as I remembered it. The old mill equipment loomed overhead and was still attached to the side of the warehouse. As we pulled into the lot, I noticed the crosses carved into each of the double wooden doors leading inside.

"Brett, I don't want to go in without you." I said.

When we entered, my husband was shocked that the building was actually broken up into three levels. He thought I had embellished that part. As he gazed into the bar labeled *Purgatory*, he was undeniably upset at the mockery of the crosses he saw inside. The establishment's intention was not to worship our Lord and Savior.

From "Purgatory," you can look up through the wooden staircase planks and see almost all the way into what they call "Heaven." The stairs were not stable, and with a good quaking, looked like they would crumble into dust. The whole club had a ready-to-fall-down appearance.

Despite my curiosity about the albino man or about whether my tiara was still lodged in the air vent, I did not want to climb those steps. My crowns are being stored in Heaven now, awaiting my arrival. Someone had pasted a picture of the typical depiction of the devil, horns and all, on the wall halfway up the staircase. The air was hard to take; the odor was disgusting (just as I remembered it), and a thick haze hung in the place.

My husband turned to leave and I followed him. We literally could not stay in the place. As we exited, I looked back; the marquee displayed the words *devil* and *burn*. I thought the building would have been burned by now or at least leveled by a wrecking ball. But I know that God's all-consuming fire is still waiting. He loves them and wants them to turn from their iniquity and accept His Son. He is waiting for them to get off that rickety staircase and get on His stairway to Heaven.

My past was no better than their present. It was not so long ago that I ignorantly walked the stairs of The Masquerade. I, too, was trapped in its deceptive embrace. Now the fire in my bones could not get me out of the parking lot fast enough. As our car pulled out, I felt freedom and peace.

I also felt sadness for all the lost souls seeking relief in that dry well. I knew firsthand how truly dry it was. I was not in judgment. I felt the pain of knowing the power of God's love and realizing the lack of acceptance for His love in that place. It reeked of lust, rebellion, and injustice.

I felt the pain of all the children God created who tread those barren stairs in and out of hell, up and down from emptiness to emptiness. They can say what they want, but when they are all alone after The Masquerade closes down, their love remains unfulfilled. They know that deep inside.

Now that we have moved closer to God, we can better sense the pain of others and pray for them in love. For the spark is in them. God created them, and He placed His love there. The problem is that they are trying to light it with a blowtorch when all they need to do is step out of denial, relinquish control, and allow God to ignite the fire of the Holy Spirit that leads to a stairway and Kingdom that can never be shaken to dust.

Therefore, since we are receiving a kingdom that cannot be shaken,
let us be thankful, and so worship God acceptably with reverence
and awe, for our "God is a consuming fire" (Hebrews 12:28-29).

We can accept with faith that our journey in Him is always upward, regardless of what we feel. We will praise Him and rejoice because our position in Him is a purposeful and necessary part of His Kingdom. We thank Him for our testimony and the souls that we can reach because of what He did. The people who are stuck where you used to be need you.

Once we resolve never to tread the shaky stairs again, we can accept, in our newfound freedom, the fact that even our failures are nothing more than valleys. Satan's favorite trick is to make us believe we are capable of stepping out of God's love. We are not going to listen to his lies. If we have been sealed in the Holy Spirit (see Eph. 1:13) and are seeking Him, we are irrevocably in His love.

The valley is where transformational work occurs. If you feel weak, let me promise you that stepping back to where you came from will not help. That place has not changed. What has changed is you. You have left your past powerless over you by stepping out of Egypt. That place is still no good. The musty smell hovers, and its occupants still breathe the wrong air for the wrong reasons.

Remember what First Corinthians 15:33 says: *"Bad company corrupts good character."*

Stepping up in the Valley

We are either in a valley of pain or a valley of the Lord's rebuke. If you have slipped back into sin or have stepped into new sin, you will soon find yourself in a valley. Step out of it by starting over with the stairs as quickly as possible.

Sometimes, you will feel that all is well, yet you feel down and out and cannot put your finger on the reason. When opposition is the strongest, you are usually at your weakest. Your awareness of His strength is imperative during this type of transition. This may be a valley of refinement, or, as I like to call it, the Lord's training camp. Seek God and keep stepping for Him in this life to attain your crown that is awaiting you in heaven.

The hardest thing I had to accept was the fact that I will always be in need of God's healing, regardless of how much I have healed. That is the absolute truth. Our consistent need for Him is a flame that we need to keep ablaze within us. That is why this book is not just about the steps to healing; it is also about the steps to staying healed.

A visual I like to picture is of a huge mountain range like the Alps. Imagine a beginning point at the very bottom, at sea level. As you begin to climb, you take some upward and some downward steps, but your trajectory is consistently upward. There are little valleys nestled between the peaks along the way. Even when you find yourself in a valley, you are still well above sea level.

When we took the trip to Atlanta right after we unexpectedly revisited The Masquerade, we traveled up into the Appalachian Mountains. We could tell we were gradually climbing as the topography and climate changed. We arrived at my mother's home up on the stunning crest of a hill. We stepped out of the car. I felt the slope of the ground and steadied my balance as we acclimated to the land. Our trip up had been beautiful and in my mind, I had a picture of where we were on this grand mountainside.

When we left, we drove out of town taking the opposite direction. We went into the mountains instead of out. As we traveled, I had to rethink my mountainside position. As we turned the corner off the road leaving my mother's home, we saw a beautiful valley full of water. My eyes felt glazed over as my mind raced to try to catch all of the unexpected treasures. I was amazed at how God had scooped out a bowl on the tippy top of this huge peak and filled it with water.

Jewel for the Journey

Make sure your valleys are God's enhancements, not sin traps, and remain in Him regardless of your natural circumstances.

I continued looking around and realized that as we consistently gained altitude, we took amazing dips and dives into little valleys and gorges along the way. The valleys and gorges only made the trip more interesting and adventurous!

I want to touch on the hard times in healing because they do happen, and I do not want anyone to feel they are alone in this challenge. Being healed and healing is a powerful place to be, but we are still human and will always have struggles. I want you to know that what you have accomplished in Christ is mighty. We can only get mightier as we step up, even when we pass through a valley.

Christ came and overcame. He tells us we will have tribulation but that He that is in us is stronger and that while we are in the world we are not of the world (see John 16:33; 1 John 4:4). We have total protection from destruction, regardless of our circumstances.

In the valley, we will submit to God, resist the devil, and he will flee (see James 4:7). His departure is not always as swift as we would like, but in the waiting period called perseverance, God makes us better. Sometimes all we can do is stand on His Word, believe for truth, and wait. Neither our devotion to Christ nor our efforts to follow Him are in vain. Paul wrote, "...hold out the word of life—in order that I may boast on the day of Christ that I did not run or labor for nothing" (Philippians 2:16).

During a stint in the valley, you may be a little weaker than usual. The devil knows this, so stay out of the realm of emotions as best you can. The devil likes to manipulate; he wants you to believe that your stairs have become a moving sidewalk taking you quickly downhill. Do not let the devil run a demon carnival through the middle of your valley.

The Cruise

Speaking of carnivals, I am reminded of the first time I laid eyes on a Carnival cruise ship. I almost fell off the pier. The magnitude of the thing was astounding; the amount of metal used, the height, width, and length of the massive ship—it was unimaginable. The enormity was completely lost in print and TV ads I had seen. Live and in person, this structure was beyond description. The fact that it stayed afloat was inconceivable.

The overwhelming scale of the ship reminds me of the way I felt when I began to open my heart to God. I was in love but I did not know why or really with what—just that it was enormous. In my newness and uncertainty, it was the mystery of what it held. I saw the vast creation and wondered how I could be kept safe.

The whole thing amazed me. Many times, we look upon His love with wonder, but are unsure of the mystery and how things will end up. We have to step into His Spirit and allow His Spirit into us in order for His love to carry us on the waters of life.

The air was fresh and salty blowing into the room from the open balcony door. My eyelids grew heavy as I turned over in the cool embrace of the feather bed. The rocking motion lulled me to sleep as the churning waters hummed in my ears. I was full from the buffet's endless provision as my mind drifted toward the next day's journey in a new land.

I remembered standing on the pier in awestruck fear and in my own might trying to determine how this all worked. Now as I lay encapsulated inside the ship allowing it to move me safely to abundant blessing, I felt a peace and a safety that cannot be explained by rational thought. God's power and love are beyond measure and understanding and they take us to places we would never see had we stayed on the pier.

The one thing I always noticed when floating into island ports was that you could see the valleys as well as the mountain peaks all at once. It gave us discernment to strategize and plan.

From the Valley With Faith

We have come so far, and I want you to know in your heart that it is still OK to have struggles and issues. These steps can be implemented daily if necessary. We know the devil is not resting when things are quiet. He is planning; so we need to be ready.

You will be in a valley again at some point, for the Lord must mold us. Many times, we put ourselves there. It is so funny because a valley with God is not the same as a valley without God. A valley without God is why this journey began. We have come a long way from those trenches of darkness. They left us with evil consequences and pain; they kept us dropping from valley to valley.

A valley with God may feel uncomfortable for a time, but He loves us so much that He is willing to go into the valley with us. The valley with God leaves us with blessing, strengthens us, and brings us closer to His likeness. His valley carries us to healing, freedom, and glory. We use our tried and true stairs, jewels, actions, principles and prayer. By the Spirit and through the Word, we will win.

We have just emerged from the valley, my sweet princess. Remember not to reside in your emotions, but to reside in His love, always (PP). Now step out onto the peak and praise Him for your life restored and your purpose exposed.

Standing Still on the Peaks

Those who trust in the LORD are like Mount Zion, which cannot be shaken but endures forever. As the mountains surround Jerusalem, so the LORD surrounds His people both now and forevermore (Psalms 125:1-2).

Psalm 125 is a song for pilgrims ascending to Jerusalem. Sojourning is exactly what we are doing; we are consistently ascending unto the temple of the heavenly Jerusalem.

My beautiful sister in Christ, with Christ in you, look how far you have climbed! You are described in Revelation 12:11: *"And they overcame him by the blood of the Lamb, and by the word of their testimony; and they loved not their lives unto the death"* (KJV). He shared with you all His pain; He wants you to share yours with others as He leads (PP).

To me, functioning in God's love is the epitome of a healthy life. It just happens to be our last Life Application Action. Why is the step and the action the same? Because everything cumulates in love, the very reason God sent His Son to heal us.

[God] *made us alive with Christ even when we were dead in transgressions—it is by grace you have been saved. And God raised us up with Christ and seated us with Him in the heavenly realms in Christ Jesus, in order that in the coming ages He might show the incomparable riches of His grace, expressed in His kindness to us in Christ Jesus* (Ephesians 2:5-7).

God has authorized us to be on these steps. With much authority comes much responsibility: in one word, our responsibility is *love*.

Satan wants us to believe that it would be arrogant of us to assume God's power. Society wants us to follow its controlling pharaoh-like powers. Scripture clearly states that God's power goes opposite to the world's. His authority is ours by grace and the activation of that authority is seeded in the transference of His love (see 2 Cor. 10).

You are so beautiful to our gracious Father. He adores you and He is healing you and imparting authority to you right now. Step up, take the scepter, and reign with Him.

When we fail to reside in His love, the scepter of our power lies inactive. We cannot escape God's love. His love is omnipresent and omnipotent. However, we can step out from under His blessing, power, anointing, honor, and authority if we are not in total surrender to His love.

Jewel for the Journey

Your title is *Princess of the Most High,* and you are empowered for your journey with His love.

When we revisited The Masquerade, I saw in my mind a sparkle from within a dust-covered air vent. I heard God speak to me saying, "Regardless of how far you think you have strayed, you are still in My love."

He loves me so much that He wanted to show me that my crown still exists as far as He is concerned. Your crown still exists, *"for God's gifts and His call are irrevocable"* (Romans 11:29). Still in the wreck of our lives, our crowns still sparkle to Him, even when we choose to chuck them down the air vent because of one little roach.

No, not anymore! We know now that all we have to do is flick that thing off, saying, He who is in me *"is far stronger than anything in the world"* (1 John 4:4 MSG). He dusts them off and refines them into glorious crowns of nobility in His Kingdom if we surrender. Then back into His love we go, stepping all the way.

We can be saved, infilled to fullness, and activated in every office with every gift, but if we are not aware of how much God loves us, all of it is still tainted. His love bought you with a price. You are His beautiful daughter and He created you. You are so precious to Him. He wants to bestow a crown of worth on you that no man can remove. Let Him place a crown of His everlasting, indestructible and undeniable love on your head, power from on high. He really, really loves you. His amazing love covers you and keeps you healthy.

Keep Climbing

Our eyes land on the gentle current flowing through the river in the base of the valley. We know that there is climbing involved, but He tells us He will carry us the whole journey. The low, rolling hills cradling the river blend softly away, graduating as they rise into jagged mountain peaks. We realize that we are much higher than we expected because He exceeds our expectations. We are resting on the peaks of His love now, and we know our passage has been is, and is being blessed.

This is one of those moments again; the kind where you realize all the amazing things He has done in your life. Realize now how He loved you on every step and before every step. Consider the words of Psalms 139:13-14:

> For You created my inmost being; You knit me together in my mother's womb. I praise You because I am fearfully and wonderfully made; Your works are wonderful, I know that full well.

A powerful witness is born when healing brings us into His completion and God's love becomes our ultimate motivation (PP). You have decided to put Him first, and in making that decision you have subjected yourself to a power that will supersede the lowest valley by countering it with the highest peak.

> Those who accept My commandments and obey them are the ones who love Me. And because they love Me, My Father will love them. And I will love them and reveal Myself to each of them (John 14:21 NLT).

Just as Job learned during his pain and trials, you will see in abundance your hurt counterbalanced in the blessing of where you are going.

God's peaks are endless because He has abundant wisdom and blessing for us to attain. We will travel through our valleys with the reminder of His peaks in our hearts and His love as a current to guide our steps. When we arrive in the valley we will picture stairs leading us up out of the canyon; we will begin to climb with hope and faith, knowing the assent is never easy but always blessed.

> *Now we see but a poor reflection as in a mirror; then we shall see face to face. Now I know in part; then I shall know fully, even as I am fully known. And now these three remain: faith, hope and love. But the greatest of these is love* (1 Corinthians 13:12-13).

He loves you more than any words I can say. Step into His love and then step up, up, up in faith. One day, we will smile from the mountain peak in the heavenly Jerusalem and all our pain will subside. In the meantime, may these steps guide you to the power of His glorious loving gift of heaven on earth ascending until we meet on the peaks of His glory.

THE PRINCESS PRINCIPLES PRACTICE

Stepping Into God's Love

- Know that you were bought with a price and are dearly loved by God.

- Accept your worth in the truth that you were created in the image of God.

❧ Find your identity and purpose only in Christ.

❧ Be willing to love mankind through His Son's blood, regardless of fleshly preferences.

❧ Give service, humility, purity, repentance, and glory, above all else and all unto Him.

❧ Yearn to reflect His glory.

❧ Desire to worship, praise, and adore the Lord with all your heart, mind, strength, and soul.

Life Application Action

Functioning in God's Love

Whoever has My commands and obeys them, he is the one who loves Me. He who loves Me will be loved by My Father, and I too will love him and show Myself to him (John 14:21).

Journal how God's love has changed your past into a future with a hope and a purpose:

Study First Corinthians 13 and allow it to permeate every cell of your being. Live it, not just on good days and with those who are lovable, but every day and especially with your enemies.

Also reflect daily on First John 4:7-8,18:

Dear friends, let us love one another, for love comes from God. Everyone who loves has been born of God and knows God. Whoever does not love does not know God, because God is love....There is no fear in love. But perfect love drives out fear, because fear has to do with punishment. The one who fears is not made perfect in love.

Remember that the place where we receive more of His love and healing is in His presence. Love Him above all else and stay in constant worship and prayer.

Summary of Princess Principles

 His love comes in the minute you concede to it and you cannot conceive of all the glorious riches it will bring to you.

However, as it is written: "No eye has seen, no ear has heard, no mind has conceived what God has prepared for those who love him" but God has revealed it to us by his Spirit. The Spirit searches all things, even the deep things of God (1 Corinthians 2:8-10).

Journal about what you have experienced in His love through His Spirit:

 The true purpose of God's healing is for us to forgive and love one another guiding each other in unity towards Christ likeness.

Bear with each other and forgive whatever grievances you may have against one another. Forgive as the Lord forgave you. And over all these virtues put on love, which binds them all together in perfect unity (Colossians 3:13-14).

Write down all the people you have forgiven and pray for them: In this transaction you will be gathering more of the Father's love for yourself!

Remember not to reside in your emotions, but to reside in His love, always.

Love is patient, love is kind. It does not envy, it does not boast, it is not proud. It is not rude, it is not self-seeking, it is not easily angered, it keeps no record of wrongs. Love does not delight in evil but rejoices with the truth. It always protects, always trusts, always hopes, always perseveres. Love never fails... (1 Corinthians 13:4-8).

List the things that Scripture says love is and journal about how those things are prevailing over negative emotions you used to see surfacing:

He shared with you all His pain; He wants you to share yours with others as He leads.

They overcame him by the blood of the Lamb and by the word of their testimony; they did not love their lives so much as to shrink from death (Revelation 12:11).

Journal your testimony:

 A powerful witness is born when healing brings us into His completion and God's love becomes our ultimate motivation.

Dear friends, since God so loved us, we also ought to love one another. No one has ever seen God; but if we love one another, God lives in us and His love is made complete in us (1 John 4:11-12).

Write about what being complete in Christ means to you and how His love makes everything possible:

Explain your understanding of His agape love:

Congratulations! You have successfully made it up to the temple and into His Holy of Holies: You understand how to stand firm in the valley seasons of life and soak up the blessings on the peaks of His love. You are ready to share as God leads, while you reside in His agape love. Do not forget to step up in Him forever.

But the eyes of the LORD are on those who fear Him, on those whose **hope** *is in His unfailing* **love**... (Psalms 33:18, emphasis added).

Appendix A

Godly Steps for Healing

Step out of Denial

Relinquish Control

Surrender

Accept Godly Guidance

Stop the Cycle of Hopelessness

Excavate the Roots

Step Into Obedience

Seek Isolation With God

Find God's Balance

Manifest God's Fruit

Step With Consistency

Step in Wisdom

Do Everything in Love

Appendix B

Life Application Actions for Healing

Hope Isaiah 40:30-31

Faith Hebrews 11:1

Pray Philippians 4:6

Read Romans 10:17

Worship Psalms 100:2

Rest Matthew 11:28-30

Fast Matthew 6:16

Listen Proverbs 12:15

Give Acts 20:35

Serve Matthew 20:28

Study His Word 2 Timothy 2:15

Function in Your Purpose Philippians 2:2

Function in God's Love John 14:21

Appendix C

Read the Bible in One Year

___ Sep 1: Gen 1-3	___ Sep 19: Exod 4-6	___ Oct 7: Lev 16-18
___ Sep 2: Gen 4-7	___ Sep 20: Exod 7-9	___ Oct 8: Lev 19-21
___ Sep 3: Gen 8-11	___ Sep 21: Exod 10-12	___ Oct 9: Lev 22-23
___ Sep 4: Gen 12-15	___ Sep 22: Exod 13-15	___ Oct 10: Lev 24-25
___ Sep 5: Gen 16-18	___ Sep 23: Exod 16-18	___ Oct 11: Lev 26-27
___ Sep 6: Gen 19-21	___ Sep 24: Exod 19-21	___ Oct 12: Num 1-2
___ Sep 7: Gen 22-24	___ Sep 25: Exod 22-24	___ Oct 13: Num 3-4
___ Sep 8: Gen 25-26	___ Sep 26: Exod 25-27	___ Oct 14: Num 5-6
___ Sep 9: Gen 27-29	___ Sep 27: Exod 28-29	___ Oct 15: Num 7
___ Sep 10: Gen 30-31	___ Sep 28: Exod 30-32	___ Oct 16: Num 8-10
___ Sep 11: Gen 32-34	___ Sep 29: Exod 33-35	___ Oct 17: Num 11-13
___ Sep 12: Gen 35-37	___ Sep 30: Exod 36-38	___ Oct 18: Num 14-15
___ Sep 13: Gen 38-40	___ Oct 1: Exod 39-40	___ Oct 19: Num 16-17
___ Sep 14: Gen 41-42	___ Oct 2: Lev 1-4	___ Oct 20: Num 18-20
___ Sep 15: Gen 43-45	___ Oct 3: Lev 5-7	___ Oct 21: Num 21-22
___ Sep 16: Gen 46-47	___ Oct 4: Lev 8-10	___ Oct 22: Num 23-25
___ Sep 17: Gen 48-50	___ Oct 5: Lev 11-13	___ Oct 23: Num 26-27
___ Sep 18: Exod 1-3	___ Oct 6: Lev 14-15	___ Oct 24: Num 28-30

___ Oct 25: Num 31-32	___ Nov 25: 1 Sam 1-3	___ Dec 26: 2 Kings 18-19
___ Oct 26: Num 33-34	___ Nov 26: 1 Sam 4-8	___ Dec 27: 2 Kings 20-22
___ Oct 27: Num 35-36	___ Nov 27: 1 Sam 9-12	___ Dec 28: 2 Kings 23-25
___ Oct 28: Deut 1-2	___ Nov 28: 1 Sam 13-14	___ Dec 29: 1 Chron 1-2
___ Oct 29: Deut 3-4	___ Nov 29: 1 Sam 15-17	___ Dec 30: 1 Chron 3-5
___ Oct 30: Deut 5-7	___ Nov 30: 1 Sam 18-20	___ Dec 31: 1 Chron 6
___ Oct 31: Deut 8-10	___ Dec 1: 1 Sam 21-24	___ Jan 1: 1 Chron 7-8
___ Nov 1: Deut 11-13	___ Dec 2: 1 Sam 25-27	___ Jan 2: 1 Chron 9-11
___ Nov 2: Deut 14-16	___ Dec 3: 1 Sam 28-31	___ Jan 3: 1 Chron 12-14
___ Nov 3: Deut 17-20	___ Dec 4: 2 Sam 1-3	___ Jan 4: 1 Chron 15-17
___ Nov 4: Deut 21-23	___ Dec 5: 2 Sam 4-7	___ Jan 5: 1 Chron 18-21
___ Nov 5: Deut 24-27	___ Dec 6: 2 Sam 8-12	___ Jan 6: 1 Chron 22-24
___ Nov 6: Deut 28-29	___ Dec 7: 2 Sam 13-15	___ Jan 7: 1 Chron 25-27
___ Nov 7: Deut 30-31	___ Dec 8: 2 Sam 16-18	___ Jan 8: 1/2 Chron 28/1
___ Nov 8: Deut 32-34	___ Dec 9: 2 Sam 19-21	___ Jan 9: 2 Chron 2-5
___ Nov 9: Josh 1-4	___ Dec 10: 2 Sam 22-24	___ Jan 10: 2 Chron 6-8
___ Nov 10: Josh 5-8	___ Dec 11: 1 Kings 1-2	___ Jan 11: 2 Chron 9-12
___ Nov 11: Josh 9-11	___ Dec 12: 1 Kings 3-5	___ Jan 12: 2 Chron 13-17
___ Nov 12: Josh 12-15	___ Dec 13: 1 Kings 6-7	___ Jan 13: 2 Chron 18-20
___ Nov 13: Josh 16-18	___ Dec 14: 1 Kings 8-9	___ Jan 14: 2 Chron 21-24
___ Nov 14: Josh 19-21	___ Dec 15: 1 Kings 10-11	___ Jan 15: 2 Chron 25-27
___ Nov 15: Josh 22-24	___ Dec 16: 1 Kings 12-14	___ Jan 16: 2 Chron 28-31
___ Nov 16: Judg 1-2	___ Dec 17: 1 Kings 15-17	___ Jan 17: 2 Chron 32-34
___ Nov 17: Judg 3-5	___ Dec 18: 1 Kings 18-20	___ Jan 18: 2 Chron 35-36
___ Nov 18: Judg 6-7	___ Dec 19: 1 Kings 21-22	___ Jan 19: Ezra 1-3
___ Nov 19: Judg 8-9	___ Dec 20: 2 Kings 1-3	___ Jan 20: Ezra 4-7
___ Nov 20: Judg 10-12	___ Dec 21: 2 Kings 4-5	___ Jan 21: Ezra 8-10
___ Nov 21: Judg 13-15	___ Dec 22: 2 Kings 6-8	___ Jan 22: Neh 1-3
___ Nov 22: Judg 16-18	___ Dec 23: 2 Kings 9-11	___ Jan 23: Neh 4-6
___ Nov 23: Judg 19-21	___ Dec 24: 2 Kings 12-14	___ Jan 24: Neh 7
___ Nov 24: Ruth 1-4	___ Dec 25: 2 Kings 15-17	___ Jan 25: Neh 8-9

Jan 26: Neh 10-11	Feb 26: Ps 78-79	Mar 29: Isa 5-8
Jan 27: Neh 12-13	Feb 27: Ps 80-85	Mar 30: Isa 9-12
Jan 28: Est 1-5	Feb 28/29: Ps 86-89	Mar 31: Isa 13-17
Jan 29: Esther 6-10	Mar 1: Ps 90-95	Apr 1: Isa 18-22
Jan 30: Job 1-4	Mar 2: Ps 96-102	Apr 2: Isa 23-27
Jan 31: Job 5-7	Mar 3: Ps 103-105	Apr 3: Isa 28-30
Feb 1: Job 8-10	Mar 4: Ps 106-107	Apr 4: Isa 31-35
Feb 2: Job 11-13	Mar 5: Ps 108-114	Apr 5: Isa 36-41
Feb 3: Job 14-16	Mar 6: Ps 115-118	Apr 6: Isa 42-44
Feb 4: Job 17-20	Mar 7: Ps 119:1-88	Apr 7: Isa 45-48
Feb 5: Job 21-23	Mar 8: Ps 119:89-176	Apr 8: Isa 49-53
Feb 6: Job 24-28	Mar 9: Ps 120-132	Apr 9: Isa 54-58
Feb 7: Job 29-31	Mar 10: Ps 133-139	Apr 10: Isa 59-63
Feb 8: Job 32-34	Mar 11: Ps 140-145	Apr 11: Isa 64-66
Feb 9: Job 35-37	Mar 12: Ps 146-150	Apr 12: Jer 1-3
Feb 10: Job 38-39	Mar 13: Prov 1-3	Apr 13: Jer 4-6
Feb 11: Job 40-42	Mar 14: Prov 4-6	Apr 14: Jer 7-9
Feb 12: Ps 1-8	Mar 15: Prov 7-9	Apr 15: Jer 10-13
Feb 13: Ps 9-16	Mar 16: Prov 10-12	Apr 16: Jer 14-17
Feb 14: Ps 17-20	Mar 17: Prov 13-15	Apr 17: Jer 18-22
Feb 15: Ps 21-25	Mar 18: Prov 16-18	Apr 18: Jer 23-25
Feb 16: Ps 26-31	Mar 19: Prov 19-21	Apr 19: Jer 26-29
Feb 17: Ps 32-35	Mar 20: Prov 22-23	Apr 20: Jer 30-31
Feb 18: Ps 36-39	Mar 21: Prov 24-26	Apr 21: Jer 32-34
Feb 19: Ps 40-45	Mar 22: Prov 27-29	Apr 22: Jer 35-37
Feb 20: Ps 46-50	Mar 23: Prov 30-31	Apr 23: Jer 38-41
Feb 21: Ps 51-57	Mar 24: Eccles 1-4	Apr 24: Jer 42-45
Feb 22: Ps 58-65	Mar 25: Eccles 5-8	Apr 25: Jer 46-48
Feb 23: Ps 66-69	Mar 26: Eccles 9-12	Apr 26: Jer 49-50
Feb 24: Ps 70-73	Mar 27: Solomon 1-8	Apr 27: Jer 51-52
Feb 25: Ps 74-77	Mar 28: Isa 1-4	Apr 28: Lam 1-3:36

___ Apr 29: Lam 3:37-5:22	___ May 30: Zech 1-7	___ Jun 30: Luke 14-16
___ Apr 30: Ezek 1-4	___ May 31: Zech 8-14	___ Jul 1: Luke 17-18
___ May 1: Ezek 5-8	___ Jun 1: Mal 1-4	___ Jul 2: Luke 19-20
___ May 2: Ezek 9-12	___ Jun 2: Matt 1-4	___ Jul 3: Luke 21-22
___ May 3: Ezek 13-15	___ Jun 3: Matt 5-6	___ Jul 4: Luke 23-24
___ May 4: Ezek 16-17	___ Jun 4: Matt 7-8	___ Jul 5: John 1-2
___ May 5: Ezek 18-20	___ Jun 5: Matt 9-10	___ Jul 6: John 3-4
___ May 6: Ezek 21-22	___ Jun 6: Matt 11-12	___ Jul 7: John 5-6
___ May 7: Ezek 23-24	___ Jun 7: Matt 13-14	___ Jul 8: John 7-8
___ May 8: Ezek 25-27	___ Jun 8: Matt 15-17	___ Jul 9: John 9-10
___ May 9: Ezek 28-30	___ Jun 9: Matt 18-19	___ Jul 10: John 11-12
___ May 10: Ezek 31-33	___ Jun 10: Matt 20-21	___ Jul 11: John 13-15
___ May 11: Ezek 34-36	___ Jun 11: Matt 22-23	___ Jul 12: John 16-18
___ May 12: Ezek 37-39	___ Jun 12: Matt 24-25	___ Jul 13: John 19-21
___ May 13: Ezek 40-42	___ Jun 13: Matt 26	___ Jul 14: Acts 1-3
___ May 14: Ezek 43-45	___ Jun 14: Matt 27-28	___ Jul 15: Acts 4-6
___ May 15: Ezek 46-48	___ Jun 15: Mark 1-3	___ Jul 16: Acts 7-8
___ May 16: Dan 1-3	___ Jun 16: Mark 4-5	___ Jul 17: Acts 9-10
___ May 17: Dan 4-6	___ Jun 17: Mark 6-7	___ Jul 18: Acts 11-13
___ May 18: Dan 7-9	___ Jun 18: Mark 8-9	___ Jul 19: Acts 14-15
___ May 19: Dan 10-12	___ Jun 19: Mark 10-11	___ Jul 20: Acts 16-17
___ May 20: Hos 1-7	___ Jun 20: Mark 12-13	___ Jul 21: Acts 18-20
___ May 21: Hos 8-14	___ Jun 21: Mark 14	___ Jul 22: Acts 21-23
___ May 22: Joel 1-3	___ Jun 22: Mark 15-16	___ Jul 23: Acts 24-26
___ May 23: Amos 1-5	___ Jun 23: Luke 1	___ Jul 24: Acts 27-28
___ May 24: Amos 6-9	___ Jun 24: Luke 2-3	___ Jul 25: Rom 1-3
___ May 25: Obad-Jonah	___ Jun 25: Luke 4-5	___ Jul 26: Rom 4-7
___ May 26: Mic 1-7	___ Jun 26: Luke 6-7	___ Jul 27: Rom 8-10
___ May 27: Nah 1-3	___ Jun 27: Luke 8-9	___ Jul 28: Rom 11-13
___ May 28: Hab-Zeph	___ Jun 28: Luke 10-11	___ Jul 29: Rom 14-16
___ May 29: Hag 1-2	___ Jun 29: Luke 12-13	___ Jul 30: 1 Cor 1-4

_____ Jul 31: 1 Cor 5-8

_____ Aug 1: 1 Cor 9-11

_____ Aug 2: 1 Cor 12-14

_____ Aug 3: 1 Cor 15-16

_____ Aug 4: 2 Cor 1-4

_____ Aug 5: 2 Cor 5-9

_____ Aug 6: 2 Cor 10-13

_____ Aug 7: Gal 1-3

_____ Aug 8: Gal 4-6

_____ Aug 9: Eph 1-3

_____ Aug 10: Eph 4-6

_____ Aug 11: Phil 1-4

_____ Aug 12: Col 1-4

_____ Aug 13: 1 Thess 1-5

_____ Aug 14: 2 Thess 1-3

_____ Aug 15: 1 Tim 1-6

_____ Aug 16: 2 Tim 1-4

_____ Aug 17: Titus-Philem

_____ Aug 18: Heb 1-6

_____ Aug 19: Heb 7-10

_____ Aug 20: Heb 11-13

_____ Aug 21: James 1-5

_____ Aug 22: 1 Pet 1-5

_____ Aug 23: 2 Pet 1-3

_____ Aug 24: 1 John 1-5

_____ Aug 25: 2 John-Jude

_____ Aug 26: Rev 1-3

_____ Aug 27: Rev 4-8

_____ Aug 28: Rev 9-12

_____ Aug 29: Rev 13-16

_____ Aug 30: Rev 17-19

_____ Aug 31: Rev 20-22

About Jennifer Rani Barham

TO listen to Jennifer's teachings and testimony go to i-tunes or you tube. To contact Jennifer for speaking engagements or book interviews, e-mail her at jbm3@rocketmail.com or write to her at the address below. You can follow JBM on facebook, twitter, blogger and on her Web site below.

Jennifer Barham Ministries

P.O. Box 2912
Madison, MS 39130
www.jenniferbarhamministries.com
www.theroachprincess.com

IN THE RIGHT HANDS, THIS BOOK WILL CHANGE LIVES!

Most of the people who need this message will not be looking for this book. To change their lives, you need to put a copy of this book in their hands.

> *But others (seeds) fell into good ground, and brought forth fruit, some a hundred-fold, some sixty-fold, some thirty-fold* (Matthew 13:8).

Our ministry is constantly seeking methods to find the good ground, the people who need this anointed message to change their lives. Will you help us reach these people?

> *Remember this—a farmer who plants only a few seeds will get a small crop. But the one who plants generously will get a generous crop* (2 Corinthians 9:6).

EXTEND THIS MINISTRY BY SOWING
3 BOOKS, 5 BOOKS, 10 BOOKS, OR MORE TODAY,
AND BECOME A LIFE CHANGER!

Thank you,

Don Nori Sr., Publisher
Destiny Image
Since 1982